For our Grandparents

Anna and Philip Fuchs   *Frank and Rosetta Wenner*
Kate and Samuel Leffler   *Brainard and Frances Legro*

IN UNCERTAIN TIMES

American Foreign Policy after the
Berlin Wall and 9/11

**Edited by Melvyn P. Leffler
and Jeffrey W. Legro**

CORNELL UNIVERSITY PRESS   ITHACA AND LONDON

Published in association with the University of Virginia's Miller
Center of Public Affairs

First published 2011 by Cornell University Press
First printing, Cornell Paperbacks, 2011
Printed in the United States of America

Library of Congress Cataloging-in-Publication Data

In uncertain times : American foreign policy after the Berlin Wall and 9/11 / edited
by Melvyn P. Leffler and Jeffrey W. Legro.
    p. cm.
  "Published in association with the University of Virginia's Miller Center of
Public Affairs."
  Includes bibliographical references and index.
  ISBN 978-0-8014-4909-3 (cloth : alk. paper)
  ISBN 978-0-8014-7619-8 (pbk. : alk. paper)
  1. United States—Foreign relations—1989–   2. National security—
United States.   I. Leffler, Melvyn P., 1945–   II. Legro, Jeffrey W., 1960–
III. White Burkett Miller Center.
  E840.I46 2011
  327.73009'049—dc22   2010053588

Cloth printing   10 9 8 7 6 5 4 3 2 1
Paperback printing   10 9 8 7 6 5 4 3 2 1

IN UNCERTAIN TIMES

Contents

Acknowledgments

We wish to thank our contributors—influential officials and scholars—who took the time to come to the Miller Center of Public Affairs at the University of Virginia to discuss these matters, to reflect on the recent past, and to draft and refine these illuminating essays. We, the editors, are also grateful to the William and Carol Stevenson family, to Governor Gerald Baliles, the director of the Miller Center, and to Cornell University Press for providing the resources to hold our conference and to support the publication of this book. And we happily acknowledge the work of our collaborator, Anne Carter Mulligan, who has been indispensable in bringing this book to fruition.

IN UNCERTAIN TIMES

NAVIGATING THE UNKNOWN

Melvyn P. Leffler and Jeffrey W. Legro

On November 9, 1989, the Berlin Wall came down. Hardly anyone had foreseen this event. When President Ronald Reagan had challenged Soviet leader Mikhail Gorbachev in June 1987 "to tear down this wall," he never anticipated that Berliners themselves would have the opportunity and courage to bring about such dramatic change. We now know that the Wall came down as a result of accidental circumstances, a series of mistaken statements and understandings among officials of the German Democratic Republic. No one had planned for this to happen, and no one had plans to deal with a new landscape that might have been dreamed about but had never been imagined as an imminent possibility.[1]

Not all surprises are so benign. On a clear, sunny, beautiful morning in New York City and Washington, D.C., on September 11, 2001, the familiar landscape of American thinking and American living was shattered. Jets, hijacked by terrorists, rammed into the twin towers of the World Trade Center in lower Manhattan, into the Pentagon just outside of Washington, and into the countryside in Shanksville, Pennsylvania. Flames engulfed the upper floors of the twin towers, and they collapsed inward. Billowing dark smoke belched out of the buildings; dust blackened the sky, turning day into night. Almost three thousand Americans lost their lives. As their loved ones mourned and the nation looked on mesmerized, if not terrified, officials in Washington struggled to provide reassurance and wreak revenge. The looming threat had now become an existential crisis akin to the one produced by the surprise attack on Pearl Harbor in 1941. Policymakers now had to plan for a future they had not dared to consider; but looking through a glass darkly, they had to chart strategy in an international landscape clouded by dust and debris. What was once clear and predictable was now opaque and uncertain.

November 9, 1989, was a dream come true; September 11, 2001, was a nightmare come true. The events of both days stunned U.S. officials. November 9 was a harbinger of a new era of opportunity; although the future was fraught with uncertainty, it seemed likely to be so much better than the past. September 11 was a day of a different sort. It shattered complacency, eradicated myths of invulnerability, and engendered unprecedented fear. America would never be the same, thought many of its leaders. Their fears were heightened and their anxieties magnified when letters laced with anthrax were found in the mail a few weeks later. Some officials were informed, wrongly, that they themselves had been exposed to substances that endangered their lives. Their sense of threat was palpable.[2] The times were not simply uncertain; they were bleak and portentous.

Understanding the Past, and Looking Forward

This book is an effort to cast light on American strategic planning in uncertain times, both good times and bad times. After 1989, new opportunities and new dangers appeared with unprecedented speed, including the collapse and rise of major powers, the assaults of terrorists, the proliferation of missile technologies and nuclear capabilities, the spread of disease, and the meltdown of financial markets and polar ice caps. U.S. officials had to navigate in these fluid international circumstances. When the Berlin Wall collapsed and the USSR disintegrated, the administrations of George H. W. Bush and Bill Clinton confronted a geopolitical map that had to be completely redrawn. The Soviet Union, major nemesis and focal point of American foreign policy for forty years, disappeared. American policymakers had to reassess threats and opportunities and reexamine goals, priorities, interests, missions, and tactics. What should the United States do in a newly reconfigured international arena?

Twelve years after the Berlin Wall came down, a small group of terrorists assaulted the symbols of America's economic and military power and murdered thousands of innocent civilians. Evacuating the Pentagon, defense officials and the military chiefs watched impotently and fumed. Gone, instantly, was the notion that the "hyperpower" United States had somehow mastered the universe. Now, decision makers faced a new set of dilemmas: How should the United States respond to the new threat of transnational terrorism in a world of porous borders, mobile people, instant communication, and proliferating weapons of mass destruction?

In both cases—when the walls fell—U.S. policymakers had to figure out what kind of world they faced, what type of world they wanted, and how to manage it, if only they could. Although these were very different events, they involved a similar set of planning challenges, ones that continue to haunt U.S. foreign policy. In this book, we seek to explore how officials went about reconfiguring foreign policy in the wake of events that suddenly and dramatically altered the global arena. We want to interrogate how U.S. leaders mapped strategy when the international landscape was inchoate and dramatically shifting.

Leaders grappled with uncertainty that came in different forms and presented different challenges. They had to evaluate and designate the priority and immediacy of threats. They had to look for new possibilities to further interests. They had to glean the intentions of other important actors, be they allies or potential foes. They had to assess the utility and reliability of international institutions and law. They had to estimate how economic affairs affected security and vice versa. And they had to figure out how domestic politics would shape and be shaped by these elusive circumstances.[3] What did U.S. officials do? How well did they do?

To address these matters we have brought together leading scholars and practitioners to recount, analyze, and reflect on how the United States responded to the fall of the walls. They have been asked to tackle the following issues:

- How did U.S. officials and bureaucracies interpret the events surrounding 11/9 and 9/11?
- How did their understanding of these events shape their subsequent thinking and planning for foreign policy or international order? Did they accurately grasp the international landscape they were about to encounter?
- Were they successful in conceptualizing and implementing their policies?
- What factors accounted for their success or failure? What lessons can be derived for meeting future challenges in making foreign policy in uncertain and shifting strategic circumstances?

The aim of this book is to extrapolate from the aftermath of the most dramatic events in recent international history for the purposes of improving strategic thinking and strategic planning. Managing uncertainty is a challenge that will not go away. In his inaugural National Security Strategy statement, President Barack Obama reminded the American people that in a new century "whose trajectory is uncertain," the United States "must be ready to lead once more."[4]

What We Thought We Knew

For the most part, journalists, historians, and scholars of international relations have not looked kindly on the making of U.S. strategy and the practice of U.S.

diplomacy in the post–Cold War era, an era that began with carefully managed euphoria that morphed into a benign indifference to most matters international, an apathy that was punctured only by the bold assault on America's most vital organs on September 11, 2001. In *War in a Time of Peace,* a best-selling book about the era between 11/9 and 9/11, William Halberstam, the Pulitzer Prize–winning journalist, writes that perhaps he should have employed the subtitle "Why America Napped" to describe policy making during these years.[5] Similarly, in a standard account of U.S. foreign policy since the end of the Cold War, Warren Cohen, one of the nation's most prolific and venerable diplomatic historians, states that the elder Bush and his chief advisers—National Security Adviser Brent Scowcroft, Secretary of State James A. Baker, and Secretary of Defense Richard "Dick" Cheney—had "neither the time nor the inclination to ponder grand theory." Clinton did little better, Cohen claims, "the sum of [his] foreign policy [was] bad but not disastrous." And the younger Bush, George W. Bush, argues Cohen, sought to "exercise American power without restraint." Historians, Cohen concludes, "will not be kind to him."[6]

These views are commonplace. They are not written without admiration for the prudence, tactical dexterity, and realism of Bush 41, without respect for the restless brilliance, keen insight, and political acumen of Clinton, and without empathy for the tragic circumstances that Bush 43 was forced to handle.[7] But for the most part, these presidents are not viewed as having had much interest in or commitment to careful strategic planning. In his diary on the day after the Berlin Wall fell, President Bush ruminated, "The big question I ask myself is how do we capitalize on these changes? . . . The bureaucracy answer [*sic*] will be, do nothing big, and wait to see what happens. But I don't want to miss an opportunity."[8] But the consensus among many observers is that an opportunity was missed. Notwithstanding the deftness and insight of Bush and Scowcroft, argues Bartholomew H. Sparrow, "the administration could not lay out a new strategic course for the United States."[9] Likewise, in a very fair-minded, thoughtful account, the historian Hal Brands concludes, "Throughout the 1990s, U.S. officials wrestled with the challenges and opportunities of a new order. At times, they overcame the complexity that confronted them, managing crises successfully and devising policies that were well suited to a fluid international environment. More often, it seemed the complexity overcame them."[10] Rapidly moving events, concludes Mary Sarotte, "resulted in imperfect choices and costly consequences."[11]

In many of these sympathetic yet critical portrayals, post–Cold War officials are pictured as struggling to find a unifying strategic theme to define their foreign policy. They are compared unfavorably with many of their predecessors who are said to have heroically carried out a forty-year struggle against the forces of Soviet-led communism with a consistent framework—the policy of containment. Only after 9/11 did the younger Bush embrace a coherent strategy—the global war on terror.[12] Articulated in a series of speeches and in a famous National Security Strategy statement, disseminated in September 2002, Bush and his advisers dismissed the policies of deterrence and containment and embraced a strategy of unilateralism, preemption or prevention, and regime change.[13] In his celebrated second inaugural address in 2005, Bush declared that it was America's mission to end tyranny and create a democratic peace.[14] Although the strategy is said to have been coherent and to have been the result of a vast array of scholarship that claimed that democratic states do not wage war against one another and, therefore, the United States would be safer in such an environment, most writers conclude that the strategy was deeply flawed for simplifying the world and overextending American power. Many of these critics claim that it was the product of a relentless neoconservative campaign to embed their views in official policy. Although these neocons (such as Paul Wolfowitz, Lewis "Scooter" Libby, and Eric Edelman) are said to have failed in their efforts in 1992 to get the ideas and polices of their Defense Policy Guidance institutionalized in subsequent policy, they are said to have triumphed in 2002.[15]

Reassessment: The Policymakers' Perspectives

This book was designed to interrogate the veracity of currently prevailing views and to develop a better appreciation of the challenges that inhere in designing strategy. We asked several influential officials of the Bush 41, Clinton, and Bush 43 administrations—whose memoirs and recollections have not yet been published—to reflect on their actions, motivations, challenges, and accomplishments. What emerges in the chapters that follow is an assault on many of the established wisdoms.

Robert Zoellick, who was arguably the closest adviser to Secretary of State Baker, provides a rich and textured summary of what amounts to a very clear strategy indeed. He acknowledges that this strategy was not scripted in a single document, but he argues that it was widely shared and that it infused coherence and direction into dispersed policies that were carried out throughout the globe, from the Americas to Asia. In an arresting paragraph that defies prevailing scholarship, he writes: "The strategic concept we sought to advance in 1989 integrated foreign, security, economic, business, and trade policies." It sought to "link security and economic interests within a political framework. It was based on U.S. interests. It valued open societies. It sought to foster economic growth and opportunity. And it promoted the development of institutions, regimes, and alliances that could evolve to meet changing circumstances. This approach was a continuation of the post–World War II tradition of U.S. international engagement through multilateral institutions, alliances, and frameworks for partnerships."[16]

Whereas Zoellick seeks to reconfigure our thinking about the overall coherence of policy, Paul Wolfowitz, the under secretary of defense for policy, illuminates the purposefulness that undergirded the evolving strategic thinking of his boss, Dick Cheney, and of his colleagues and assistants. They wanted to preserve old alliances and reassure traditional allies by promising a continuation of America's "forward presence." They appreciated the magnitude of change that occurred after the dissolution of the USSR and struggled to reconfigure the nation's nuclear posture. They believed that "history was flowing in our direction," adjusted to legislators' demands for cuts in the defense budget, reorganized their office and administrative capacities, and sought to configure forces to shape an environment that they understood was fraught with uncertainty.[17]

One of Wolfowitz's key assistants, Eric Edelman, further develops this line of thinking. He provides a very original analysis of the origins, evolution, and consequences of the famous 1992 Defense Planning Guidance (DPG). Rather than seeing it as a singular effort by a cabal of neocons to preserve military primacy for the United States, he explains that it was an attempt to bring defense policy into line with the president's expressed wishes and in response to the lessons learned from the war in the Persian Gulf. The document, Edelman argues, "attempted to move the discussion of U.S. strategic interests from the global challenge represented by the Soviet Union to the more likely regional threats to American security."[18] Although its leakage to the press exposed it to criticism and highlighted the difficulties of making strategic plans, Edelman insists that the basic axioms of the DPG were widely shared by Democrats as well as Republicans.

Walter B. Slocombe, the under secretary of defense for policy in the Clinton administration, illuminates the challenges that inhered in making policy toward Russia. Contrary to much that has been written about the president, Slocombe says that Clinton grasped the strategic landscape, defined his goals carefully, and tried to allocate resources in commensurate fashion. He shows, however, that a focused strategy does not ensure strategic success. Clinton failed to achieve his goals because they were overly ambitious, bedeviled by conflicting imperatives, subject to political controversy, and ultimately supported by too few resources. Moreover, Clinton's partner in Russia—Boris Yeltsin—was unreliable. In a basically benign security environment, Slocombe concludes, governments often have greater difficulty "exploiting opportunities . . . than staving off threats."[19] Nonetheless, there was strategic thinking that shaped the contours of the Clinton administration's policies.

Philip Zelikow was on the National Security Council (NSC) staff during the Bush 41 administration and operated in 2002 as an unofficial confidante to

Condoleezza Rice, President George W. Bush's national security adviser. In his essay in this book he turns conventional wisdom upside down. After making the claim that the strategic goals of Bush 41 were radical—that he wanted "to support change and fashion a new international system"—Zelikow says that the younger Bush actually possessed more modest aims. Inspired by fear, "W" and his aides tried to control risk in order to enhance the system's resistance to a potentially deadly threat, terrorism. Confronted with novel challenges, the younger Bush "chose methods that were experimental and unfamiliar." The global war on terror, Zelikow writes, "was predominantly reactive and defensive." Although the "core mission was relatively limited in relation to world politics . . . the policy instruments and actions felt surprising and even shocking." When "these experiments succeeded," they encouraged "new habits of thought and action."[20]

Contrary to established thinking once again, Zelikow claims that he, John Bellinger, and Rice, not Wolfowitz and other neocons in the Defense Department and the Office of the Vice President, were the principal authors of the National Security Strategy statement of 2002. Moreover, he emphasizes that the focus on preemption was a belated semantic adjustment and "had little to do with grand strategy." But preemption nonetheless had important consequences for strategy, especially in an administration that was sundered by bureaucratic conflicts and personal animosities. Outcomes, however, were not predetermined, particularly because of the patchiness and uncertainty of Bush's thinking and the messiness of the policy process. Officials at State and Defense cordially detested each other: "Bureaucratic entrepreneurs struck out in every direction, latching onto favored ideas or controversies in a fractious administration staffed by plenty of veteran intriguers and their allies." In this context, the decision to go to war against Saddam Hussein was more contingent that we usually think it was, and it certainly was not a foregone conclusion before 9/11. "Bush and his top advisers," Zelikow concludes, "did not enter office with an ambitious agenda for changing the world." Inspired by fear, intoxicated with a sense of resolve that 9/11 engendered, officials improvised. "It was a potent compound of anxiety mixed with . . . hubris."[21]

The chapters written for this book by former policymakers not only introduce new information; they also present new ways to think about strategic planning in the aftermath of 11/9 and 9/11. Zoellick, Wolfowitz, Edelman, and Slocombe depict the policy that was pursued in a more favorable light. Zelikow, although critical of the policy process, is nonetheless sympathetic to the extraordinary pressures under which officials labored. "War," he emphasizes, "was not a metaphor or a conflict being handled by distant generals and armies. It was real; the threats could come directly into their homes; the judgment calls that might save lives were theirs to make." The absence of solid information about potential threats was terrifying. "People do not understand how goddamn dangerous we thought it was," confided one senior CIA analyst.[22] Overall, then, these contributions by policymakers encourage us to see more coherence and more intelligence behind the policies that unfolded than is usually thought to be the case in the existing literature. Strategy is hard to make even in ordinary times, let alone in the unexpected landscapes that emerged after 11/9 and 9/11. We see officials fighting with one another, reacting to leaks, seeking to balance discordant priorities, struggling to mobilize resources to support goals, and worrying about engendering legislative and popular support for their initiatives.

Reassessment: The Views of Scholars

In turbulent times, the right and the wrong things to do are far from clear for analysts as well. A superb group of scholars offers views both supportive and critical in their assessment of U.S. policy making under uncertainty. In the opening chapter of this book, Mary Sarotte, a prize-winning historian, calls 1989 a "punctuational" moment—a moment of dramatic and unexpected change. The events surrounding the fall of the Wall, she writes, "were fraught with uncertainty and risk." They arose independent of American will. Critical decisions "about the future of U.S. foreign policy" emerged "not as a result of thoughtful deliberation but in haste and in response to external pressures; once sanctioned, they [became] very hard to change."[23] In such an atmosphere, chance and contingency dominated. Sorting through feasible options and predicting what would be efficacious depended on a host of variables, many of which were beyond the control of policymakers.

But lest we be tempted to be too sympathetic to the worldviews and prescriptions of the policymakers, we are forcefully reminded of their shortcomings in the incisive chapter by Sarotte as well as in those by John Mueller, Bruce Cumings, and Odd Arne Westad. Sarotte does praise President Bush and Secretary of State Baker for their imaginative improvisation, for their support of German chancellor Helmut Kohl's initiatives, and for their capacity to bring about Germany's unification inside NATO (North Atlantic Treaty Organization). U.S. officials were right, she notes, to worry about the potential for violence and to be wary about experimenting with new security institutions. But her overriding conclusion is that Bush and Baker missed a unique opportunity to configure new institutions for the post–Cold War era, institutions that might have fostered the integration of Russia into a new international order. "Unlike 1945," Sarotte stresses, "American leaders in 1990 sought to maintain established structures rather than create new ones."[24]

Like Sarotte, John Mueller, a prolific and iconoclastic political scientist, draws a series of deft comparisons between U.S. policy making during the Cold War and after the Cold War. American officials, he acknowledges, compiled a good record integrating former enemies into a vibrant democratic capitalist community. He refers to Germany and Japan after World War II and to Eastern Europe—but not Russia—after the Cold War. Policymakers did less well, however, extrapolating lessons from the past, grasping the essentials of the evolving international landscape, and gauging the degree of threat. They tended to exaggerate American vulnerabilities and, therefore, designed policies that wasted resources and lives in a struggle to overcome insecurities that did not exist. Mueller raises fundamental questions about how to interpret threats and asks why officials exaggerate dangers.

For Bruce Cumings, the answers are rather clear. A renowned and provocative historian of modern Korea and a penetrating analyst of the international political economy and U.S. foreign economic policy, Cumings believes that people's basic assumptions do not change easily; these assumptions often trump new knowledge and are resistant to new information "particularly when something entirely unanticipated happens." Cumings examines, among other things, why U.S. officials persisted in exaggerating the danger of the North Korean threat while stressing the vulnerability of the regime, views that changed little over the decades. Why, for example, did John Deutsch, Clinton's director of Central Intelligence, and Paul Wolfowitz, Bush's deputy secretary of defense, continue to predict the "coming collapse" of Korea even as they dwelled on the portentous nature of the regime's nuclear ambitions? Their errors, argues Cumings, are fundamental because they derive from officials' core assumptions. These policymakers (and their favorite pundits) continue to see North Korea "entirely through the lenses of Soviet and East European communism and therefore cannot grasp the regime's very different history, the pragmatic shrewdness of its post-Soviet foreign policy, the desperate and cruel survival strategies it is willing to undertake, let alone the anticolonial and revolutionary nationalist origins of this regime."[25] These officials, concludes Cumings, cannot avoid speaking in metaphors, metaphors that are grounded in unconscious illusions and that are shaped by emotions that have little to do with reality.

Odd Arne Westad, one of the most eminent historians of the Cold War, offers a probing critique of U.S. policy in Iraq and Afghanistan. He emphasizes that in times of uncertainty, officials draw on the lessons of the past, on their core values, and on their most basic ideological predilections. Examining U.S. actions in the aftermath of 9/11, he argues that American policymakers drew the wrong conclusions from their victory in the Cold War, misconstrued the role of technology, underestimated the dislocation and anguish caused by the globalization of world financial and commercial markets, exaggerated the universal appeal of their own values, and tried to impose societal change from without. "Unlike Eastern Europe in 1989," he writes, "the two states [Afghanistan and Iraq] in which the United States intervened in the 2000s had no history of democracy, no tradition of functioning capitalist economies, and no national leaders who could overcome ethnic and religious divisions. . . . The idea of a domino-like spread of democratic change in the Middle East after the invasion of Iraq was therefore a chimera."[26]

The dilemmas of decision making in uncertain times are beautifully illuminated in the chapter by William Wohlforth, a leading scholar of international relations. He shows that his colleagues in the academy often prescribed solutions to such matters as German unification and NATO expansion that, at least in retrospect, were likely to have been less wise than those adopted by the policymakers. Those of us who are historians of American foreign policy and scholars of international relations should be chastened by our own record. "The style of reasoning" that adds gravitas to the "analytical power [of independent experts] in normal times," Wohlforth suggests, "may hamper their ability to update quickly when the underpinnings of a long established strategic equilibrium come unhinged."[27]

Reexamining Strategy in Uncertain Times

The critiques of official U.S. strategic thinking and action in the Sarotte, Mueller, Cumings, and Westad chapters raise profound questions about whether U.S. strategy actually changed in consonance with the rapidly evolving international landscape. Fears did not abate, values did not change, ideas did not mutate, and U.S. goals and interests did not change all that much. What seems clear from the chapters—and from the discussions at the conference at which drafts of these chapters were discussed—is that in the immediate aftermath of 11/9, George H. W. Bush and his advisers still remained wary of the Soviet Union and uncertain of Gorbachev's intentions. They reacted cautiously yet improvised brilliantly to bring about German unification inside NATO. Rather than disbanding the alliances of the Cold War and the multilateral institutions and networks of global capitalism, they sought to build upon them.

Only in 1991–92, in the aftermath of the Persian Gulf War and the dissolution of the USSR, did officials really come to grips with the astounding changes in the international landscape that had been wrought by Gorbachev's reforms and failures. "In a blink of an eye," Scowcroft recollected, the assumptions, institutions, and defense strategies became outdated. "We were suddenly in a unique position, without experience, without precedent, and standing alone at the height of power. It was, it is, an unparalleled situation in history, one which presents us with the rarest opportunity to shape the world and the deepest responsibility to do so wisely for the benefit of not just the United States but all nations."[28]

The challenge, then, was how to make strategy in this vastly changed world. Zoellick was trying to do so in the State Department and Wolfowitz, Edelman, and their colleagues were forging ahead in the Office of the Secretary of Defense. They seem to have discussed their ideas with one another rather little, but this does not necessarily mean that they defined the nation's aims, goals, and interests in conflicting ways. But whether they adjusted effectively to the vastly altered environment and whether they took advantage of the "unparalleled situation in history" to forge the new world order that President Bush liked to talk about, but never carefully defined, is open to question.

As Scowcroft said, they had the "rarest opportunity" to make strategy and shape the world in what they and their successors in the Clinton administration regarded as a benign environment. But benign environments present peculiar problems of their own, especially in a democratic pluralist polity where domestic constituencies looked inward and parochial interests predominated. Moreover, basking in the triumphalism of the immediate post–Cold War era, Republican and Democratic officials alike were less prone than ever to reevaluate prevailing ideas about political economy and strategy; indeed in many respects Zoellick's plans and those of his colleagues in the Defense Department were extrapolations and extensions of long-term U.S. aspirations to invigorate global capitalism, open commercial and financial markets, thwart rivals from dominating regions of perceived vital interest, and extend prevailing alliances and institutions. In a benign environment where threats seemed muted, new ideas did not percolate and policymakers were not inclined to be as bold and experimental as circumstances might have allowed.

In fact, if strategy involves accurate threat perception as well as shrewd assessment of interest, perhaps in the 1990s looming threats were not sufficiently appreciated. Bush 41 and Clinton administration officials sought to squeeze all they could from their old Cold War enemy—for example, pressing rapid NATO enlargement—and discounted worries about mounting Russian resentment. Focused on great power rivals and fearful of rogue threats in Asia and the Middle East, policymakers tended to ignore or downplay warnings of terrorist activity from radical Islamic fundamentalist groups with transnational ambitions. Suddenly, then, when a different set of walls came down on 9/11, the strategic environment appeared drastically altered. Rather than benign, it was portentous. As Zelikow notes, anxiety and hubris, in equal degrees, shaped policymakers' reactions. They scrambled to design an effective strategy to deal with a vastly transformed international landscape, but their performance was not commensurate with their aspirations.

In the conclusion, we will return to these matters. But for now, we seek to invite our readers to revisit the post-11/9 and post-9/11 eras with our group of policymakers and scholars. In their different ways, they force us to rethink and reassess familiar historical territory. They invite us both to look more sympathetically on the making of strategy after these transformative moments, and to ask more critical, probing, and perhaps even embarrassing questions about the nature of grand strategic formulations in eras of uncertainty. How does the nature of the environment, threatening or promising, affect the ability of officials to adapt? Can they measure threats and opportunities accurately? Are policymakers more effective in reacting to immediate dangers and opportunities than in formulating long-term analyses and plans? Are they capable of changing their strategic ideas and values to match evolving international circumstances? How does public opinion and domestic politics shape their responses? Can officials mobilize resources in ways proportionate to the aims they seek without vastly exaggerating dangers or hopes? Can complex bureaucracies and democratic polities actually forge grand strategies?

As we reexamine the history of the post–Cold War era, we have a unique opportunity also to rethink some of the most fundamental challenges that inhere in the making of strategy. In this book, we invite readers to reexamine these events from the perspectives of policymakers who actually had to grapple with making strategy in uncertain times and from those of scholars who can take a more retrospective view. The years that have followed the collapse of the Berlin Wall have been far more turbulent and perilous than anticipated. We have been witnessing a lone superpower trying to adapt to a world that had not been foreseen. In this book, chastened by events, we see policymakers and scholars alike seeking to learn from the recent past in order to advance both historical understanding and strategic thinking.

1

THE WALL COMES DOWN

A Punctuational Moment

Mary Elise Sarotte

How did those in charge of U.S. foreign policy respond when a wall came, quite literally, tumbling down? Initially, they were as stunned by the events in Berlin on November 9, 1989, as the rest of the world. No evidence available to date suggests that any senior leader in Washington expected the opening of the inner-German border in November 1989. This opening caught the relatively new George H.W. Bush administration on the back foot, as it had been trying throughout 1989—its first year in office—to slow down what it viewed as former President Ronald Reagan's irresponsible rate of change to the Cold War status quo. However, when faced with strategic uncertainty after November 9, administration officials had to find a different response, since slowing matters down was no longer an option. Bush decided to back Chancellor Helmut Kohl in the German leader's quest for the rapid unification of his divided country; Kohl, in exchange, would foot the bill. In other words, Bonn, not Washington, would provide what Deputy National Security Adviser Robert Gates referred to as the "bribe" to get the Soviets out of Europe—large amounts of deutsche marks either given or loaned on easy terms to Moscow.[1] The response of U.S. foreign policy to November 9 was therefore one of inspired improvisation, as policy making in times of change so often is. Washington's main success lay not in shaping all events itself, but in backing a reliable ally—West Germany—and in trusting it to act in the interest of the United States.

This essay will examine the opening of the Berlin Wall and its consequences in detail, but, before doing so, it is worth suggesting what this particular case study can contribute to our broader understanding of decision making in times of rapid change. Scholars need to pay more attention to what G. John Ikenberry and Daniel Deudney have insightfully termed "ordering moments."[2] These are moments when dramatic change happens rapidly. They are rare, and brief, but extremely significant. In conceptualizing them, the theory of "punctuated equilibrium" from evolutionary biology may be helpful.[3] This theory, as developed by Stephen Jay Gould and Niles Eldredge, maintains that great changes do not evolve slowly.[4] Rather, after extended periods of stasis, they appear rapidly, but then give way to a new stasis.[5] The theory is not uncontroversial, and has received a number of challenges.[6] It provides, however, a useful means of understanding moments of contingency and dramatic change as punctuational moments, demanding policy responses. Once leaders make their choices in an immediate response to the punctuational event, they thereby choose a path that largely determines and shapes subsequent events.[7]

The Contingent Events of November 9, 1989

How did the punctuational event under study here—the opening of the Berlin Wall—happen on the night of November 9? A number of historical accounts mistakenly assume that there was a conscious decision on the part of the leaders of the German Democratic Republic (GDR, or East Germany) to do so.[8] The evidence, however, shows that the opening was an unplanned and highly contingent event. It was also one of the best stories to emerge from the Cold War. How did it happen?

In fall 1989, the ruling East German Socialist Unity Party (or SED, as it was known in German) still believed that it could ride out Gorbymania—international enthusiasm for the liberalization in the Soviet Bloc endorsed by its leader, Mikhail Gorbachev—by offering a few concessions but basically holding on to its repressive ways. In contrast, the East German population kept turning out in increasingly large numbers in street protests to demand real liberalization. These protests were a counterpart to the massive emigration to the West flowing over the Hungarian border (opened in August) but with an important difference: the protesters wanted to force change at home, not flee. None of them dreamed how quickly change would come, in the form of a historical accident on November 9, 1989.

In an effort to appease the crowds without actually conceding very much, the SED, under its leader Egon Krenz, decided to issue "new" travel regulations in early November 1989. However, these "new" rules still included the fine print that had always prevented foreign travel. East Germans had, in theory, always enjoyed the right to leave their country. The GDR had a written constitution and it included this right de jure; but de facto "national security" exceptions—still in place in the November 1989 regulations—stopped the exercise of that right. Partly for this reason, when formulating the "new" rules, no one in the SED bothered to discuss such seemingly basic issues as consulting the Soviets about opening the border, or even informing the border guards. The latter omission would have particularly fateful consequences. In short, there were no signs that anyone realized that the new regulations were actually going to open the Berlin Wall immediately.[9]

On the evening of November 9, at 6:00 p.m., a member of the East German Politburo, who also served as its media spokesman, Günter Schabowski, was scheduled to hold a press conference. Shortly before it began, he received a piece of paper with an update on the "new" travel rules and the suggestion that he mention them publicly. Schabowski had not been present at the discussions about these rules and did not have time to read them carefully before he had to begin his appearance before the media. The Politburo had only very recently started holding press conferences—also as a means to assuage the anger of the crowds—and Schabowski was clearly unskilled at them. Neither he nor anyone else in the Soviet Bloc had ever had any incentive to develop skills in managing the media, and it showed that night.

Schabowski's hour-long press conference was, for fifty-five minutes, an exercise in tedium and boredom. He mumbled through a number of uninteresting announcements. U.S. television anchorman Tom Brokaw, who had travelled to East Berlin to be present and to interview Schabowski afterward, remembered that he was so "bored" that he nodded off at points. Then, just as it was about to end, an Italian journalist's question about travel seemed to spur Schabowski's memory about the piece of paper that he needed to read aloud.

In response to the Italian reporter, the East German spokesman picked up the paper that he had been given just before the start of the press conference and tried to summarize its unfamiliar contents. He did so in a wordy and confused fashion. His incomplete sentences mostly trailed off incoherently. However, sprinkled among his long-winded phrases—"Anyway, today, as far as I know, a decision has been made, it is a recommendation of the Politburo that has been taken up, that one should from the draft of a travel law, take out a passage"—there were unclear but exciting snippets like "exit via border crossings" and "possible for every citizen."

Schabowski was surprised to see that every journalist in the room suddenly wanted to ask questions: "When does that go into force?" shouted a reporter. "Excuse me?" Schabowski replied, puzzled. "Immediately?" shouted someone else before he could answer. The Politburo spokesman became visibly unsettled and irritated. He started flipping through the papers in front of him and looking helplessly to colleagues in the room in search of an answer. Someone shouted out the question again: "When does that go into force?" Clearly rattled and mumbling to himself as he tried to concentrate on his disorderly papers, Schabowski uttered the phrase "immediately, right away."

Years later, Brokaw still remembered that it felt as if "a signal had come from outer space and electrified the room." Commotion ensued. Some wire journalists rushed out to file reports, having heard enough. The race was now on to be the first to report what they thought they had heard, and every minute counted.

The journalists still in the room shouted out a number of questions. Someone yelled: "What will happen to the Berlin Wall now?" Seriously alarmed, Schabowski decided to switch to damage control mode and stop saying anything else that might cause trouble. He replied: "It is 7:00 p.m. This is the last question." Evasively, he wrapped up the misbegotten press conference by waffling: "The question of travel, of the permeability therefore of the wall from our side, does not yet answer, exclusively, the question of the meaning, of this, let me say it this way, fortified border of the GDR." In a belated attempt to make clear that the matter was unresolved, he added that any discussion of the border required that "many other factors . . . must be taken into consideration." In particular "the debate over these questions could be positively influenced if the Federal Republic and if NATO would commit themselves to and carry out disarmament."

His attempt to pour cold water on this speculation about the Wall came too late, though. Already by 7:03 p.m., the first wire journalists had reported the most favorable possible interpretation: the Berlin Wall was open. One of the main West German television channels, ARD, had to decide what to broadcast on its evening news show at 8:00 p.m. At first, the show decided to take a relatively cautious approach, guessing that the Wall "should become permeable." For its big news program at 10:30 p.m., however—briefly delayed that evening to 10:42 p.m. by a late-running soccer match—the ARD staff decided to gamble on a bigger claim. The moderator, a man named Hanns Friedrichs, solemnly intoned at the opening of the show: "This ninth of November is a historic day." East Germany "has announced that, starting immediately, its borders are open to everyone." He announced this despite the fact that attempts to find exciting images from Berlin to broadcast failed.

East Germans had the ability to watch Western shows such as this one and listen to radio reports, despite the fact that doing so was theoretically forbidden. Hearing such coverage in the early evening and then seeing increasingly more confident announcements like that of Friedrichs' later broadcast, East Germans became convinced that they could in fact cross the border. As a result, the Cold War division of Germany ended sometime around 11:30 p.m. on the night of November 9.

Where and how did it end? It happened not at the Brandenburg Gate but at the Bornholmer Street border crossing in East Berlin. No prominent American or Soviet officials were there; indeed, no senior representatives of any of the four occupying powers, still in Germany as a result of World War II, were present, nor were there East or West German politicians.

Senior border guard Harald Jäger was there, however. He had been on the job since 1964 and had never dreamed that what was about to happen was even possible.[10] He was inside the station that night, on the job as usual, eating dinner during his late shift and watching Schabowski's press conference on television. What he heard just before 7:00 p.m. made him choke on his food. He was shocked by Schabowski's remarks, which came as news to him. After telling his fellow guards that Schabowski's words were "deranged bullshit," Jäger started calling around to find out if anyone knew what was going on. Superior officers assured him that travel remained blocked as always. Within half an hour, however, Jäger and his team were busy trying to wave back would-be crossers, telling them that the border was not open.

The guards even received reinforcement. A police van with a loudspeaker pulled up and started announcing the same message. The crowds just kept swelling. An enormous group of agitated people amassed, and the situation grew increasingly ugly. Jäger and his colleagues were armed and in theory could use deadly force if they chose. Oral orders to avoid bloodshed had circulated among some border guards earlier that fall, but now they were heavily outnumbered and police efforts to dispel the crowd were failing. Moreover, this situation was repeating itself at other checkpoints: the guards at the Invaliden Street crossing called up reinforcements—forty-five men armed with machine guns. The situation was fraught with danger.

It was at Bornholmer Street that events came to a head. In the hopes of easing the pressure, and after more useless phone calls, Jäger and his team started to let a trickle of people through, a few at a time. They would check each person individually, take names, and then refuse the rowdiest reentry later; the sign that border crossers should be kept out was a stamp placed directly on the face of their passport photos. Jäger and his fellow guards managed this for a couple of hours, by which time the overwhelming crowd was ominously chanting "open the gate, open the gate!"

By the time that Friedrichs was going on air just before 11:00 p.m., the border guards at Bornholmer Street were realizing that their plan was not working. The crowds kept growing larger and more menacing. After more phone calls and debate among themselves, Jäger and his fellow guards decided that the only course of action other than mass violence was to open the barriers, and Jäger told his men to do so. A massive surge ensued. Later, Jäger would estimate that several thousand people had pushed their way out within just thirty minutes. The division of Germany was over.

Other border crossings opened in the course of the night in much the same way: individual guards, fearing the crowds and unable to get clear instructions, decided to raise the traffic barriers. And every opening meant more people flooding into the West in front of cameras, which meant more images beamed back into the East, which in turn sent more people out into the streets to see for themselves; it became a self-reinforcing feedback loop. Fortunately for those crossing, nearly every senior East German official was locked in crisis meetings and the senior Russians were asleep. As a result, those who might have ordered bloody reprisals were uninformed and unaware. No resistance was organized that night, although futile orders to reseal part of the border were issued in the next few days.

Washington and Bonn Respond

How did the two most important groups of Western foreign policymakers—the U.S. and West German governments—experience these events? What happened in the immediate aftermath of the Wall's opening? It is important to look at *both* Washington *and* Bonn, since, as mentioned before, the U.S. foreign policy response that emerged was closely coordinated with West Germany. The evidence shows that, unsurprisingly, leaders in both countries viewed the Wall's opening with a mixture of shock, happiness, and deep concern.

On November 9, Kohl was in Poland for a visit meant to mark the fiftieth anniversary of the start of the Nazi occupation. Neither Bonn nor Warsaw could ignore the tragic anniversary of the start of World War II, so they organized a West German state visit to promote improved German-Polish relations in the future.

At the state dinner that evening Kohl got confirmation that something was definitely happening at the Wall. He seems to have realized immediately that he was on the verge of what could potentially be the biggest crisis of his chancellorship. As a student of history, he was not about to make the same mistake that his predecessor Konrad Adenauer had made. On the advice of the Western allies, Adenauer had not gone to Berlin in 1961 in the midst of his own major crisis, when the Wall went up. The elder chancellor had endured heated criticism for staying away from the scene of the action, and Kohl did not want to face the same reaction. Kohl decided that he had to go back—not to divided Berlin, but rather to Bonn.

He decided that he had to find a way to extract himself from Poland without insulting his hosts. Even as he attempted to do so, however, Kohl got more unsettling news. The mayor of West Berlin, Walter Momper, a member of the opposing Social Democratic Party of Germany (SPD), had organized the first major press event for 4:30 p.m. that very afternoon. It would be held at the Schöneberg Rathaus, or town hall, in West Berlin—the location where U.S. president John F. Kennedy had famously spoken in 1963. Missing it would make Kohl and his party, the Christian Democratic Union (CDU), seem as though they were not in control of events. Horst Teltschik, Kohl's most trusted adviser on foreign and security policy, thought that was precisely the point of holding the event on short notice with the chancellor out of the country. With difficulty, they managed to make it back to West Berlin in time.[11]

When he finally got on stage, the chancellor had to face a wave of catcalls and boos from the audience. West Berlin was known for its vocal and active left-wing political organizations as well as its regional pride. Even if it had been a less dramatic moment, a left-wing West Berlin rally would not have been an event at which a conservative Catholic politician (that is, Kohl) would be welcome. Now, with emotions running high, the audience had no patience for him whatsoever. The crowd tried to drive him off the stage with continuous noise.

Ignoring their deafening catcalls, Kohl focused on the millions who would be watching on television, both in East Germany and foreign capitals. "I would like to call out to everyone in the GDR: You are not alone! We stand at your side! We are and will remain one nation, and we belong together!" It had been a long time since a leader of West Germany had spoken that way, and it signalled what Kohl's response was going to be.

Washington was listening. Just like Kohl, Bush and his advisers were trying to make sense of what had happened. Secretary of State James Baker got the news about the Berlin Wall as he was hosting Philippine president Corazon Aquino at a luncheon. Soon thereafter, he began receiving pages of press reports from around the world. Baker wrote on top of them in thick black pen a phrase—"Europe whole and free"—that had been the theme of a major address by Bush given in Mainz in May 1989. The administration would repeat it often in the wake of the opening of the Berlin Wall, considering it a better idea than Gorbachev's "common European home" in which the Americans had no room.

Baker spoke multiple times with the U.S. ambassador in Bonn, Vernon Walters, who assured him that the situation remained peaceful. As all of this was going on, Baker made time to appear on a number of television shows, partly to counteract what commentators were calling a lackluster response from Bush himself. Lesley Stahl, interviewing President Bush on the CBS Evening News on November 9, was puzzled by his lack of jubilation. "You don't seem elated and I'm wondering if you're thinking of the problems," she had asked. Bush had responded, "I'm not an emotional guy, but I'm very pleased." He had admitted that developments had caught him by surprise and had said that he was determined not to incite a Soviet backlash by acting in a triumphalist manner.

The administration was in fact trying hard to figure out exactly what its policy response should be. Upon coming into office earlier that year it had decided to slow down the rapid pace of change that had characterized the end of the Reagan era. As Robert Hutchings, a National Security Council member under Bush, put it, an "entirely new team came in, representing foreign policy approaches fundamentally at odds with those of the Reagan administration." Although many commentators had used the phrase, there was in fact "no such thing as a 'Reagan-Bush' foreign policy. Before 1989 there was Reagan; afterwards there was Bush."[12] Indeed, some scholars have used the Reagan-Bush transition as a prime example of how vicious an intraparty White House handover can be. As one transition expert noted, "George H. W. Bush fired everybody."[13] There was a sense in 1989 that Reaganite wild-eyed idealism about nuclear disarmament and relations with Moscow had started to outstrip practical realities, and now the time for sober policy making had returned. Gates found that not only Reagan but also his secretary of state, George Shultz, "had sped past both the U.S. military's analysis of the strategic implications and the ability of U.S. intelligence" in their bid for glory before the clock ran out on their administration in 1988.[14]

Now that it was their watch, Bush and Baker wondered whether there was any reason that the United States should continue to support the Soviet desire to change the status quo. As Baker wrote in a summary of U.S.-Soviet relations in early 1989, the Russians "have to make hard choices. We do Gorbachev no favors when we make it easier to avoid choices." Baker believed that necessity had been the mother of virtue in Gorbachev's case: "He made a choice in Afghanistan because he saw the need for it. He made a choice in arms control because there was a need for it." Baker kept these thoughts private, but Secretary of Defense Richard Cheney told CNN bluntly that Gorbachev would "ultimately fail." Eduard Shevardnadze later responded to Cheney's comments by calling them unsurprising: "I know that the Secretary of Defense needs money. How would he finance his defense programs if there were no Soviet threat?"[15]

Contemporaries nonetheless soon sensed the differences between Reagan and Bush. In a one-on-one meeting in June 1989, Kohl and Gorbachev compared the two presidents, to the benefit of the latter. Kohl recalled meeting Reagan when the former actor was still a presidential candidate in 1979. Helmut Schmidt, the West German chancellor at the time, had refused to meet the American because he considered it a waste of an hour. Kohl, however, made time to see Reagan, and was deeply disappointed by the experience. Reagan, he was shocked to discover, "knew practically nothing about Europe." Kohl asked himself at the time "what consequences that would have." The situation with Bush was "completely different," fortunately. "To a great extent, Bush sees many problems with European eyes . . . he understands more about Europe than Reagan."[16]

The differences between the Reagan and Bush approaches became obvious on February 15, 1989. On that date, Bush announced that he was calling for a large interagency study on U.S. foreign policy, known as National Security Review 3.[17] This announcement served to manage expectations because it bought the new administration a few months of time during which both domestic and foreign audiences knew they should not expect anything. It sent a clear message that the Bush administration was not as interested as the Reagan administration had been in thawing Cold War relations with the Soviet Union.

In policy terms it produced little. Gates admitted later that "there was never much expectation that the policy reviews would result in a dramatic departure." Brent Scowcroft, the national security adviser, found the whole exercise to be a big disappointment. He began working on a replacement study immediately thereafter.[18] And Baker, who agreed that the result of the review was useless "mush," assigned the blame for its failure to the fact that it "was run by Reagan holdovers . . . these officials found themselves incapable of truly thinking things anew."[19] Yet Gates defended this much-criticized exercise on one account: precisely because of its failure to produce any new initiatives or approaches, the top-level officials in the Bush administration knew that they would have to come up with them personally. As a result, policy would come solely from "Bush, Baker, Scowcroft, and their respective inner circles working in harness together."[20]

Strategy in the Face of Uncertainty in 1989–90

In early 1989, the administration had intentionally stepped back. This cautious attitude initially put the United States on the back foot during the drama of fall 1989, but it was obvious to all senior leaders in Washington that the opening of the Wall was a dramatic event—a punctuational moment, although that phrase was not used at the time—that would demand a strategic U.S. response. After the initial surprise, Bush signalled that his preferred approach was to work closely with Bonn and indeed follow its lead.

Bush indicated to Kohl that he agreed with the latter's plans to push for unification as rapidly as possible, as long as a united Germany remained in NATO.[21] The two men discussed the challenges involved in person in December 1989, when they met on the fringes of a NATO summit, then subsequently on the phone, and then in person once again at a bilateral meeting at Camp David in February 1990. This February summit represented the first time that a West German chancellor had been given the honor of an invitation to Camp David, which allowed visiting leaders to have more extensive personal contact with the president and his family than a White House visit. During the visit, Bush and Kohl came to the conclusion that they would be able to convince Gorbachev to allow a unified Germany to become part of NATO, but that the Soviet leader would want to be paid for it. "It will come down in the end to a question of cash," Kohl predicted to Bush at Camp David. The president replied that Kohl and West Germany had "deep pockets," meaning presumably that they could handle paying the necessary price.[22] As Gates would later summarize matters, Bonn and Washington had realized that their best strategy was "to bribe the Soviets out" of East Germany using the wealth of West Germany.[23]

U.S. foreign-policy makers could have chosen differently. The last major transatlantic ordering moment at the end of World War II had resulted—after numerous false starts and debates—in a policy oriented toward inclusion where possible. Although it evolved haphazardly, Washington ultimately settled on a policy that assigned priority to the integration of defeated enemies, particularly occupied regions of Germany, into structures that would cooperate with the West. Ultimately, this belief resulted in the Marshall Plan and, later, West German integration into the military alliance of NATO.[24]

In 1989–90, however, Washington's aim was to capitalize on the unexpected opportunity at the expense of the dying USSR. Obviously, the situation in 1989–90 was different from the 1940s. There had been no superpower shooting war, and no new enemy comparable to the Soviet Union arose to concentrate the minds of U.S. foreign-policy makers. But the example of the post–World War II era remained. There may not have been an equivalent to Stalin in 1989, but there was the example of success in the past. Indeed, historians Campbell Craig and Fredrik Logevall call the Marshall Plan "the most successful single foreign policy initiative ever undertaken by the United States."[25] Had those in charge of U.S. foreign policy in 1989–90 been more inspired by the history of U.S. policy making, they might have emphasized the integration of their Cold War enemy into post–Cold War structures.

One way to work with Gorbachev and to integrate a former foe into a comprehensive settlement might have been to create alternatives for collective European security. In 1990, Gorbachev persistently tried to interest Bonn and Washington in new political and economic structures that would include the United States, Western and Eastern Europe, and the USSR. The evidence shows, however, that Gorbachev's thinking stayed vague, and he was dealing with too many problems at home to focus his attention on making them more specific. Indeed, one of the very reasons that Bonn and Washington intentionally picked up the pace was precisely because they feared such plans might begin to come into focus. In order to prevent Gorbachev and his aides from getting their bearings and thinking through the future more carefully, they intentionally kept moving at a breakneck rate, and thereby succeeded in keeping Moscow off balance.[26]

Baker consistently advised the president that there was no reason to help the Soviet Union solve its own problems. Bush agreed, and made clear to Kohl during the Camp David summit in February 1990 how he felt about the idea of the West doing more to help Gorbachev and the USSR: "To hell with that! We prevailed, they didn't. We can't let the Soviets clutch victory from the jaws of defeat."[27] Although undoubtedly an accurate analysis, such an attitude did not assign priority to the integration of the USSR into post–Cold War institutions.

There were many twists and turns along the way, but Bonn and Washington ultimately achieved the goals agreed upon in February 1990. Over the next six months Kohl secured permission from Moscow for Germany to unify rapidly and within NATO. In return, Bonn—not Washington—provided Moscow with aid in the form of billions of deutsche marks to help shore up the crumbling Soviet economy and Gorbachev's crumbling political position. Gorbachev proved to be unable to save himself; but the dramatic events of 1991, namely the August "coup" and the December dissolution of the USSR, did not affect German unification. It had already been accomplished by the time of Gorbachev's departure from office.

The Legacy of the Punctuational Moment of 1989–90 for 2001

Fifteen years after the Wall opened, in another punctuational moment— September 11, 2001—policymakers looked backward to find reasons why the attack had succeeded. The *9/11 Commission Report* concluded that "the national security institutions of the U.S. government are still the institutions constructed to win the Cold War."[28] The report meant this remark as a critique, but the survival of Cold War institutions beyond the end of the conflict that created them was not an accidental oversight. It was the result of concerted effort on the part of Bonn and Washington in 1990 to ensure that old structures, rather than new post–Cold War institutions, not only survived but also dominated the post–Cold War era.

In maintaining these institutions, Bonn and Washington defended them against a number of calls for new international security structures. Gorbachev had not been the only one to call for new institutions. Both elite political leaders (such as French president François Mitterrand) and popular groups (such as the pacifist dissidents who had caused the revolutionary events in the first place) proposed either significantly changing old or creating new collective security institutions.[29] Working together, Bonn and Washington successfully outmaneuvered such plans. Of course, the new institutions would not have automatically prevented the attacks of September 11, 2001; but the old ones—the ones that failed in 2001 and which were the object of criticism in the *9/11 Commission Report*—were a conscious policy choice.

This outcome did not have to be the result of the opening of the Berlin Wall. The punctuational moment of November 9, 1989, demonstrated that the Cold War order had ended. Of course, it had not ended all at once; the opening of the Wall revealed that long-term trends had come to fruition. But once the Berlin Wall was open, it was no longer possible to deny the changes. The collapse of that order required a response: either the creation of a new order or the reassertion of the old.[30] Unlike 1945, American leaders in 1990 sought to maintain established structures rather than create new ones. There are no serious parallels in 1990 to the creation of the United Nations, the Marshall Plan, or, a few years later, NATO.

Of course, it is always easier to judge events in hindsight. The events of November 9 were fraught with uncertainty and risk. Both Bush and Kohl worried greatly about potentially violent outcomes, if East German troops or secret police were to seek protection with the occupying Soviet forces. Whether the Soviet troops would fire on German civilians, and whether or not Gorbachev could control his military, were open questions. Experimentation with new security institutions while violence threatened and Gorbachev's hold on power grew ever more tenuous did not seem like a desirable idea. The decisions and actions of Bonn and Washington were understandable and, indeed, successful.

But as Baker himself has pointed out, "almost every achievement contains within its success the seeds of a future problem."[31] He was right. As a result of Bonn and Washington's preferences, the basic security institutions remained throughout the 1990s very much as the *9/11 Commission Report* described them in 2004. In other words, the U.S. foreign policy response to the punctuation of the Wall's collapse was an energetic effort to ensure the perpetuation of Cold War institutions, specifically NATO, in the post–Cold War world. This successful effort ensured that institutions that the United States dominated would continue to play a significant role in international order. Although the institutions themselves changed and expanded, the fact of their existence was no longer in doubt after 1990. The possibilities for change inherent in the punctuational moment faded.

Conclusion: Looking Forward

What insights from the brief analysis provided here are potentially useful to U.S. policy making in future punctuational moments? There are three in particular. The first is that the time period in which critical decisions can be made is extremely brief. Such decisions arise, of necessity, in immediate response to a crisis; the U.S. government could hardly fail to respond to the fall of the Wall. The actors or institutions capable of quickly advancing a coherent vision after a crisis arises therefore have an advantage, regardless of whether that vision is suitable or not as a crisis response. Second, in times of dramatic and unexpected change, critical decisions about the future of U.S. foreign policy often emerge not as the result of thoughtful deliberation but in haste and in response to external pressures; once sanctioned, they become very hard to change. Third, punctuational moments show the power of chance and contingency. Great events, and great shifts in U.S. foreign policy, do not necessarily arise from long-term causes. If the severely sleep-deprived East German press spokesman had continued to forget for five more minutes to mention the "new" travel regulations, the Berlin Wall would not have opened on the night of November 9. Of course, the Berlin Wall would have opened eventually, but not as easily, not for free, not when all Soviet and East German leaders of any significance were incommunicado or asleep, and not at a time when a cooperation-minded Gorbachev still had sufficient authority to manage the Soviet reaction before his authority and the state he governed dissolved. But the Wall did open. Thanks to the mumbling of the Politburo member giving the press conference on the night of November 9, journalists believed that the Wall was open. The combination of their over-eager reporting with the willingness of the East German population to risk a trip to the Wall, not the conscious decision of their dictatorial leaders, led to an unexpectedly swift and peaceful end to the Cold War division of Europe.

When thinking about strategic planning it is worth remembering that U.S. decision makers will not control the punctuational moments. These moments arise independently of U.S. will and they provide fleeting opportunities for major institutional shifts. The events of 1989–90 demonstrate that crises are terrible things to waste; they constitute rare chances for dramatic change.

2

AN ARCHITECTURE OF U.S. STRATEGY AFTER THE COLD WAR

Robert B. Zoellick

This chapter, adapted from a speech, offers my perspective about strategy and policy at the end of the Cold War. Governments, of course, act as a collective. My thoughts are those of just one participant, although they were shared by others in varying degrees. Future historians and policymakers can provide a more independent assessment of the influence of these ideas and their consequences.

By and large, historians of the end of the Cold War have concentrated on political-security matters, with a narrow geographic focus on the European and transatlantic theaters. I will include political economy dimensions as well as U.S. policies toward the Asia-Pacific and Western Hemisphere.

The strategic concept we sought to advance in 1989 integrated foreign, security, economic, business, and trade policies. The approach reflected six principal ideas.

First, the strategy adopted by the United States between 1989 and 1992 sought to link security and economic interests within a political framework. It was based on U.S. interests. It valued open societies. It sought to foster economic growth and opportunity. And it promoted the development of institutions, regimes, and alliances that could evolve to meet changing circumstances. This approach was a continuation of the post–World War II tradition of U.S. international engagement through multilateral institutions, alliances, and frameworks for partnerships.

Second, the strategic framework was linked to but not constrained by a geographic perspective. With an emphasis on a North American base, which had not been a U.S. priority since early in the twentieth century, the strategy attempted to bolster development and democracy in the Western Hemisphere, a goal of U.S. policy in the nineteenth century. The strategy acknowledged the need to transform transatlantic relations in order to maintain strong ties between the United States and a more integrated and enlarged European Union. It recognized the growing importance of the Asia-Pacific region. In the aftermath of the first Persian Gulf War, the administration also sought to utilize economic development as a tool to improve security in the Middle East and Persian Gulf region, and there were renewed efforts to pursue this course in George W. Bush's administration.

Third, the strategy at the end of the Cold War recognized shifts in power—economic and political as well as military. It anticipated the rising importance of the Asia-Pacific region, a trend that is obvious in 2009 but which was not a foregone conclusion in 1989. The strategy also perceived an opportunity for the Western Hemisphere to play a more significant role in the global political economy. And it recognized that a Europe whole and free had the potential to be a new power not only in Europe's borderlands, but in other regions as well.

Fourth, this was a multilateralist strategy. But it did not view multilateralism solely through the lens of United Nations structures or hierarchies. This multilateral model sought to position the United States at the center of intersecting political, security, military, and economic networks. The approach sought to build partnerships and encouraged shared responsibility that would be fostered through institutions, treaties, political accords, customs of behavior, and even negotiated rules. UN bodies—the Security Council, specialized agencies, the General Assembly—were part of this network, but not "monopolists of multilateralism." The concept of sharing responsibility through multilateral networks was the seed of the "responsible stakeholder" idea I later developed for China and other emerging powers at the start of the twenty-first century.

Fifth, the international strategy was connected to the "home front." The goal was to help Americans adapt to change and compete in what was becoming a globalized economy. A sustainable foreign policy strategy requires a mutually supportive interconnection between the international and domestic agendas. Sustainable and successful U.S. foreign policy strategies have combined the pursuit of interests and the promotion of values. This strategy would seek to draw the American public's attention to evolving international interests—including security, but ranging beyond—by emphasizing agreements and institutions to further regional and global ties. Values were advanced through economic openness and development guided by the rule of law and democracy.

Sixth, the strategy built in adaptive flexibility—not only for governments, but also for private parties and individuals. It recognized that political and economic liberties lead to innovations and developments that governments cannot foresee. These changes need to be integrated into a flexible system, with institutional adaptation. In a sense, the approach tried to reconcile Friedrich von Hayek's "spontaneous order" of markets with international governmental cooperation.

Reuniting Europe and Modernizing a Transatlantic Community

As the Cold War was ending in 1989, U.S. officials were at a great disadvantage compared to subsequent scholars: We could not be sure that the Cold War was in fact ending! Therefore, we needed to navigate through a sea of dramatic changes, while being prepared to adjust to "counterrevolutionary" winds and even storms. Circumstances required us to articulate our plans and expectations clearly and directly, despite uncertainties. We had to explain what we were seeking to do, with different time frames, to a variety of publics: Germans, East and West; Central and Eastern Europeans; Western Europeans; Americans; and, of course, the Soviets. Stating policy directions and goals to broader publics was important because the momentum for our diplomacy in 1989–90 came from publics in the Federal Republic of Germany (FRG), the German Democratic Republic (GDR), and Central and Eastern European countries.[1] The United States had to move quickly to deal with fast-paced events. At the same time, we were seeking to steer a course in a constructive way within a strategic context. And the course we were steering had to be flexible enough to allow for adjustments for events we could not foresee.

We were thinking in terms of changing architectures and structures. But we had to lay the foundation for new possibilities while the ground was still being shaken by political earthquakes. Some ideas took hold; others did not. We needed "feedback" loops to build on the positive, discard false starts, and modify tactics as needed. Policy implementation could not be on "autopilot."

The strategy drew on three existing but changing institutions. The first was the North Atlantic Treaty Organization (NATO), the primary security link between North America and Europe. NATO emphasized security, not just defense, and was not a traditional alliance. NATO is an alliance and partnership that is based on common values as well as interests, and its missions need to evolve as the challenges facing that democratic security community change. Second, the European Community (EC), then on its way to becoming the European Union (EU), was a critical piece of the strategic architecture. And third, the Conference on Security and Cooperation in Europe (CSCE), which later became the Organization for Security and Cooperation in Europe (OSCE), offered a wider geographical reach that included the Soviet Union.

Why did we think in terms of structures? It was partly a lesson drawn from their absence in the breakdown in the 1920s and 1930s. We also recognized that patterns of partnership could be reinforced by norms of behavior and customs of cooperation that help manage military, economic, and political integration. Institutions and processes can reduce the cost of cooperative action. They do so by helping participants share information and prepare possible responses in advance. They help build a sense of mutual interest. And they can encourage negotiations and mediation of differences, which are inevitable, even among the closest partners.

Moreover, these existing institutions reflected democratic values that stemmed from the Cold War struggle. We believed that these values should guide the world in the future.

Secretary of State James Baker gave a speech in Berlin in December 1989 titled "A New Europe, a New Atlanticism: Architecture for a New Era." The title is a good example of our strategic perspective. We recognized that a unified Germany needed to take its place within a free and integrated Europe, a Europe that remained part of a transatlantic partnership. The strategic perspective in Secretary Baker's speech focused on Central and Eastern Europe, a unified Germany firmly anchored in Europe, and the Soviet Union's interest in a prosperous, peaceful, and secure Europe.

The speech was a diplomatic tactic as well as a strategy. It was designed to reassure other countries at a moment when Germany seemed to be in a headlong rush to unify. Yet the speech was also intended to reassure the German people of our commitment to unification, and to establish the United States as a leader in ideas as well as influence. Although our approach sought to achieve these objectives in the near term, we tried to design it in a way that could adapt to medium- and longer-term change.

The strategy presented in the speech emphasized four core ideas. First, the future needed to respect free men and women who would create free governments. Self-determination was going to be crucial to supporting German unification. Backing self-determination by the German people as well as the populations of Central and Eastern European countries would also provide the United States with diplomatic leverage vis-à-vis the Soviet Union.

Second, we needed to change NATO's role and the perception of it by past foes. We stressed NATO's political and security dimension over its military purpose, while making clear that a future U.S. military presence in Europe, which many Europeans wanted, depended on NATO. Therefore, we suggested NATO play a key role in the negotiation and verification of the Conventional Forces in Europe (CFE) Treaty, in other arms control negotiations and verification for weapons of mass destruction, in cooperation on regional conflicts, and even in political and economic issues. The attention to weapons of mass destruction and regional conflicts looks prescient today.

Further, in 1990 the U.S. and German governments recommended creating the North Atlantic Cooperation Council (NACC) to enable NATO to reach out to Central and Eastern Europe. Our thought was to assist these states to become partners of NATO and potentially members. The next administration let NACC wither. But they eventually revived it with a different name: the Partnership for Peace (PfP), which has become the pathway to NATO membership for former members of the Warsaw Pact.

Third, we called for an enlarged and more integrated European Community. As events turned out, French president François Mitterrand worked with Jacques Delors, president of the European Commission, to urge Germany and others to create a European Union to bind a united Germany more closely to its neighbors.

In 1989, there was considerable uncertainty in the U.S. government about deeper European integration. At that time, the main idea driving European integration was the creation of a single European market by 1992. For President George H. W. Bush, 1992 would also be the year of his reelection campaign. President Bush was concerned that the European single market could turn out to be a protectionist exercise. In 1989, there were anxieties about the dangers of a "fortress Europe" that could undermine liberalization of the international economy. The late Manfred Wörner, the well-respected German secretary-general of NATO and also a strong believer in European integration, played an important role in allaying President Bush's worries. He explained how concerns about a unified Germany among its neighbors could be eased by firmly connecting Germany into a deeper European integration. Nevertheless, this course created tension with Margaret Thatcher, who was concerned about German unification but did not wish to use deeper European integration as a complementary means of reassurance.

We recognized that Central and Eastern Europe would offer an opportunity for an enlarged EC. I also suspected that the single European market would actually open the EC to more competition, as it indeed has done.

As the EC integrated and enlarged, it was my hope that the United States could keep pace with the institutional changes accompanying European integration. The United States should have special ties with the EC/EU and its new institutions as well as with its member states. Therefore, in his Berlin speech in December 1989, Secretary Baker called for a new treaty to achieve stronger institutional and consultative ties between the United States and the changing EC.

Most Europeans seemed to welcome stronger U.S.-EC ties, which they viewed as affirming the importance of Europe's integration and institutions.

President Mitterrand, however, resisted this idea, because he was concerned about the United States being too closely connected to (and influential with) European institutions. Nevertheless, working with Italy, which held the European presidency, we completed a U.S.-EC framework accord that was to be announced at the 1990 Paris CSCE summit. At the summit, President Mitterrand insisted on paring back the language, but we worked with the Italians to preserve a procedural accord. The framework called for a series of consultations at different levels to achieve common aims, with the most important being two summits a year between the U.S. president and the presidents of the European Council and the European Commission. In recent years, the United States has reduced this to an annual summit.

U.S.-EU cooperation continues today, for example with the European Central Bank, European Council, European Commission, and European Parliament. EU enlargement has also broadened the perspectives of countries within a deeply integrated Europe to include a wider region.

Fourth, Secretary Baker's speech used the CSCE to describe a broader notion of security. We were trying to reach out to the Soviet Union in order to avoid a "Versailles victory" at the end of the Cold War: a success that would invite its own destruction. We also needed to counter initiatives such as Gorbachev's "Common European Home," which marginalized the United States in Europe. This idea had some backing in France. Yet the CSCE component of the architecture was not just a focus on interests or power. Baker's speech suggested we should build on the CSCE's record with human rights, support elections with observers, encourage confidence-building measures for security, and expand economic ties. The OSCE did eventually take on some of these tasks, although its role waned in the years that followed.

Some revisionist historians have suggested that a "Third Way" should have eliminated the Cold War institutions and started anew.[2] Despite the dreams of East German protest leaders in 1989–90, the GDR's population wanted to be part of the West and not part of a Third Way experiment. Moreover, the geopolitical consequences of a neutral Germany, a new Mitteleuropa, were frightening to the rest of Europe. There is also a principled objection to these critics: What is wrong with Western democracy and market economics? Why not build on those values as advanced and safeguarded by Western institutions? Why not utilize them and modify those institutions as appropriate? This might be called an American "constitutionalist" perspective: build on frameworks and then adapt them, while benefiting from the cohesion and customs that those constitutions and traditions create.

There was also a powerful logic for the EC to enlarge. Despite some tensions, the EU's enlargement has been one of the great late-twentieth-century successes.

An enlarged NATO has offered a broader security in transatlantic relations. We definitely rejected the notion that Central and Eastern Europe should be left as a buffer zone between the West and the East. Our aim was to overcome the ideological division of the Cold War through supporting open, democratic, market economies, while recognizing national interests would still differ and require mediation and compromises. Today, NATO faces the larger tests of mission and purpose, some of which we were anticipating in 1989.

Finally, I hope scholars will recall that during the twentieth century "revolutionary visions" have led to terrible outcomes. Edmund Burke's cautions bear recalling: the legal, economic, and democratic traditions of the transatlantic partnership, while always in need of reexamination and extension, should not be lightly cast aside for well-intentioned utopias.

The revisionists' reveries also should not obscure large changes that were taking place within the traditional structures. For example, in May 1989 President Bush made a very far-reaching proposal to reduce conventional forces through a CFE treaty. It was so ambitious that the chairman of the Joint Chiefs of Staff, Admiral William J. Crowe, opposed it.

Until 1989, nuclear weapons had been the central focus of arms control negotiations. The received wisdom stemming from the Mutual and Balanced Force Reduction (MBFR) talks left people exceedingly skeptical about counting tanks and armored personnel carriers. But President Bush's initiative went to the heart of the logic for nuclear deterrence in Europe. His premise was that it would be easier to reduce and perhaps even eliminate nuclear forces in Europe if NATO and Warsaw Pact conventional forces levels were slashed to much lower and equal levels.[3] In addition, since we wanted to support calls for change in Germany and Central and Eastern Europe, what better way to show change than by getting the Soviet forces to go home after forty years?

Of course, the offer of extending transatlantic and European structures to the East had to be seized by others. We could encourage them, and we could create incentives, but ultimately other countries and peoples had to decide. The violent breakup of Yugoslavia showed that some people chose a different and disastrous path. Ironically, those states now look to the EU and NATO for the opportunity and security first offered twenty years ago. Indeed, the potential positive influence of the EU, NATO, and OSCE continues today, for Russia, Ukraine, and others in Eurasia.

At the 1990 G-7 Economic Summit, the G-7 leaders encouraged Russia to work with the International Monetary Fund (IMF) and the World Bank. In 1991–92, Presidents Mikhail Gorbachev and later Boris Yeltsin attended the G-7, which became the G-8 (though today it is being overtaken by the G-20).

Russia's economic transformation then and now is not mainly a matter of money. The transition to a diversified market economy, to the rule of law, and to property rights was always going to be extremely difficult for Russia.[4] The breakup of the Soviet Union created an environment of political upheaval that made the transition even harder. Today, eight years after China's accession to the World Trade Organization (WTO), Russia still has not managed to complete its negotiation. However, Russia is a constructive member of the World Bank and the IMF. The opportunities for integration or partnership with its former foes in the transatlantic community and with others remain active and potentially beneficial to all.

North America and the Western Hemisphere at the End of the Cold War

It seems that most scholars of the end of the Cold War never consider the strategic shifts and possibilities that occurred in North America and the Western Hemisphere during those years. Yet there are important interconnections, especially from a U.S. perspective.

In 1987, Howard Baker, the White House chief of staff and former Senate majority leader, asked Secretary of the Treasury James Baker to step in to save the fading and failing negotiations for a U.S.-Canada free trade agreement (FTA). Secretary of State George Shultz was strongly supportive.

It certainly was unusual to have a secretary of the treasury in charge of a trade negotiation. Yet a few of us perceived the U.S.-Canada FTA as much more than a trade agreement. It was a political and legal recognition that trade and economic integration could be the foundation for deepening a host of other ties. I recall discussing with Richard G. Darman, deputy secretary of the treasury, in 1987 whether I should press Secretary Baker, with all the other demands on his time, to take up the Canada FTA negotiation. And I recall Darman saying, "If Bismarck were around, this is the type of opportunity he would seize."

Against tight congressional deadlines, we completed the FTA negotiations; the U.S.-Canada FTA was passed in the summer of 1988, defying the conventional wisdom that it is impossible to approve big trade agreements in an election year. Equally important, the U.S.-Canada FTA became a key issue in Canada's election late in 1988. The governing Progressive Conservatives supported the FTA and the opposition Liberal Party rejected it. Many Canadians of all parties have told me that the Progressive Conservatives' victory in 1988 decisively turned Canada toward free trade, strengthened ties with the United States, and led to a much stronger economic competitiveness for Canada. Indeed, the reforms Canadian companies carried out as a result of the FTA made them—and Canada—more influential globally.

In 1989, we hoped for an opportunity to build on the Canada FTA by negotiating free trade with Mexico, possibly creating a North American Free Trade Agreement (NAFTA). For historical reasons, the initiative had to come from Mexico. As it turned out, opportunity struck: Mexican president Carlos Salinas de Gortari was concerned that Mexico would be left behind by the end of the Cold War. After a Davos meeting that focused the attention of investors on Central and Eastern Europe, Salinas decided to compete by proposing an FTA with the United States. Yet the negotiation was far from foreordained. The Office of the U.S. Trade Representative was working very hard on the Uruguay Round of the General Agreement on Tariffs and Trade (later the World Trade Organization) and its "organizational culture" was to resist bilateral or regional free trade agreements. I spent a lot of back-channel time overcoming that position, but enjoyed strong support. The fact that the president, secretary of state, and secretary of commerce were all from Texas clearly helped. Fortunately, President Bill Clinton shared the commitment to NAFTA, because his administration had to persuade Congress to enact the accord after Ambassador Carla Hills completed the negotiations in 1992.

NAFTA was a huge transformation with implications then, today, and I believe beyond. In most basic terms, it connected Mexico to North America. The timing was important, because the old "corporate state" of the ruling Partido Revolucionario Institucional (PRI), created in the 1920s and '30s, was breaking down. The question was where would the pieces of the "corporate state"—the political groups, businesses, military, unions, police, universities, and judiciary—reattach themselves? This transformation of institutions is still going on in Mexico today with the need to build law enforcement and judicial systems to fight against narco-traffickers. NAFTA's orientation toward North America, and the opening of Mexican society, were definitely part of Mexico's transition to democracy. Former president Ernesto Zedillo, the last president of the old PRI era, was willing to let the PRI lose power through the ballot box in 2000.

NAFTA also led to changes in Mexico's foreign policy. Traditionally, Mexico would instinctively oppose U.S. foreign-policy positions. Given its strong neighbor to the north, the political tensions of the past, and the fact that Mexico lost about half of its territory to the United States in the nineteenth century, opposition to U.S. foreign policy was the way to signal independence and distance. Also, it placated the political intelligentsia of the Left in Mexico while domestic policy was controlled by the conservative ruling elites of a corporate state.

Today, if one examines issues from trade to Central America to global climate change, Mexico is one of the most natural partners of the United States. Mexico now is like a close European ally that the United States can turn to as a partner on many issues. Although there are differences, just as there are with Canada, geography and shared interests create a basis for partnership and mutual cooperation. Yet again, opportunity is not assurance. Mexico still needs to undertake significant structural economic reforms to take full advantage of geography and NAFTA. It has to compete with East Asia.

Moreover, proximity creates additional problems that can lead to tensions, such as illegal immigration, narcotics trafficking, and weapons sales. But these issues will not be addressed successfully from just one side of the border. Deeper partnership and cooperation are essential.

Today, therefore, there's a vital North American agenda that needs attention: immigration, environment, energy, infrastructure, narcotics and crime, terrorism, Central America and the Caribbean, and cooperation in all of Latin America. Both presidents Clinton and George W. Bush sought to advance this agenda, building on deepened interdependence. But a U.S. administration cannot deal effectively with any of these issues without congressional support. Most of the U.S. foreign policy establishment has been a little slow to recognize both the importance of the North American relationship and how "foreign policy" in this sphere can be exercised only through legislative efforts with the Congress.

Ronald Reagan and George H. W. Bush were strong proponents of free trade throughout the Americas. But free trade was not only an economic policy. It was also part of strategic thinking at the end of the Cold War.

After World War II, freer trade and economic integration generated growth and prosperity in Western Europe. U.S. support for Europe's economic integration and liberalization through the Marshall Plan, the OECD, and the European communities was crucial to the political, economic, and security success of Western Europe. The nature of this transatlantic political economy partnership also offered a stark contrast with the Soviet empire's hegemony over Eastern Europe.

Economic liberalization and integration also strengthened democracy, the rule of law, and—under NATO's security umbrella—ensured the longest period of peace in contemporary European history.

During the Cold War, the United States had also promoted regional security organizations—ASEAN (Association of Southeast Asian Nations), SEATO (Southeast Asia Treaty Organization), CENTO (Central Treaty Organization), ANZUS (Australia, New Zealand, United States Security treaty)—on other continents, backed by bilateral trade and security agreements. The U.S.-Japan and U.S.–Republic of Korea security treaties were backed by successful development models of export-led growth. The economic weaknesses of other countries undermined their capabilities as security partners or even their internal strength.

The George H. W. Bush administration sought to use trade and economic ties to modernize linkages in a new and changing economic context, thereby building a stronger underpinning for future security. We also believed more open economies were more likely to spur more open societies and political institutions.

The collapse of Communism did not bring about the end of history and the undisputed triumph of democracy and free markets as some hoped at the time. But fostering free trade and economic liberalization and integration could help advance those aims, while better connecting America's economic and security interests.

To that effect, in 1991 the U.S. Treasury Department launched the Enterprise for the Americas Initiative (EAI) to develop trade facilitation agreements throughout the hemisphere so as to plant seeds for free trade agreements. EAI connected debt forgiveness to environmental protection through debt-for-nature swaps. It also proposed steps to foster the investment climate.

In 1991–92, working from the State Department, I tried to encourage the Office of the U.S. Trade Representative to follow NAFTA with a U.S.-Chile free trade agreement. I was unable to do so at the time, but history sometimes gives second chances; in this case, it did. During the George W. Bush administration we enacted the U.S.-Chile FTA in 2004.

In 1991, we were able to conclude the Andean Trade Preference Act (ATPA), which awarded trade preferences to the four Andean countries to support their fight against narcotics. The ATPA laid the foundation for eventual FTA negotiations with Peru and Colombia in the George W. Bush administration.

With Secretary Baker's support, we also fostered economic integration in Central America during the George H.W. Bush administration. Central America was emerging from its bloody civil wars of the 1980s, with the help of U.S. diplomacy. In 1989, we decided to test Gorbachev's "new thinking" in foreign policy by urging the USSR to help resolve regional conflicts—in Central America, Angola, and elsewhere. In particular, we wanted the Soviets to signal the withdrawal of their support for the Sandinista regime in Nicaragua; this issue was even on our agenda with the Soviets at the Malta Summit in December 1989. With the loss of its economic mainstay, the Sandinista regime felt compelled by international pressure to hold free elections. They lost, and we worked with international partners to ensure a transfer of power.

Some commentators questioned whether the Soviets in fact had curtailed their support to the Sandinistas, but years later I had an opportunity to ask an important figure in the Sandinista regime how he had perceived the situation. There was no doubt, he asserted, that the Sandinistas had to accept elections because they recognized that the Soviets were halting their support and backing elections.

El Salvador and Guatemala were also overcoming brutal civil wars during this period and holding democratic elections. We wanted to bolster the peace process and democracy in all these countries with improved economic opportunity. One idea was for a Central American FTA that would combine regional cooperation and integration with development assistance. But we ran out of time in 1992.

After I returned to the U.S. government in 2001, we enacted an FTA with the five countries of Central America and the Dominican Republic (the United States–Dominican Republic–Central America Free Trade Agreement, or CAFTA). We passed FTAs with Chile and Peru. We concluded FTA agreements with Colombia and Panama as well, although unfortunately Congress has not acted on them. In sum, all the U.S. FTAs in the hemisphere cover two-thirds of the Western Hemisphere's GDP and population, not including the United States. We were well on the way to Ronald Reagan's vision.

As I left the U.S. government in 2006, I urged the next step, namely to consolidate NAFTA, CAFTA, and FTAs with Chile, Peru, Colombia and Panama, as well as with the Caribbean trade preferences. We could use the accords as a foundation for deeper cooperation in business, the environment, education, and trade facilitation. My proposal included a headquarters in Miami to foster ties of all types, including academic ones.[5]

In September 2008, President George W. Bush and the leaders of the U.S.'s FTA partners launched the Pathways to Prosperity in the Americas (Pathways) initiative. The foreign and trade ministers of the fourteen Pathways member countries held a ministerial conference in Panama in November 2008. The Obama administration has embraced the Pathways initiative. In 2009, Secretary of State Hillary Clinton attended a Pathways ministerial conference in El Salvador and a Women Entrepreneurs Conference was held in Washington, D.C., in October 2009.

Some critics contend that bilateral and regional free trade agreements interfere with the WTO. This is a frustrating argument. It ignores both the economic and political-economy evidence, which show that partners in comprehensive FTAs are actually more prone to reduce trade barriers with third countries. It also is dismissive of foreign policy interests, including fostering cooperation on topics ranging from energy and the environment to the rule of law and democracy.

It is also ironic that the critics decry the interconnection of American foreign and international economic policies. U.S. policy reflected a keen awareness of the overlap throughout the nineteenth century. In the first half of the twentieth century, there was "Dollar Diplomacy" and government encouragement of financiers to work out debt plans with Europe and Mexico. President Franklin D.

Roosevelt used the Reciprocal Trade Agreements Act of 1934 to work back from the protectionism of the Smoot-Hawley Tariff Act. After World War II, the Marshall Plan very successfully connected economics with politics and security. In 1961, President John F. Kennedy launched an "Alliance for Progress with Latin America."

Research carried out by the World Bank and other institutions demonstrates that comprehensive FTAs—such as the ones the United States negotiates—in fact support economic reforms and openness to nonmembers.[6]

The FTA countries support global WTO liberalization, too. There is a very good political economy reason for this. The FTA partners of the United States believe in liberalization. They view an FTA with the United States as a way to "lock in" reforms. FTAs enable them to counter political opposition at home—usually of protected groups—with real benefits of openness. Chile offers a good example: it has signed more FTAs than any other country and is a strong supporter of WTO negotiations.[7] From 2001 until 2005, when the United States negotiated FTAs we also required our partners to support the global negotiations.

Moreover, facts are stubborn things for theorists to dismiss. While the United States was negotiating NAFTA in 1989–92, it was also achieving a breakthrough in the Uruguay Round of GATT, which President Clinton completed right after passing NAFTA. After George W. Bush's election in 2001, we launched the Doha negotiations in 2001, and got them back on track with a framework agreement in 2004, while at the same time completing FTAs with sixteen countries in Latin America, Asia-Pacific, and the Middle East. Today, on the other hand, the United States is not negotiating FTAs, and the WTO Doha Round is stalled. Periods of advancement of FTAs in U.S. policy making are also the periods of aggressive trade liberalization globally.

The End of the Cold War, APEC, and Asia-Pacific Security

In 1989, U.S. security alliances with Asia-Pacific countries were described as spokes of a wheel. The United States had separate security treaties with Australia, Japan, the Republic of Korea, Thailand, and the Philippines. We perceived possible competitive tensions, but also significant economic opportunities for the United States in the Asia-Pacific region. We wanted to show the American public the economic opportunities, while helping to counter a potential resurgence of U.S. economic isolationism. More positively, we wanted to better align economic interests with security interests and vice versa.

Before Secretary Baker left the Treasury Department in August 1988 to head George H. W. Bush's campaign for president, Baker had been planning to launch a new meeting of finance ministers for the Asia-Pacific region. We viewed the Asia-Pacific group as a complement to the G-7, emphasizing the growing economic importance of the region. We felt it would be harder to gain U.S. public support for Asia-Pacific security ties if the public did not perceive those ties as benefiting U.S. economic interests.

Shortly after George H. W. Bush took office in January 1989, we had an opportunity to advance this concept through a different guise. Australian prime minister Bob Hawke had just launched the idea that would lead to the creation of the Asia-Pacific Economic Cooperation (APEC) forum. But Hawke had excluded the United States and Canada, prompting a swift rebuke from Washington. We turned rapidly to the creation of APEC, which required allaying the fears of Southeast Asian ASEAN countries that APEC would overwhelm ASEAN. Australia hosted the first meeting of APEC in late 1989. Singapore, a member of ASEAN, hosted the second APEC ministerial in 1990.

APEC was a different type of multilateral association; it incorporated new ideas and Asian preferences. It complemented intergovernmental participants with private-sector business and academic groups. To avoid bureaucratization, we initially organized policy cooperation by various sectors, relying on officials from capitals, not diplomats posted to an organization. As opposed to negotiating fixed agreements or rules, APEC identified issues of common concern, and then discussed ways of cooperating and sharing experiences. Some countries tested solutions as "pathfinders." Discussions among ministers were designed more to expose one another to contending views and concerns, not to take votes or press for agreement.

One early example of APEC's importance as a "mediating" body came in 1991–92. Since 1989, China had been subject to sanctions and international isolation. But officials in China were seeking to restart economic reforms. APEC became a vehicle to open relations and support reforms. Working closely with the Republic of Korea, which at that time did not have diplomatic relations with the People's Republic of China, the United States helped negotiate the entry of the People's Republic of China, Taiwan, and Hong Kong into APEC. In 2001, we utilized a similar compromise to bring the People's Republic of China and Taiwan into the WTO, while retaining Hong Kong as a member.

APEC became a vehicle through which China could gain confidence in multilateral cooperation. In the past, China had been wary of most multilateral agreements and institutions, perhaps fearing constraints on its sovereignty, much as the United States has at times. After World War II, the United States embraced multilateral alliances and institutions to help rebuild a shattered world, counter

Communism, and avoid the types of systemic breakdowns that had contributed to disaster in the 1930s. Since the 1990s, China has also recognized the benefits of multilateralism. Indeed, it has engaged in skillful multilateral diplomacy. APEC membership was one of the first steps that led to China's accession to the WTO in 2001 and to China's effective insertion in the multilateral economic system.

APEC also embraced the idea of "open regionalism." APEC's members recognized that the benefits of regional integration needed to be linked to participation in an open, global economy. Indeed, the creation of APEC, along with the negotiation of NAFTA, sent a salutary signal to European states that were resisting the completion of the Uruguay Round of GATT/WTO negotiations: if the global round faltered, Europeans might be left behind by North American and Asia-Pacific integration. Similarly, after the breakdown in the WTO negotiations at Cancún in late 2003, one of our first steps to revive the process was through an APEC statement that helped re-create momentum and eventually led in July 2004 to a framework accord, a necessary "way station" on the way to a final deal.

Economic Multilateralism and Foreign Policy

The strategic perspective I have outlined emphasizes the links between free trade and economic integration on the one hand, and political and security interests on the other. Yet we did not believe that economic integration or free trade were inextricably linked to peace or democracy. Instead, we believed that well-designed political economy policies could enlarge the realm of economic liberty, strengthen the role of the private sector, open up societies, break down old oligarchies and oligopolies, and contribute to global growth and development. In addition, we had seen that policies that support economic integration can help expand patterns of cooperation, sharing of information, trade and investment, innovation, negotiation and mediation of disputes, and cooperation on transnational issues such as the environment. They encourage a valuable search for mutual interests and win-win opportunities. And they foster peaceful management of differences.

The history of European integration in the second half of the twentieth century provides an excellent example of the ways economic integration can help build a larger political order. European integration served larger strategic ends. It encouraged a union of democracies. It built and relied on a supportive infrastructure of rules and institutions.

Secretary Baker's tenure at the Treasury Department (1985–88) emphasized G-7 economic coordination, which resulted in the adoption of the Plaza and

Louvre accords. Most of the public attention focused on currency intervention, but the policy underpinnings of the accords were a recognition of economic interdependence and a pursuit of common interests. This approach to multilateral economic cooperation was rejected, mainly by economists, in the 1990s, partly as a result of the 1987 market crash.

Secretary Baker's concept of economic cooperation involved asking the G-7 finance ministers (in the company of central bankers) to share their forecasts so they could be assessed—by countries and the IMF—for consistency. Over time, the IMF was supposed to spur deeper debate and cooperation by offering its independent assessment, including identification of inconsistencies among national forecasts. To help reconcile differences—and perhaps seize opportunities—the G-7 finance ministers would report to the G-7 summit leaders. The idea was that heads of governments would help to resolve—if they could be resolved—the political economy choices that would inevitably be raised by the coordination exercise. Although macroeconomic coordination would be the centerpiece of the effort, the ministers—and heads of government—might also cooperate on other international economic topics, such as global trade negotiations or debt crises.

It is interesting to note that the economic crisis of 2008–09, and the rise of the G-20, revived interest in managing economic interdependence through multilateral cooperation. Indeed, the IMF and World Bank have now been asked to contribute mutual assessments of the world economy that parallel the ideas Secretary Baker was advancing twenty-five years ago. The effectiveness of the G-20 and multilateral economic cooperation will be one of the important challenges of coming years.

Strategic Coherence of Foreign and Domestic Policies

In August 1992, James Baker left the State Department to become President Bush's chief of staff. As part of the campaign of 1992, we presented a reform agenda that linked America's foreign engagement with domestic interests: it was published in a campaign plan, *The Agenda for American Renewal,* and highlighted by President Bush at a speech to the Detroit Economic Club.

The *Agenda* sought to develop a coherent strategy that integrated economic, domestic, and trade policy. That strategic coherence also provided a foundation for America's international security engagement.

The core objective of the *Agenda* was to link domestic policy reforms to the U.S. push for global economic openness and competitiveness. The American public perceived President Bush as skillful in foreign policy, but detached from domestic problems. The polls showed that Americans wanted him to apply his international capabilities to *their* concerns. This "refocus" would seem more credible if it were connected to the president's international expertise. And the challenge of this interconnection would only grow over time.

In essence, the theme of *The Agenda for American Renewal* was helping the American public adapt to change. The term globalization had not yet come into wide circulation. But we recognized that in order to benefit from liberalization of trade, investments, and financial markets, the United States would have to increase its competitiveness. Increased competitiveness required improved health care policies, better quality education based on competition and choice, more effective worker training, pension mobility, research and development, entrepreneurial capitalism, legal reforms, and more efficient and effective government performance. The *Agenda* advocated policies that drew on market incentives, choice by families, competition, property rights, private sector involvement, and targeted government safety net support.

The underlying premise of *The Agenda for American Renewal* was that the United States' greatest asset is its openness as a society and its openness to goods, capital, people, and ideas. But it also recognized that to sustain openness, government needed to help people manage change.

The Agenda for American Renewal called for comprehensive trade liberalization. In addition to seeking a conclusion to the Uruguay Round of the GATT, it called for expanding NAFTA by adding a free-trade agreement with Chile, a free-trade agreement between the United States and Central America, and a strategic network of FTAs with ASEAN members, the Republic of Korea, and Australia. President George W. Bush's administration accomplished many of these goals, a connection not recognized by scholars.

The challenge the United States faced during the George H. W. Bush administration and continues to face today is how to help people adjust to change and uncertainty. Without public support, any U.S. administration will not be able to maintain a strategy of global American engagement. In effect, we were trying to explain the changes in the world, articulate American interests, and advocate how we could advance our values while helping citizens to cope with the changes. Economic interests—and fears—had to be a cornerstone of this explanation.

The initial public and press reaction to the Detroit Economic Club speech and the *Agenda* was positive. One Clinton campaign strategist later said it was the one moment when they worried about a reversal of momentum: Bush had "a plan." But other issues soon dominated the election. It was "the economy, stupid." And after twelve years of Republican presidents, voters opted for change.

Concluding Thoughts

My purpose in presenting this piece of history is to give scholars another perspective on the end of the Cold War to consider. As time has passed, I could see that while elements of this story have been available to students of the period, the interconnecting intellectual tissue was lost. This sketch is preliminary and far from complete. I recognize that other colleagues in the George H. W. Bush administration placed a higher priority on other agendas, and some of these also reappear after 2001. Scholars will be the ones to judge whether these strategic concepts were useful, followed, or worth reconsidering.

Unlike grand designs such as NSC-68, this strategy will not be found in one interagency paper. But as I have sought to demonstrate through references to speeches and publications (including a political campaign document!)—and equally important, to actions—these strategic concepts were a very real part of policy in 1989–92.

Indeed, as I have noted, some of the concepts—whether or not recognized as part of a strategic design—were pursued by the Clinton administration and given a new burst of energy, especially in trade, under President George W. Bush. Many of the questions the strategy sought to address remain alive for President Barack Obama.

Equally important, I hope this brief review of the past will prompt scholars— as well as policymakers—to examine more closely policy interconnections both across regions and the dividing lines of security, economics, and political disciplines. Too often the specialization of careers or research may lead one unintentionally to narrow one's focus.

"Grand strategies" may be overambitious. But 1989–92 was a period when some of the key U.S. participants were trying to avoid the dangers of incrementalism and ad hoc responses by developing a barebones design that could guide decisions made in the face of opportunities and dangers.

The focus of this book is "strategy in uncertain times." The end of the Cold War was certainly an uncertain period. It was my belief then—and today—that the likelihood of achieving positive outcomes at that time, or any time, is much higher if one has in mind a strategic perspective of what one wants to achieve. That is what we tried to do.

3

SHAPING THE FUTURE

Planning at the Pentagon, 1989–93

Paul Wolfowitz

In the first half of the 1980s, the ice dividing East and West seemed permanently frozen. Why did it crack open so suddenly and so peacefully? Was it the product of inevitable historical forces, such as the internal weaknesses of the Soviet empire and the economy that supported it? Did Mikhail Gorbachev's unsuccessful attempt to adapt Soviet communism to those forces lead eventually to the peaceful end of the Cold War? Or did President Ronald Reagan's deliberate strategy to shape those forces bring about a situation where a reformist leader such as Gorbachev could emerge? Or was it some combination of all of these?

Around the middle of 1992, a young Russian, who had created his country's first association of disabled persons, came to visit Secretary of Defense Dick Cheney and mentioned that he was heading to California to meet with Reagan, "the father of perestroika." He explained this unusual description of the former U.S. president this way: "The Soviet military had thought that it was invincible. But then came stealth [the B-2 bomber]. And then SDI [the Strategic Defense Initiative or Star Wars]. And they realized that the system had to change in order for them to compete. But when small changes didn't work, they had to resort to larger and larger changes and eventually the system broke down."

What caused the Cold War to end will be debated for a long time, but it is important to recognize that Reagan did indeed have a strategy, one that recognized the important difference between what can be controlled and what is the product of uncontrollable forces.[1] Reagan's strategy recognized that there were fundamental forces at work, but he labored to shape those forces, particularly through pressure on the Soviet system (and not just through stealth and SDI).

It was a strategy that sought to create opportunities, and also took advantage of opportunities when they presented themselves, as they did in Poland. And it was a strategy that assisted historical forces when they were flowing in the right direction.

Nautical metaphors are common in discussions of strategy, perhaps because the basic question of strategy—how do you get from point A to point B—is fundamental to navigation as well: as the Cheshire Cat explained to Alice, "If you don't know where you're going any road will get you there." Chinese strategists, however, prefer a different kind of water image, that of the sea or a large river collecting the smaller tributaries that flow into it: "The way that large rivers and the sea can reign over all other water courses is through their ability to position themselves below them." From this way of thinking comes Sun Tzu's classic statement of strategic excellence: "To win a hundred victories in a hundred battles is good but belongs to the order of that which is not good. The height of excellence is to manage to overcome the enemy without having to fight."[2]

If the ice dividing East and West seemed permanently frozen in the early 1980s, by 1989, when I went to work as undersecretary of defense for policy under Secretary Dick Cheney, it had cracked almost completely and we were now in a rushing torrent.[3] Although Michael Beschloss and Strobe Talbott title their book about that period *At the Highest Levels,* equally important was the activity taking place among millions of less-exalted Central and East Europeans and—perhaps most importantly—Russians, who seized the opportunity to break free from oppressive rule.[4]

By 1989, the forces of change inside the Soviet empire were almost unstoppable. Still, the possibility of figuratively capsizing or hitting the rocks in the river was real. Probably, no Soviet leader could have held the empire together—but a different leader could have made the result more violent. Similarly, an American president less skillful than George H. W. Bush could probably have presided over the end of the Cold War—but the result might well have been a less stable Europe and a fractured Atlantic alliance. The diplomacy of President Bush and his team, led by Secretary of State James Baker, achieved something that was far from inevitable—persuading the Soviet leadership to accept a unified Germany as a member of NATO and even to recognize that this change actually served the Soviet interest in maintaining peace in Europe.[5]

President Bush also faced the first major crisis of the "post–Cold War era," when Saddam Hussein invaded Kuwait. He met that challenge with remarkable resolve and political courage, qualities that are frequently underestimated in historical hindsight because the feat seemed much too easy after the fact.[6] However, that impressive victory, coming on top of the victory in the Cold War, contributed to a widespread feeling that the United States no longer faced serious dangers in the world or else that the problems we faced could be handled by a newly invigorated United Nations. Rhetoric from the administration about "A New World Order"—or comments that we had "no dog" in fights such as those in the former Yugoslavia—did nothing to counter that complacency.[7]

Indeed, it is odd that Bush, Brent Scowcroft, his national security adviser, and Baker, who understood well the need for U.S. leadership, should have produced rhetoric that sounded so like those who thought that the need for such leadership had passed. Virtually alone among the top officials in the administration, Secretary of Defense Cheney warned of the danger of repeating the mistake, so often made after previous victories, of discarding the capabilities needed to deal with future conflicts. Out of that concern, Cheney developed the Regional Defense Strategy that enabled the United States, at affordable cost, to preserve the stability gained by those victories.

Redirecting Arms Control

Odd as it may sound now, in early 1989 the new U.S. administration was fearful that it was NATO—not the Soviet empire—that might collapse under the challenge of Gorbachev's "peace offensive." Bush's advisers feared that the Reagan administration had been too soft. Rozanne Ridgway, Reagan's assistant secretary of state for European Affairs, was later asked by Baker, "Tell me, Roz, don't you think that you all went too fast?"[8]

At the same time, the new administration was also scornful of the Reagan administration's initiatives as not sufficiently imaginative. They wanted to go even faster, seeking more dramatic arms control proposals to compete with Gorbachev. Yet, in the end the most important U.S. initiative in the spring of 1989 was based on Reagan's Conventional Forces in Europe (CFE) proposal.

A number of interagency studies undertook ambitious reviews of strategy but—predictably—they produced little that was new, since large interdepartmental reviews inevitably tend to kill innovative ideas. Formal reviews are useful to subject new ideas to critical examination, but without high-level backing, any new initiative is likely to be smothered in the cradle. The "pause" to undertake these strategic reviews, although intended to buy time, instead increased the pressure for dramatic initiatives, by raising doubts about the Bush administration's policy direction. Adding to that pressure was NATO's controversial plan to modernize the short-range tactical nuclear Lance missiles, which lacked a compelling rationale when the Soviet threat appeared to be declining.

One of the more surprising departures proposed that spring was the suggestion by National Security Adviser Brent Scowcroft for an agreement to withdraw all U.S. and Soviet ground forces from the territory of their European allies. When he introduced the idea in a small meeting with the president, Scowcroft reports, "Cheney looked stunned."[9]

No doubt Cheney was astonished, but not because he failed to recognize the significance of the changes under way in Europe. He had described himself as a "believer" that Gorbachev was "serious" about cutting military spending and about making changes in the Soviet economy that would demand "certain political reforms."[10] But Scowcroft's astonishing proposal ignored the geographic asymmetry—with Soviet troops just a short drive away and U.S. forces moved to the other side of the Atlantic—and even worse the political asymmetry between NATO and the rapidly expiring Warsaw Pact. Encouraging the withdrawal of Soviet troops made sense, but doing so at the price of equating Soviet troop presence with U.S. presence in NATO was unnecessary and potentially dangerous. Fortunately, this idea *was* smothered in its cradle, partly by Cheney's opposition.[11]

Cheney wanted instead to test Gorbachev's declared willingness to reduce conventional forces in Europe, which was the underlying cause of insecurity and the reason for NATO's tactical nuclear weapons.[12] The Reagan administration's CFE proposal was ideal for this purpose. It was a radical departure from NATO's earlier approach in the Mutual and Balanced Force Reduction (MBFR) negotiations, which merely sought equal percentage reductions in military manpower. For fifteen years the Warsaw Pact had rejected that proposal, even though it would have retained its conventional superiority. In CFE, NATO was proposing reductions to lower *and equal* levels of tanks, artillery, and armored personnel carriers. That would substantially eliminate the conventional military threat in Central Europe, but some State Department officials believed the proposal was unrealistic because the Warsaw Pact would reject it. They pressed instead for negotiations on short-range nuclear forces (SNF), as urged by German foreign minister Hans Dietrich Genscher, to deal with the Lance controversy.[13]

We should have been pleased when, during Baker's visit to Moscow on May 11, Gorbachev accepted the idea of reductions of conventional arms to equal levels, with numbers that were strikingly close to NATO's for tanks, artillery, and armored personnel carriers. However, Baker was unhappy that Gorbachev unveiled "his customary 'surprise,'" announcing a unilateral reduction in Soviet tactical nuclear weapons in a "clear attempt to . . . score public relations points with European publics."[14] Moreover, the Soviet CFE proposal appeared more ambitious because it also included reductions in aircraft, helicopters, and personnel.

My recollection of what came next differs somewhat from other accounts. At a White House meeting following Baker's Moscow trip, Cheney pointed out that the Soviet numbers were very close to our own in the three key ground force categories. When Baker responded that Gorbachev's proposal was more ambitious than ours, Cheney surprised the meeting by saying there was no reason not to include aircraft and helicopters, even though we could expect some objections from Margaret Thatcher and François Mitterrand.

We spent the next several days debating how large a manpower reduction to offer, but the inclusion of dual-capable aircraft—part of NATO's theater nuclear deterrent—was the dramatic change.[15] When Deputy Secretary of State Lawrence Eagleburger and Deputy National Security Adviser Robert Gates were dispatched to consult with Thatcher and Mitterrand, that aspect of the proposal made Prime Minister Thatcher particularly unhappy. But that was also what made the proposal compelling both to Gorbachev and to European publics.

En route to the NATO summit with President Bush—which I was attending as Cheney's representative—the White House and State Department continued to press for Cheney to agree to begin SNF negotiations. However, when the dramatic news broke about the president's conventional arms control initiative, the SNF controversy faded into the background—as Cheney had predicted it would. In a late-night negotiating session, Baker fashioned a compromise between the Germans and the British to postpone SNF negotiations until after initial progress in the CFE talks. The priority for conventional arms reductions had been established.

Organizing for Strategic Planning

Reflection and action are qualities that do not sit comfortably together. Successful practical men must necessarily be decisive, efficient, and able to act quickly. Yet strategic thinking requires reflection. Paul Nitze referred to this as the "tension between opposites," between theory and practice.

Cheney was one of those rare senior officials who are able to do both. In a decision meeting he was all business, but on other occasions he could step back and entertain a discussion that had no immediate conclusion, the kind of discussion that would often leave some of the department's senior people shaking their heads. Cheney responded readily to the suggestion that we set aside time outside normal business hours to listen to experts debate fundamental issues, a practice that I had learned earlier from Secretary of State George Shultz.

Cheney wanted our first session to address the historic changes taking place in the Soviet Union. The discussion was so useful that afterwards he would periodically say, "let's round up the usual suspects" for another Saturday meeting. The participants, a diverse group, varied from meeting to meeting. The regulars included outside experts, such as Jeremy Azrael, Ric Ericson, Paul Goble, Marshall Goldman, Rose Gottemoeller, Arnold Horelick, Peter Reddaway, and Steve

Sestanovich, along with the CIA's George Kolt and Fritz Ermarth. These discussions helped Cheney anticipate the extraordinary changes in the Soviet Union and to appreciate earlier than his colleagues the importance of Boris Yeltsin and the strength of the demand for change in Russia and the other Soviet republics.

Another organizational innovation that helped us address the new environment was restructuring the office of the undersecretary of defense for policy. That position had been established ten years earlier, largely to manage bilateral defense relationships and arms control negotiations. I created a new division devoted to strategic planning and persuaded Lewis "Scooter" Libby—a deeply thoughtful and dedicated public servant—to return to government and lead that division as principal deputy undersecretary for strategy and resources.

His division had three new offices:

An Office of Resources and Plans to analyze the budget implications of policy options (critical for our strategy reviews) and to review military contingency plans (which became important during Operation Desert Storm), headed by retired Lieutenant General Dale Vesser, a former head of plans and policy for the Joint Staff.[16]

A Policy Planning Office, headed initially by Naval War College professor Al Bernstein and later by Zalmay Khalilzad, a leading RAND analyst (who served more recently as U.S. ambassador to Afghanistan, Iraq, and the United Nations).

An office of Soviet Union and East European affairs, to fill a gap in the Office of the Secretary of Defense (OSD) created by the absence of bilateral relations with Warsaw Pact countries. That had left thinking about the Soviet Union largely to the intelligence community—with the important exception of Andy Marshall's small but remarkable Office of Net Assessment. The new office was headed by Eric Edelman, an outstanding Russian-speaking foreign service officer. Together, Edelman and Marshall gave us exceptional understanding of developments in the Soviet Union and Warsaw Pact.

Defining Objectives after the Fall of the Berlin Wall

When the Berlin Wall came down, my State Department colleague, Ambassador Reginald Bartholomew, and I created an informal working group to think through our objectives in this unprecedented situation. This was not a conventional interagency committee to debate formal departmental positions, but rather an opportunity to discuss issues freely before those positions were set in stone.[17]

However, one issue was taken off the table very quickly. President Bush's early embrace of German unification silenced those skeptics in the bureaucracy who shared the Anglo-French desire to slow down movement toward unification. The president had set the policy clearly and boldly and policy thinking followed suit.

It took somewhat longer to abandon earlier accepted wisdom that unification would require conceding to the Soviets some measure of German neutrality. However, our discussions concluded that Germany might feel compelled to rearm—if it were deprived of NATO's guarantees—in ways that would be destabilizing for all of Europe and threatening to the Soviet Union itself.

General Klaus Naumann, a senior West German official, expressed the thought compellingly: a neutral Germany, he told us, would be like "a loose cannon rolling around on the deck of Europe." Collective defense, through an alliance such as NATO, enables its members to achieve security both at lower cost and without threatening the security of others. A Germany anchored in NATO would be good for the Soviets, and hopefully they could be convinced of that.

Our consensus proved useful at the NATO summit on December 4 when President Bush presented the U.S. conditions for German unification. When Bartholomew and I saw the draft of the president's statement, one of the crucial conditions for German unification spoke only of Germany's "continued association with" NATO.[18] We agreed that this suggested something short of NATO membership and presented our concerns to Baker. After noting that the Soviets might oppose German membership in NATO, he observed that this was, after all, a negotiation and decided to take a strong opening position. The language was changed to say that unification needed to be in the context of Germany's "continued commitment to" NATO.

Over the following six months, Baker and Bush did persuade the Soviets of the value of keeping Germany in NATO. This was a major diplomatic achievement for which they deserve great credit. It helped that we had achieved some consensus about the objective at the outset, through those informal interagency discussions. That consensus was also important for a different exercise that Secretary Cheney had initiated very quietly at that time, the planning that produced the new "Regional Defense Strategy" and the "Base Force."

Defense Planning in a Period of Uncertainty

Not long after the fall of the Berlin Wall, Secretary of Defense Cheney called General Colin Powell, the chairman of the Joint Chiefs of Staff, and myself to his office for a small meeting with himself and Deputy Secretary of Defense Donald Atwood.

Cheney's message was very direct. He said he would have to go to Congress that year with "one more Cold War budget" and would be criticized for a lack of "new thinking." But he was prepared to live with that in order to buy time to think through a new strategy. He wanted us to use that time to undertake a fundamental reexamination of our defense policy, strategy, force posture, and budget. The Joint Staff and my civilian staff were to work independently. And there should be no leaks.

Our two staffs worked largely independently and out of the public eye, thanks to the cover that Secretary Cheney provided us. On the civilian side, Libby, working with my front office, divided the work among separate teams on his staff that examined: (1) alternative futures for the Soviet Union and the former Soviet Bloc, Western Europe, East Asia, the Middle East, and elsewhere; (2) the impact of technology and other factors on future U.S. military capabilities; (3) alternative U.S strategies in different future environments; (4) strategies other countries might pursue, including responses to U.S. strategies; and, (5) significantly, the budget and force structure implications of alternative strategies.

The subsequent six months witnessed one of the most thorough reexaminations of defense strategy—including budget and force structure implications of alternative strategies—since the creation of the Defense Department in 1947. The work was reviewed privately by Cheney as it progressed. At his request, we presented ways to shift, if necessary, from one strategy to another if circumstances changed, particularly if our assumption that the global threat from the Soviet Union was disappearing were to come into question. This intense effort produced a dramatic revision of the U.S. defense posture that, I believe, served the country well for the next decade and longer.

General Powell and I presented our conclusions to the Defense Policy and Resources Board (DPRB) in May 1990. Our independent recommendations for the new force structure were not too far apart. Both envisioned substantial reductions from Cold War levels. Despite grumbling from the service chiefs, Powell recommended a "Base Force" that reduced force structure by roughly 25 percent (from an active duty force of 2.1 million to 1.6 million) and lowered defense spending by more than 10 percent over the course of the Five Year Defense Program (FYDP). Our recommendations were similar.

Powell's strong leadership to get the chiefs to accept such dramatic changes was critical. His analysis was based heavily on a military judgment about how much and how fast U.S. forces could be reduced without "breaking" the all-volunteer force. That consideration was critical, but Cheney also wanted a strategic basis for the new force recommendations. On that point, Powell's presentation fell short, suggesting that the future security environment was simply one of disappearing threats. He even quipped at one point that Kim Il Sung might soon be the only threat he would have left.[19]

Cheney was pleased by Powell's recommendations for force structure changes and by the fact that our conclusions were similar. However, he focused much more on the question of strategy, so much so that my strategy presentation was extended into a second session. In the end, the recommendations Cheney took to President Bush were a combination of Powell's force structure recommendations and Libby's strategy work.

The first element of the new strategy was *forward presence,* the military capability to assure our allies that we would meet our commitments. It reflected the consensus reached earlier that a framework of collective defense had great benefits for all parties. Particularly the NATO alliance and the U.S.-Japan Security Treaty enabled the members of those alliances to achieve security at lower cost and without the need for destabilizing rearmament.

In light of the later controversy over the leaked draft of the 1992 Defense Planning Guidance, it is significant that our allies agreed with that conclusion. Germany and Japan, in particular, had no desire to become major military powers, nor would our other allies in Europe and Asia have welcomed such a development.

The objection came instead from those who believed that our prosperous allies were getting a "free ride." That argument was pressed most strongly by Deputy Secretary Atwood, a former vice president of General Motors, who believed that Japan benefited unfairly from the U.S. commitment to its defense. However, Secretary Cheney was persuaded that we would eventually spend more—and face a more dangerous world—if we withdrew those defense commitments and left our allies to fend for themselves.

The second element of the new strategy was *crisis response,* the capability to deal with two regional contingencies in critical parts of the world. Under the Cold War strategy, it was assumed that the forces we needed for unforeseen contingencies elsewhere in the world would be a part of the much larger force needed in the event of a global war with the Soviet Union. With that large force-sizing construct gone, the question was what if anything should replace it.

Asked, in February 1990, who NATO's adversary was, now that the Soviet enemy had gone away, President Bush had replied that "the enemy is *unpredictability.* The enemy is *instability.*" There was wisdom in that response, although it was mocked by some.[20] But for the U.S. military, *unpredictability* was in fact too vague a basis for planning forces. Something more concrete was needed. After lengthy discussion, the conclusion from our strategy review was that we should retain the capability to respond to sudden threats in Korea, where we had traditional alliance commitments, and in the Persian Gulf, against the possibility of Iraqi aggression against the weaker states of the Arabian Peninsula.

Earlier planning treated requirements for a Persian Gulf contingency as covered by the much larger requirements for a global war with the Soviet Union. In the summer of 1989, with the Soviet threat receding, the JCS chairman, Admiral William Crowe, wanted to remove any mention of the Persian Gulf from the Defense Guidance. I argued against the change and Cheney overruled Crowe.[21] My reasoning was based on analysis we had done in 1979 when, as deputy assistant secretary of defense for regional programs in the Office of the Assistant Secretary for Program Analysis and Evaluation, I had created an office to analyze Persian Gulf requirements. One of our conclusions was that the threat to U.S. security interests in the Persian Gulf was not a naval threat—as had often been assumed—but rather the threat of a land or air attack by the Soviet Union or by a major regional power.

People had been slow to accept that conclusion, until the Soviet invasion of Afghanistan forced a dramatic change in thinking about threats to the Persian Gulf. However, with the Soviet threat disappearing, we now had to be explicit about threats from regional powers. This was an essential feature of the new strategy. We were not predicting an Iraqi invasion of the Arabian Peninsula, but we did recognize that Iraq's military strength, the record of its conduct, and the importance of U.S. interests in the region made it a serious danger.

The new strategy had two other elements. One was *nuclear deterrence,* which obviously had to remain a key element of U.S. strategy. Equally obvious, we needed to rethink nuclear deterrence. However, we had been asked to focus primarily on U.S. conventional forces, so we did not undertake a significant reexamination of nuclear forces at this stage.

The fourth and final element was a new concept, *reconstitution,* designed to deal with uncertainties about the future Soviet role in Europe. In hindsight, that looks overly cautious. However, the possibility of a leadership change was not fanciful, as the August 1991 coup attempt showed. To guard against a possible reversal, we proposed developing cadre divisions and other "skeleton" forces that could be reconstituted in the event that a significant Soviet threat reemerged. Reconstitution in that form ceased to be an important part of the strategy, but the importance of reserve forces for unforeseen contingencies has been demonstrated powerfully over the last decade.

In June 1990, Secretary Cheney took General Powell and myself to the Oval Office to present the new strategy and force reductions to President Bush and General Scowcroft. The president was pleased and decided to unveil the new strategy in a major speech at a conference in Aspen on August 2, which Prime Minister Thatcher would be attending.

But history had more surprises. The following month, even as we were preparing a speech for the president that would highlight the defense of the Arabian

Peninsula as a principal focus of the new Regional Defense Strategy, Saddam Hussein mobilized his army on the Kuwaiti border. In the end, Saddam invaded Kuwait on the very day of the president's speech and the radical changes that Bush was proposing in that speech became lost in the drama of the crisis.

The Gulf War itself demonstrated how important American strength was for successful diplomacy. The invasion of Kuwait demonstrated the continuing importance of deterrence, and the Saudi decision to stand up to Saddam rested not on Security Council resolutions but on U.S. resolve and capability.[22] So, too, the diplomatic success of persuading Israel to stay out of the war, in the face of repeated Iraqi Scud missile attacks, would not have been possible without the capabilities that Cheney persuaded the president to offer Israel for defense against those attacks.

A New Nuclear Posture

The Cold War "balance of terror" has so commonly come to be discussed in purely U.S.-Soviet terms that it is frequently forgotten that it originated from the conventional threat to Western Europe. Our NATO allies had no interest in reducing their dependence on nuclear weapons. To the contrary, they wanted a posture that would virtually ensure that any major war in Europe would rapidly become nuclear, believing that this was the best way to prevent war entirely, hence the need for a massive nuclear deterrent.

The collapse of the Soviet Union changed the whole basis for U.S. and NATO nuclear forces. After the failed coup attempt in Moscow, on September 5, 1991 Cheney returned from a White House meeting saying that the president had asked how we could use this opportunity to make progress, particularly in the area of nuclear weapons.

We decided this was an opportunity to reduce Soviet tactical nuclear weapons and bring them under better control.[23] It was also an opportunity to try a new approach, one that recognized the sometimes perverse consequences of protracted arms control negotiations. Too often during the Cold War negotiations had the effect of exaggerating the importance of the systems under negotiation and even forcing investment in unnecessary systems simply for negotiating leverage. One alternative, recommended by Libby, was to announce unilateral reductions and urge the other side to respond with its own parallel reductions.

Cheney responded to the president by proposing that the United States should announce its intention to eliminate short-range tactical nuclear weapons in Europe (except for dual-capable aircraft) and all tactical nuclear weapons on naval ships. The latter proposal had enormous appeal to the U.S. Navy because it removed the burden of handling nuclear weapons aboard surface ships and at-tack submarines. It could also reduce frictions over ship visits with some of our key allies, particularly Australia and Japan. The announcement of these dramatic changes would be accompanied by an invitation to Moscow to reciprocate.

Cheney also recommended significant changes in our strategic nuclear pos-ture, both through START negotiations (the Strategic Arms Reduction Talks) and through reciprocal unilateral reductions, including proposals to lower the alert level of U.S. strategic forces, thereby reducing the danger of an accidental or mistaken launch.

These proposals were well received at the White House. Brent Scowcroft—who had long disliked submarine-launched cruise missiles because of the challenge they presented to arms control verification—particularly liked the removal of tactical nuclear weapons from attack submarines.[24] At his suggestion, a proposal to ban multiple-warhead intercontinental missiles through START and a unilat-eral withdrawal of tactical nuclear weapons from South Korea were also added.

The timing of this last initiative took the South Korean government by sur-prise, but fortunately we had spent several days that summer in discussions with a South Korean delegation, headed by their national security adviser, explaining our desire to remove our nuclear weapons from Korea and clear the way for South Korea to propose a denuclearization of the peninsula.[25] Given the extraor-dinary effectiveness of U.S. conventional weaponry in Desert Storm, we no lon-ger needed tactical nuclear weapons in Korea for deterrence and they had become an unnecessary burden on our forces.

Within days of President Bush's announcement of his nuclear initiative on September 27, Gorbachev and Yeltsin responded with separate and similar re-sponses of their own, paving the way for eliminating many Soviet tactical nuclear weapons, consolidating the remaining ones in central locations, and giving new impetus to strategic arms control negotiations. The result, as Powell has sum-marized, was that U.S. operational nuclear warheads would be reduced over ten years by 65 percent from the level at the time he became chairman of the JCS, a total reduction of fifteen thousand.[26]

Stability versus Change in the Soviet Empire

The disagreements within the Bush administration over policy toward German unification and related issues of arms control were largely tactical and easily re-solved. Indeed, there was considerable admiration in the Cheney Pentagon for the way Secretary Baker secured agreement to a unified Germany remaining a member of NATO.

There was substantial disagreement, however, concerning change in Central Europe and Eastern Europe, and particularly in the Soviet Union itself. It seemed to us that State and the NSC staff had a peculiar attachment to the status quo. One early manifestation was Baker's surprising suggestion, on the eve of Romanian president Nicolae Ceauşescu's fall, that the United States would not object "if the Warsaw Pact felt it necessary to intervene" in Romania. This suggestion of a return to the Brezhnev Doctrine, just weeks after a Warsaw Pact summit had condemned the 1968 invasion of Czechoslovakia, astonished even Gorbachev and Eduard Shevardnadze, his foreign minister.[27]

The difference manifested itself again when Boris Yeltsin emerged as leader of the Russian Federation. Here too, State and the NSC staff seemed to prefer Gorbachev to the popularly elected Yeltsin, and they reinforced this preference with personal criticisms. In contrast, Yeltsin was welcomed warmly by Secretary Cheney at the Pentagon during his visit to Washington in June 1991. In their meeting Yeltsin said memorably that "increasing the Soviet defense budget would be a crime against the Russian people, who have already suffered enough under seventy years of Communism." It was a remarkable statement coming from the former Communist Party boss of Sverdlovsk, and it clearly came from the heart.

That attitude alone would have endeared him to the secretary of defense. But Cheney also knew, thanks partly to the regular discussions with his experts, that Yeltsin was no flash in the pan. To the contrary, he represented passionate anti-Soviet feelings within Russia itself, to say nothing of the non-Russian republics.

These differences emerged more sharply, though only briefly, on August 19, 1991, the day of the failed coup attempt against Gorbachev. The initial response from the president and Scowcroft, who were in Kennebunkport, Maine, was ambiguous. Scowcroft cautioned Bush against calling the coup "illegitimate" or even "unconstitutional," suggesting the formulation "extraconstitutional" instead. He told Bush, "We may have to deal with these guys," and Bush even told the press that his "gut instinct" was that Gennady Yanayev, the nominal coup leader, had a "commitment to reform."[28] Cheney, who hurried back that same day from his vacation in British Columbia, was clear from the beginning that the United States had to come out strongly against the coup.[29] Fortunately, by the end of the day the White House came out with a clear statement condemning the coup, after an urgent message from President Yeltsin to President Bush.

Even after the coup, State and the White House were still skeptical of Yeltsin and sympathetic to Gorbachev, although increasingly aware of his weakness. The more immediate issue, however, was the U.S. attitude toward the referendum on Ukrainian independence scheduled for December 1. Visiting Ukraine in July, Bush had endorsed Gorbachev glowingly in a speech in Kiev and warned that freedom is not the same as independence. Americans will not support those who seek independence in order to replace a far-off tyranny with a local despotism. They will not aid those who promote a suicidal nationalism based on ethnic hatred.

The speech enraged Ukrainians, who saw it as opposition to independence.[30]

As the referendum approached, the administration debated how it should respond to a likely vote in favor of Ukrainian independence. At a White House meeting on October 11, Cheney argued that "support for the center puts us on the wrong side of reform," while Baker said that "we should not establish a policy of supporting the breakup of the Soviet Union into twelve republics. We should support what *they* want, subject to *our* principles."[31]

The State Department wanted a policy of "delayed recognition," insisting that an independent Ukraine meet a number of conditions to gain U.S. recognition, including a commitment to denuclearization and destruction of the nuclear weapons that were on Ukrainian territory.[32] Despite the importance of denuclearization, making that a condition of recognition undervalued the moral and strategic significance of Ukrainian independence. It would also have put at risk the very goals that we hoped to achieve, by weakening Ukraine's sense of security and possibly even encouraging Soviet opposition to Ukrainian independence.

In the end, the issue was decided on the eve of the referendum when Bush told a meeting of Ukrainian Americans that the United States would recognize independence if that was the outcome. The setting suggests that the president was thinking about U.S. domestic politics, but that is not clear. In any case, none of the subsequent accounts explain why delaying recognition would be a more principled position or more conducive to a peaceful outcome. No doubt Cheney's view was influenced by his belief that the breakup of the Soviet Union was in the U.S. interest—but certainly that was more reasonable than the opinion sometimes expressed by our State Department colleagues that the United States would be better served by preserving the Soviet Union. More important, by this time the United States could not determine the outcome, only perhaps delay it, and delay was fraught with danger. Cheney understood that history was flowing in our direction and that it would be a mistake to stand in the way.

Articulating the New Defense Strategy

In welcoming her colleagues to NATO's first post–Cold War summit in London in July 1990, British prime minister Margaret Thatcher reminded them of the disappointed optimism of earlier times. "Europe stands today at the dawn of a new era," she cautioned, "as promising in its own way as 1919 or 1945." Yet even Mrs. Thatcher probably did not expect that less than a month later Iraq would invade Kuwait.

The major cuts in U.S. force structure and budgets that President Bush had announced in his Aspen speech were postponed as we proceeded to deploy a force of five hundred thousand to the Persian Gulf. By the end of 1991, however, that force had returned home and we turned to the task of writing the Defense Planning Guidance (DPG) for the military services to prepare their budgets, taking account of the Gulf War experience, the collapse of the Soviet Union, and the massive changes in our nuclear posture.

For Cheney, the Gulf War experience reinforced his belief that "we cannot base our security on a shaky record of predicting threats." Even the failed coup attempt in Moscow, despite its positive outcome, was a reminder to expect the unexpected. The new Regional Defense Strategy that President Bush had announced in Aspen was designed to provide for an orderly reduction of the U.S. defense posture and avoid what Cheney viewed as the mistakes of the past, when the United States had to cut its defense efforts too much and too quickly following major wars. "Never in this century," he told the Congress in February 1992, "have we ever gone through one of these periods of downsizing the force and done it right":

> If we fail to maintain the necessary level of military power, we are likely to find that a hostile power will try to fill the vacuum and present us with a regional challenge once again. And this will, in turn, as it has previously, force us to higher levels of defense expenditure at a higher level of threat and a greater risk of war.[33]

However, for others, such as Congressman Les Aspin, the influential Democratic chairman of the House Armed Services Committee, the defeat of Saddam Hussein and the collapse of the Soviet Union were simply reasons to seek even bigger peace dividends. The reductions made possible by moving from a global defense strategy to a regional one were no longer sufficient. Instead of planning for two major regional contingencies, Aspin believed we only needed a capability for one or at most one-and-a-half.[34]

Working closely with Scooter Libby and myself, Cheney developed four principal arguments against Aspin's narrowly "threat-based" strategy. He presented these in congressional testimony in February 1992.[35]

First, since "the history of the Twentieth Century is replete with instances of major, unanticipated strategic shifts" and since changes in our strategic posture cannot be made quickly, "a proper appreciation of *uncertainty*" had to be "a critical part of any realistic defense strategy."

Second, in addition to allowing for uncertainty, an effective strategy should *"shape the future security environment"* rather than simply react to threats. We could even prevent threats from emerging by shaping how both friends and foes perceive "our will and our capability."

Third, we needed to preserve what Cheney called *"strategic depth,"* the fact that threats to our security were now remote geographically and also in time. The investments required "to maintain the strategic depth that we've won" are much less than the investments required in the past. But if we "fail to secure those advantages . . . eventually, these threats will not be remote . . . vague or difficult to discern, and we will not have the alliances and capabilities required to deal with them."

Fourth, *U.S. leadership* was essential for preserving this strategic depth since the unparalleled security we now enjoyed came not only from our own military superiority but from the fact that most of the other strong countries of the world were our allies. Cheney believed that we still needed allies and friends. But he did not share the view that U.S.-Soviet cooperation in confronting Iraq meant that we had entered a "new world order" in which the Security Council could, as Scowcroft put it, "perform the role envisioned for it by the UN framers" in opposing aggression.[36] Rather, the Persian Gulf coalition, impressive as it was, would not have come together without the demonstration of U.S. ability and willingness to act alone if necessary.[37]

Unfortunately, the possibility of a serious debate over the Regional Defense Strategy evaporated when the *New York Times* reported a leaked draft of the DPG before Cheney, Libby, or I had even seen it. As Eric Edelman explains in his important accompanying chapter about the DPG in this book, press characterizations of the draft gave rise to a number of myths about the new defense strategy. Far from being an extreme strategy developed by a small group of Defense Department officials, the DPG not only reflected the consensus thinking of the first Bush administration but became generally accepted defense policy under President Clinton. Like President Bush's original Aspen speech, it was not a blueprint for a U.S. military buildup but rather for a substantial drawdown.[38] Nor was it a secret plan waiting to be implemented a decade later in response to the terrorist attacks of September 11, 2001.[39]

The Regional Defense Strategy, eventually published in January 1993, was a direct product of the work Cheney initiated in late 1989, which was first announced publicly by President Bush in his 1990 Aspen speech, and elaborated in congressional testimony by Cheney, Libby, and myself in 1991–92. Yet most accounts of the draft DPG make no reference to that previous work.[40] The principal failing of the draft was that it had not yet caught up with what Cheney was saying in testimony, unlike the final guidance, which was issued in May.[41]

The Regional Defense Strategy was not a grand strategy because it covered only defense strategy, but it did more than just replace one force-sizing plan with a different one. It defined, with considerable success, the military capabilities needed to "shape the future" and preserve "strategic depth" in the face of uncertainty. Like the containment strategy at the beginning of the Cold War, it identified certain principles, geographic areas, and capabilities as key to future U.S. security. It proposed to preserve and extend the strategic depth achieved with the end of the Cold War by shaping developments in the three regions of greatest strategic significance—Europe, Northeast Asia, and the Persian Gulf—not through the use of force, but by shaping the expectations of both friends and potential adversaries. This was a direction that was very different from that suggested by either a "new world order," in which strategic competition simply disappeared, or a "sole surviving superpower" that would be able to dominate all others by itself.

The most misleading characterization of the new strategy was the allegation that it was "unilateralist." To the contrary, at its core was the notion that the United States had achieved unparalleled security not because we were now the "sole superpower," but rather because most of the other powerful countries in the world were our allies. This was the major feature of the "strategic depth" that the strategy proposed to maintain and, if possible, extend.

In fact, the strategy identified America's *alliances* as the *first* of three enduring requirements needed to "shape the future" and preserve that "strategic depth." At a time when American allies are fighting alongside us in Afghanistan, the emphasis on maintaining U.S. alliance relationships may seem like a blinding flash of the obvious. But strategic insights often look more obvious in hindsight than they did originally, and at the time many argued that our alliances were no longer necessary or not worth the effort.

In addition to the commonly recognized function of deterring aggression—which at the time seemed happily a remote possibility—our alliances had helped to develop habits of cooperation among our allies and had avoided the need for competing national defense programs. The disappearance of the Soviet Union made it necessary to be more explicit about this function of our alliances than we had been in the past. As the final document expressed it:

> Our alliances . . . represent a democratic "zone of peace," a community of democratic nations bound together by a web of political, economic and security ties. This zone of peace offers a framework for security not through competitive rivalries in arms, but through cooperative approaches and collective security institutions.[42]

This notion of a "democratic zone of peace" referred specifically to what had been achieved in Europe and Northeast Asia during the Cold War. It reflected the success of American alliances in calming historic rivalries in Europe and North-east Asia, as well as a recognition that the remarkable durability of those alliances owed much to the common democratic values of the members. It was a notion that was consistent with an emerging stream of scholarship on "democratic peace theory," but it was grounded in our actual experience in Europe and Northeast Asia.

Most boldly, the Regional Defense Strategy suggested further that the same benefits of denationalizing defense efforts through the collective efforts of a democratic alliance could be extended to the newly independent states of Central and Eastern Europe and the former Soviet Union. On this point, we were ahead of much of the thinking in the Bush administration, though not—as it eventually turned out—of the Clinton administration.[43]

Cheney won the budget fight in 1992, but the Democrats won the election and Aspin himself became secretary of defense. Nonetheless, as Edelman points out, the Clinton administration adopted much of Cheney's Regional Defense Strategy, though not by name. Several factors contributed to this somewhat surprising result.

For one thing, the logic of preserving and enlarging our democratic alliances in Europe and Northeast Asia was compelling not only to our existing allies but to the new democracies of Central and Eastern Europe. To the credit of the Clinton administration, it eventually responded positively when those new democracies made clear their strong desires to join the NATO alliance. Second, there was the logic of events in each of the three "critical regions"—crises in the Balkans, the Iraqi mobilization on the Kuwait border, North Korean and Chinese missile firings—that demonstrated the need for substantial regional capabilities. Third, it proved difficult politically to break away from the logic of planning for two major regional contingencies, although Aspin initially tried. Finally, the regional defense strategy was affordable. It permitted some reduction in defense spending, even though not as much as its Democratic critics had previously wanted.

As implemented through the 1990s, the strategy successfully shaped the security environment in the critical regions of Europe and Northeast Asia. It made it possible to avoid a renationalization of defense policies, not to mention the violent anarchy or the competition between the United States and its former allies, particularly Japan and Germany, which some self-proclaimed "realist" scholars of international relations had predicted.[44] By bringing the newly independent states of Central Europe into a U.S.-led security framework, the strategy also eased their fears of a resurgent Russia and thereby reduced potential tensions in Central Europe.

The strategic depth that has thus been acquired has made it possible to view the hardening of Russian policy with comparative equanimity.[45] So, too, did we benefit from our security structures in Northeast Asia and the Persian Gulf. Although there is much room to debate how the United States has dealt with the North Korean and Iranian nuclear issues, we are certainly better off managing them within the framework of our collective defense arrangements in those regions than if each of our allies were left to fend for themselves. And those arrangements depended on U.S. leadership.

We have no historical experience to tell us whether this stability might have been achieved if the United States had abandoned its alliances with the end of the Cold War. However, we did have experience with the ineffectiveness of the "collective internationalism" in Bosnia and Kosovo. NATO, in contrast, proved to be remarkably effective in bringing an end, although belatedly, to the fighting in the Balkans. That success, in turn, may have discouraged what might have been serious ethnic conflict elsewhere in Central Europe.

By the end of the 1990s, U.S. defense capability had been cut below the levels of the "Base Force" envisioned in the original strategy. Arguably, it was on the edge of being inadequate. During the Quadrennial Defense Review in 2001, there was pressure to cut the force even further, particularly to cut the Army from ten active divisions to eight, but fortunately those proposals were rejected by Secretary of Defense Donald Rumsfeld.

The Regional Defense Strategy did not predict anything like the attacks of September 11, but a strategy is not a detailed road map. The purpose of a strategy is rather to provide a set of principles and capabilities that enable you to deal with both expected and unexpected developments as they occur. That was particularly true in the case of the Regional Defense Strategy, which emphasized the uncertainty of the future.

Now, nearly two decades later, it can be said that the Regional Defense Strategy was realistic about the uncertainty and demands of the years ahead and about the need for America to help shape the future security environment. It proposed to meet these challenges in ways consistent with American resolve, strength, and values. The regions it identified as critical remain so today. U.S. determination and capability to provide leadership in those three regions in the coming decades—and to deal with the unexpected—will continue to be vital for international peace and security.

4

THE STRANGE CAREER OF THE 1992 DEFENSE PLANNING GUIDANCE

Eric S. Edelman

Probably no defense planning document since the end of World War II, with the possible exception of NSC-68 (which was not strictly speaking a defense document), has received as much attention and discussion as the 1992 Defense Planning Guidance. If you Google the 1992 DPG or Defense Planning Guidance you come up with over ninety-two thousand hits, one of which is a Wikipedia entry that suggests the DPG represents the "Wolfowitz Doctrine." The PBS television show Frontline, which produced the "The War Behind Closed Doors" program, devotes several pages on its website to the 1992 DPG, links it to the decisions leading to Operation Iraqi Freedom, and suggests that it was the first draft of the Bush "Grand Strategy" articulated in the 2002 National Security Strategy (NSS).[1]

Even before the beginning of Operation Iraqi Freedom, journalists Frances Fitzgerald and Nicolas Lemann had drawn attention to the views expressed in the DPG and their impact on President George W. Bush's views of the world. According to Fitzgerald, what had once been a minority view in the Bush 41 administration had become the dominant view in Bush 43. Sketching out a view that would become dominant in later writings (many influenced by the views of Colin Powell's chief of staff Larry Wilkerson), Lemann suggested that there was a cabal of senior officials in the Bush 43 administration who were "generally speaking, a cohesive group of conservatives who regard themselves as bigger-thinking, tougher-minded, and intellectually bolder than most other people in Washington." Lemann intimated that the DPG was weighing on Condoleezza Rice's mind as she sought to prepare the new National Security Strategy that was issued later in the year. "There are two ways to handle this document," Rice told Lemann, "one is to do it in a kind of minimalist way and just get it out. But it's our view that, since this is going to be the first one for the Bush Administration, it's important." Lemann concluded that Rice wanted to assert a "more dominant American role in the world" than she had previously contemplated.[2]

It is a stretch to say that Fitzgerald and Lemann are responsible for all that was subsequently written (particularly the more conspiracy-minded writings) about the DPG, but certainly they established the basic tropes. In their view, a self-conscious set of neoconservatives, bent on world domination, had taken a run at developing a U.S. grand strategy in 1991–92. Having failed to impose it on the Bush 41 administration, they returned after 9/11 to impose their agenda on Bush 43. This was evident in the language of the National Security Strategy of 2002, which allegedly bears so much resemblance to the Defense Planning Guidance.

Characterizations of the DPG, starting with the original *New York Times* article, are frequently drawn in hyperbolic terms. Eugene Jarecki calls it "one of those unsettling blueprints from the Strangelovian depths of the system." He argues that had it been adopted it would have entailed one of the "most radical expansions of American hard power since the Truman Doctrine." Even careful scholars have been unable to refrain from hyperbole in their accounts. Joan Hoff attributes the DPG to neoconservative fury at stopping the first Gulf War with the liberation of Kuwait rather than "going to Baghdad and getting rid of Saddam." She goes on to argue that "the neocons responded to this rebuff by producing from the bowels of the Pentagon a new national defense policy document called the Defense Planning Guidance." Her summary of the document intimates that the DPG called for higher defense spending as well as unilateral and preemptive action to prevent the emergence of peer competitors and eliminate weapons of mass destruction (WMD) threats. Michael Lind argues that "the hegemon strategy became official U.S. doctrine when Wolfowitz joined the George W. Bush Administration." Even a generally thoughtful critic, Francis Fukuyama, seems to regard the DPG as an unrealizable attempt to impose global hegemony in the face of a rising China (although he argued in 1992 that the "DPG established a good framework for a post–cold war strategy").[3]

This durable narrative distorts the drafting history and content of the original DPG and attributes greater influence on the 2002 NSS than is warranted. The DPG was not a plan for the United States to assume the role of "globocop," although it did seek "lessons learned" from the Gulf War and the end of the Cold War to support and extend U.S. primacy in the international system. The NSS, for its part, was drafted largely by Philip Zelikow at the direction of Condi Rice and in consultation with Deputy National Security Adviser Stephen Hadley. The "self-confident" conservatives in the Office of the Vice President and the Pentagon had no hand in it, other than the normal, bureaucratic routine of commenting on and clearing the document.

Although the drafting of the DPG has been shrouded in controversy, and discussion of the document has been shaped by the hyperpartisan atmosphere in Washington, it is, I think, well worth reconsidering the document now that the passions engendered by the Bush 43 administration and the war in Iraq are beginning to cool.

A more balanced reconsideration of the DPG is now possible since some of the documents associated with the draft have been declassified, thus allowing a more thorough and accurate account of what it actually said. In retrospect, how well did the DPG describe the future national security environment? How did it compare with many of the academic assessments written in 1990–92? Did the DPG influence the development of the 2002 Bush National Security Strategy? Did the thinking in the DPG deviate, if at all, from the broad mainstream of American strategic thinking since 1945? The story offers a rare example of officials attempting to step back and think strategically about the nation's future at a very dramatic turning point in its history.[4]

Attempts to outline a grand strategy for the United States have been infrequent. NSC-68 is the most famous case (and deservedly so). The standard Cold War history calls it "the American blueprint for waging the cold war." As two other scholars have written, "The central policy message of NSC-68 was that the United States and its allies must achieve preponderant power by a massive and rapid buildup, especially of military capacity across-the-board." A subsequent effort by President Dwight D. Eisenhower, the "Solarium" project, along with NSC-68 formed what one scholar has called the "the American strategic synthesis." President Richard M. Nixon and Henry Kissinger, his national security adviser and later secretary of state, arguably attempted to impose a grand design on U.S. foreign policy but that effort was quickly overwhelmed by Vietnam. Although the DPG was solely concerned with defense strategy (as opposed to the other instruments of national power), it was clearly undertaken in the spirit of those earlier initiatives. The fate of the DPG, in that sense, is a cautionary tale about the difficulty of making strategy in the postmodern world. If ever there was a subject that is ripe for revision, the making of the 1992 Defense Planning Guidance is it.[5]

The DPG Hits the Press: Are We "the Global Big Enchilada"?

The DPG entered the national consciousness on March 8, 1992, when Patrick Tyler published a leaked version of the draft guidance, at that time circulating for comment in the Pentagon, in the *New York Times*. The article argued that because the document focused on the "concept of benevolent domination by one power, the Pentagon document articulates the clearest rejection to date of collective internationalism." Tyler's overstated article, published amid a presidential election campaign, set the tone for all future discussions of the document.

Two days later, quoting unnamed critics, Tyler noted that insistence on maintaining America's position as the sole superpower "reflects intense pressure in the American military establishment to define a robust mission for itself in the post-cold-war era" and predicted that if the document was issued by Secretary of Defense Dick Cheney it would potentially put the Bush administration "at odds with a number of its international allies and, domestically, with the Democratic majority that controls Congress." The *Washington Post* added that "Democrats continued their assault on the Pentagon memorandum." Sen. Alan Cranston (D-Calif.) accused DoD of wanting to make the United States "the one, the only main honcho on the world block, the global Big Enchilada."

Tyler also reported that bureaucratic politics was at work: "One Administration official, familiar with the reaction of senior officials at the White House and State Department, characterized the document as a 'dumb report'" that "in no way or shape represents U.S. policy." But Tyler suggested that the draft did represent "a substantial body of opinion" in DoD that would support "a one-superpower world" and would regard aspirations for regional leadership by other nations with "suspicion." Lost in the swirl of bureaucratic backbiting was the fact that the draft had not been read or approved by Cheney, Paul Wolfowitz, or Scooter Libby.

On March 11, the *Washington Post*'s Bart Gellman reported that the DPG draft tracked with previous public comments by Cheney and General Colin L. Powell, chairman of the Joint Chiefs of Staff, and added that "like their public statements" the DPG draft highlighted the virtues of alliances and collective action, respect for international law, and "the spread of democratic forms of government and open economic systems." He also reported that Cheney and Wolfowitz had not approved the draft but concluded that it represented ideas they had developed: "'This is not the piano player in the whorehouse,' one official said."

Gellman, whose reporting on the controversy, at this stage, was more accurate and balanced than Tyler's, also noted that:

> Senior Pentagon officials angrily disputed the charge, first made in Sunday's *New York Times*, that the new strategy was "the clearest rejection to date of collective internationalism." They cited the document's pledge, on its first page, to "continue to support and protect those bilateral, multilateral, international or regionally based institutions, processes and relationships which afford us opportunities to share responsibil-

ity for global and regional security." "What is just dead wrong is this notion of a sole superpower dominating the rest of the world," a ranking defense official said. "The main thrust of what the secretary has to say and what that draft also says is that the key to maintaining the rather benign environment we have today is sustaining the democratic alliances we've shaped over 40 years."[6]

During this typical Washington feeding frenzy, the Pentagon spokesman, Pete Williams, made the valid, but generally overlooked, point that "people are responding to what's been reported about the draft, so it becomes a sort of hall of mirrors." President George H. W. Bush, when asked, said he hadn't seen the paper but was "broadly supportive of the thrust of the Pentagon document." None of this stopped an anonymous senior official from opining that "hopefully, that document's going down in flames . . . it certainly reads like the U.S. is arrogating to itself the role of world policeman."

First impressions are notoriously hard to shake but what strikes one looking back at the press coverage is how utterly routine the story was. Most of the criticism by unnamed sources simply reeks of the "not invented here" syndrome that is the mark of Washington's tribal bureaucratic culture. Critics did not generally put forward alternative strategies for securing the nation's interests but, rather, chose to comment harshly about a document that they had not read and that was still in the preparatory stage.

The Document Itself: Origins and Intent

The origins of the DPG can be found in the efforts by Secretary of Defense Cheney to adapt the U.S. defense posture to the rapidly changing international security environment at the end of the Cold War. Although many critics argued that the DPG was mainly an exercise to maintain defense spending, in reality it was drawn up specifically to cope with the looming reality of decreasing resources for defense in a post–Cold War era. A June 1991 briefing by Wolfowitz to the Defense Planning Resources Board noted that Cheney had directed consideration of "large funding reductions" and "programmatic implications of [a] new security environment" in fall 1989.[7]

At Cheney's and Wolfowitz's direction, Libby and others had specifically looked at the drafting of NSC-68 and the "Solarium" effort under President Eisenhower. In January 1990, a new DPG had been issued that foresaw a reduced Soviet conventional threat and a reorientation of force planning toward the emergence of regional threats in Southwest Asia. The result was to be a new defense strategy and "Base Force" structure that would be announced by President

Bush at Aspen in August 1990. Unfortunately, the announcement was lost in the noise of Saddam Hussein's invasion of Kuwait. In their memoir, President Bush and National Security Adviser Brent Scowcroft mention the speech in Aspen on August 2, but interestingly never mention its subject.[8]

Bush announced that day that U.S. active duty forces could be reduced by about 25 percent to the lowest level since 1950, but that "the United States would be ill-served by forces that represent nothing more than a scaled-back or a shrunken-down version of the forces that we possess right now. If we simply prorate our reductions, cut equally across the board, we could easily end up with more than we need for contingencies that are no longer likely, and less than we must have to meet emerging challenges. What we need are not merely reductions but restructuring." Bush summarized the new defense plan as follows: "Our new strategy must provide the framework to guide our deliberate reductions to no more than the forces we need to guard our enduring interests—the forces to exercise forward presence in key areas, to respond effectively to crisis, to retain the national capacity to rebuild our forces should this be needed." He also added the maintenance of what he called "a defensive strategic nuclear deterrent" and introduced the "concept of reconstitution of our forces . . . the readiness to re-build, made explicit in our defense policy, will be an important element in our ability to deter aggression." The general outline at Aspen—reduced U.S force structure; forward presence; rapid crisis response capability; nuclear deterrence; and reconstitution—became the basis on which the further refinements of the 1992 DPG would be built.[9]

A contemporaneous assessment of the "Aspen Strategy" noted that the president's announcement "appears to be a very top-down re-direction in defense strategy and force structure. From the public record, it appears that there were a handful of individuals that orchestrated the new concepts." In addition, it was clear "that despite their obvious concern with Operations Desert Shield and Desert Storm, the secretary of defense and the JCS chairman were simultaneously working the new national security strategy and force structure." Curiously, the new doctrine "had no name." It was variously referred to as "the Aspen Strategy," "the reconstitution strategy," "the strategy for the new world order," "the new strategy," or the "President's strategy." Because there was so little evident White House involvement, the degree of presidential commitment to what was an-nounced at Aspen would have to be measured by what came out in the NSS.[10]

When the NSS of 1991 did appear in August, the ideas outlined at Aspen emerged only at the tail end of a document that was intentionally watered down. According to a former Bush administration NSC staffer, "it was consciously in-tended that the 1991 NSS say as little as possible." Some of the White House staff desired to dilute the document probably because they wanted to avert controversy in an election year. The relative disengagement of President Bush and his national security adviser may reflect the fact they were preoccupied with the personal diplomacy of handling both Soviet decline and Iraqi aggression. In addition, Bush and Scowcroft lacked the inclination to engage in speculative "grand strategy" or the "vision thing." Baker, for his part, had State Department counselor Robert Zoellick working on geoeconomic strategy for promoting a world of linked open economies and free trade. That work was conducted independently of the defense reviews at DoD, but its postulates were embedded as assumptions in the DPG draft.[11]

Wolfowitz's June DPRB brief made it clear that the DPG was meant to be grounded in the defense strategy outlined at Aspen. But Wolfowitz also wanted the DPG to build on the lessons learned from the Persian Gulf War. His deputy, Scooter Libby, was leading a major, congressionally mandated study of the "Conduct of the War," from which the lessons, particularly with regard to precision guided munitions, would be derived and assessed in the context of the "military technological revolution" also known as the "revolution in military affairs."[12]

A first draft of the DPG was circulated by Lieutenant General (retired) Dale Vesser in early September 1991 with a laconic note that "work on the Russian revolution" was keeping the bureaucracy from moving at the pace originally envisaged. The anti-Gorbachev coup and final paroxysm of the Soviet Union had begun, injecting urgency to the DPG deliberations. The original plan was based on the end of Soviet empire in Europe and the decline of the conventional threat. Events on the ground were now accelerating and the environment began to look even more favorable to the United States. The Soviet Union, itself, appeared about to break up, the Communist Party's hegemony had been overthrown, and the prospect of a democratizing Russia was thoroughly changing the strategic equation. These developments demanded a rethinking of U.S. strategy. The document attempted to move the discussion of U.S. strategic interests from the global challenge represented by the Soviet Union to the more likely regional threats to American security. The language of the early drafts echoed, in some respects, the argument put forward by Francis Fukuyama in his 1989 article on "the end of history" and prefigured some of the literature on the so-called democratic peace. This was not surprising. Fukuyama had worked for Wolfowitz in Reagan's State Department and was then serving as a consultant to DoD.[13]

Time and space do not permit a full exegesis of the several drafts of the DPG and the internal memos that have now been declassified. It is definitely a project that should be on the research agenda of the historical profession. Still, one can make some preliminary observations. First, although Cheney, Wolfowitz, and Libby were providing guidance to the process, it is clear from the documents that multiple authors were involved in writing different sections of the strategy paper. Second, rather than "retreating" from the initial position taken in the first iteration, subsequent drafts were designed primarily to smooth out the unevenness caused by drafting by many hands. Third, OSD officials were seeking to transform a highly classified, internal document into something that could be released publicly in an unclassified version. They also wanted to bring it into conformity with Secretary Cheney's previous congressional testimony on the new defense strategy. Winning congressional support for the strategy and its associated budgets was an important goal of OSD policymakers.[14]

The authors of the DPG were not embracing unilateralism. The outline circulated by General Vesser in September 1991 listed "alliances generally" as the first item under the subsection "broad policy." A proposed introductory section circulated with that draft noted "in general, the US role will be that of leader or galvanizer of the world community, not of sole actor." The leaked February 18 draft stipulated that the end of the Cold War reduced "pressure for US military involvement in every potential regional or local conflict," and stated in another section that the United States would "maintain and nurture its alliance commitments in Europe, Latin America, and in the Far East." Subsequent revisions altered the original language, but the commitment to alliances remained.[15]

The authors of the DPG introduced the notion of strategic depth and discussed a widening zone of peaceful democratic nations. These insertions made the document more easily available in an unclassified form and reflected Cheney's explanations of the new defense strategy in his congressional testimony. For example, on March 20 Scooter Libby sent Secretary Cheney a revised draft (it was the second one since the leaked February 18 version), noting the new draft "is as near to an unclassified text as possible at this stage of drafting." He wrote that the text had "been significantly reworked for clarity and to emphasize the themes you struck in your testimony, including shaping the environment and providing U.S. leadership within a system of democratic alliances." Three specific points that Libby made are relevant to later developments. He underscored "the importance of striving to extend this system of collective security to the East European countries and the nations of the former Soviet Union," elaborated the conditions that might require the United States "to plan forces to enable us to act with only limited help from others, if necessary," and specified "critical interests in Europe, East Asia, and the Persian Gulf, and in areas such as freedom of the seas and honoring historic or alliance commitments—for example, Latin America and (silently) Israel."[16]

A memo from Dave Shilling, director of the Office of Strategy and Resources, to Libby outlined where the document set new directions, but was at pains to show where those areas had language that was similar to that used by Secretary Cheney in his congressional testimony. At the end of April, the late Admiral Don Pilling (at that time a director for politico-military affairs on the NSC staff) forwarded the NSC staff comments on the DPG. The comments were relatively minor edits to provide "conforming language" to some upcoming presidential speeches. One of the fixes was important, however. Appended to one of the paragraphs in the section on continued U.S. leadership was language that made explicit something that was implicit in the entire editorial process. "In the end," the NSC commentators wrote, "there is no contradiction between U.S. leadership and multilateral action; history shows it is precisely U.S. leadership [that] is the necessary prerequisite for effective international action." That editorial fix remained in both the classified document and the unclassified version released later.[17]

By May, the revised draft had been circulated, edited, and cleared by all the appropriate bureaucratic actors. Wolfowitz sent it to Cheney and noted that "there have been relatively few changes to the first half of the Draft DPG. It is still a rather hard-hitting document which retains the substance you liked in the February 18th draft." In a handwritten note, Wolfowitz wrote that although he was clearly "biased," he believed "the document faithfully reflects the direction you have set for the Department." Although the DPG remained classified (and in particular the annexes with illustrative planning scenarios), work continued on an unclassified version, not identical but very similar to the various classified versions. That document, entitled "Defense Strategy of the 1990s: The Regional Defense Strategy," was released by the Department of Defense in January 1993 as the Bush 41 administration came to an end.

The Regional Defense Strategy paper discussed the importance of integrating the newly independent nations in Europe into a "democratic zone of peace," applauded the disappearance of a global threat and hostile alliances, refocused attention on regional challenges to U.S. security interests, elaborated on the importance of maintaining America's technological edge, and pointed to the looming threat of ballistic missile and WMD proliferation. The release of the document was barely noted in the press.

The DPG's Significance: As Seen at the Time and Since

It is easy to understand, given the electoral cycle, why the leaked DPG became a subject of bitter partisan debate, but something else is needed to explain the particularly vociferous bureaucratic infighting that was sparked by the leak. One important contributing factor was the interagency dispute over the breakup of the Soviet Union. After the abortive coup attempt in Moscow in August 1991, Mikhail Gorbachev returned from his short exile to face a resurgent Boris Yeltsin, now leading the Russian Federation. When Ukraine declared its intent to leave the Soviet Union and scheduled a referendum on independence, Cheney and his subordinates believed it was a positive development, one the United States should welcome and assist, if possible.

Secretary Baker and his team, as well as the NSC staff, took a much more cautious view that reflected the outlook of Soviet foreign minister Eduard Shevardnadze. The internal debate burst into public view in November. As Baker recounts in his memoirs:

> Unfortunately, before we could even discuss our views with the President, Jeff Smith of the *Washington Post* laid out the debate in an article on Monday, November 25, headlined, 'U.S. Officials Split Over Response to an Independent Ukraine.' I was furious and felt sandbagged, not by Cheney, but by the DOD bureaucracy that clearly had been the initial source of the story. It was the only time I can remember during the Bush Administration when a real policy dispute in which I was involved was aired in the press before we could resolve it among the principals.

As this passage makes clear, the anger was real. It was still lingering the following spring when the DPG was leaked and debate was intensifying within the administration over potential NATO membership for the Central Europeans.[18]

Writing two years later, without the heat of the moment or the prism of a second Iraq War through which to view it, David Callahan made two important points about the DPG. First, the document drew on "deeply rooted traditions of American foreign policy doctrine" in arguing for U.S. leadership to avoid the emergence of potential rivals in Europe and Asia. Second, the rewritten, final version did not differ that much from the original. Callahan noted that "while the initial Defense Planning Guidance draft was strongly criticized, the revised version, containing many of the same points, was not." He also pointed out that many experts, in and out of government, on a bipartisan basis were worried about the potential renationalization of defense (particularly by Germany and Japan).[19]

James Mann, who wrote without the benefit of the declassified documents, picked up and extended Callahan's argument—that there was bipartisan support for the general approach of the DPG at the time it was finally presented to Congress. He acknowledged the claim by Paul Wolfowitz in 2000 that the 1992 DPG had "turned into the consensus, mainstream view of America's post-Cold War defense strategy." Mann concluded that this was correct and contended that "after an initial review of defense issues" the Clinton administration "preserved the general outlines and structure of the post–Cold War force structure that had been worked out under Cheney." The Clinton team embraced NATO enlargement and described the United States as the "indispensable nation." National Security Adviser Tony Lake told an audience at Johns Hopkins University's School of Advanced International Studies on September 21, 1993, that "the successor to a doctrine of containment must be a strategy of enlargement—enlargement of the world's free community of market democracies."

Furthermore, as Mann pointed out, defense expenditures remained at a level that exceeded that of the next fifteen nations combined at the end of the 1990s. The Democratic administration twice bombed Iraq unilaterally and undertook a major NATO military operation in Kosovo without UN Security Council endorsement. Mann reported that "in short . . . while Democratic leaders often accused the Republicans of unilateralism, the truth was that the Clinton Administration too gave far less weight to principles of collective security than had America's leaders from the 1940s through the 1980s." Mann may have overstated the case for U.S. fidelity to multilateralism during the Cold War, but his underlying point still stands. Mann argued that, at the end of the day, the Democrats failed to come up with any clear alternative vision of American strategy that would forswear the 1992 vision of the United States as the sole superpower.[20]

Derek Chollet and James Goldgeier have also reviewed the tempest over the DPG, situating it, appropriately, in the context of the 1992 election year. They also rightly note that the document did not really change in substance as it was redrafted. Their account, however, errs on one key point. They claim that some senior officials around the president disowned the document. They quote Brent Scowcroft as saying the DPG was "just nutty. I read a draft of it. I thought, 'Cheney, this is just kooky.' It didn't go anywhere further. It was never formally reviewed." Scowcroft is not quite right. As previously described, the revised April draft was reviewed by Scowcroft's NSC staff and cleared for release by the secretary of defense. Continued interagency disputes kept it from being formally promulgated, but it was ultimately released publicly by Secretary Cheney.[21]

Chollet and Goldgeier argue, as have many other writers, that the DPG planted the seeds of the strategy of preemptive and preventive war that were subsequently outlined in George W. Bush's National Security Strategy of 2002. Other scholars, disregarding a denial by Philip Zelikow, have asserted that "the muscular idealism revealed in September 2002 was an unabashed manifestation of well-documented neo-conservative thought." They allege, moreover, that Paul Wolfowitz had "a hand" in both documents. But the DPG documents that have been declassified so far actually don't use the term "pre-empt" at all, and it is clear from the drafting process that any discussion of preemptive or preventive action was in the context of possible battlefield use of WMD by an adversary. Wolfowitz, in any case, had only the most glancing involvement with the 2002 NSS.[22]

It is possible to see some traces of the reasoning used in the DPG in the 2002 NSS, but those hints are largely indirect and prosaic. In that sense, they validated Wolfowitz's point that the arguments of the DPG had become accepted as part of a broad consensus on national security strategy by 2002. Hence, the 2002 NSS acknowledged that "the United States enjoys a position of unparalleled military strength and great economic and political influence," but argued that, rather than seeking U.S. unilateral advantage, the United States would attempt "to create a balance of power that favors human freedom." Beyond that, a comparison of the now declassified drafts of the DPG, the unclassified Regional Defense Strategy paper of January 1993, and the NSS makes very clear that there is not much resemblance between the first two and the latter document. The lengthy discussion of preemption in the NSS finds no real earlier precursor in the DPG.[23]

The DPG and Post–Cold War Security Environment

Much of the criticism of the DPG focuses on its policy recommendations, but how did the DPG stand up as a description of the post–Cold War security environment? How did it compare to what others, particularly academic students of international politics, were writing at the time? After all, a strategy document can only be useful for policymakers if it accurately describes the likely environment for decision making. The DPG was based on the proposition that, according to an early, pre-February 18 draft, "the United States may be said to be the world's sole superpower, enjoying predominance on the world political-military stage that is unprecedented in the last century." This reflected Charles Krauthammer's declaration of the "Unipolar Moment" in *Foreign Affairs* as well as Samuel Huntington's advocacy of retaining U.S. primacy in international affairs. Huntington concluded his article with words that could have easily come from the 1992 DPG: "A world without U.S. primacy will be a world with more violence and disorder and less democracy and economic growth than a world where the United States continues to have more influence than any other country in shaping global affairs. The sustained international primacy of the United States is central to the welfare and security of Americans and to the future of freedom, democracy, open economies, and international order in the world."[24]

Interestingly, one of Huntington's main preoccupations in that article was the threat that Japanese economic policies (and potentially European economic policies as well) posed to American economic primacy. Those concerns also mirrored the worries of others about the renationalization of defense and security policies in Europe and Asia. Precluding such renationalization, of course, had been one of the more controversial parts of the leaked DPG draft, but the DPG's prescriptions—reliance on the traditional alliance treaties and structures, U.S. leadership, and extension of the democratic zone of peace—were quite different from what many academics at the time were proposing.

Jack Snyder and John Mearsheimer forecast a more multipolar, and hence, more unstable and violent Europe. Snyder proposed pan-European (rather than existing transatlantic) institutions to foreclose a predicted resurgence of praetorianism in Eastern and Central Europe. Stephen Van Evera, for his part, was more optimistic that Europe was "primed for peace" rather than war, but he urged that the best way to ensure that outcome was to "Finlandize," that is, neutralize, the newly independent states of Central Europe. Others called for a Concert of Europe to coexist with NATO until such time as the alliance could cede its collective security function to the Organization of Security and Cooperation in Europe.

Kenneth Waltz and Christopher Layne presented still more fundamental challenges to the logic of the DPG. They argued that unipolarity was doomed to be a short-lived phenomenon since the nature of the international system would guarantee that other states would rise and balance the overweening power of the United States. The failure of their predictions has spawned a cottage industry of articles in international affairs journals seeking to explain why U.S. primacy has proved so persistent.[25]

The fact that the Clinton administration seems to have relied more on the argument and spirit of the DPG than on most of what appeared in the pages of various scholarly journals appears to speak for itself. Reflecting on the twenty years since the fall of the Berlin Wall, the former editorial director of *Le Monde*, Daniel Vernet, notes that the United States "has competitors but no rivals." If that judgment is correct, it serves as a vindication, from an unlikely source, of the analysis, policy prescriptions, and strategic consensus that the DPG represented. It explains, perhaps, why James Mann characterizes the DPG as "one of the most significant foreign policy documents of the past half century," and why George Herring, who decries "the halting response of the George H. W. Bush administration to the new world order it had proclaimed," nonetheless suggests that the 1992 DPG was the "one serious effort to plot a post–Cold War strategy." If anything, the document can be faulted for not sufficiently anticipating the danger of Islamic extremism, state failure, and terrorism. Nonetheless, it outlined the defense posture that provided both the military capabilities and the rationale for a forceful response that both Bill Clinton and George W. Bush relied on when confronted with these phenomena.[26]

The Difficulty of Grand Strategy in the Postmodern Era

The DPG offers an interesting case study of what happens when a group of officials attempts to look at first-order questions in the wake of a series of major events that prompt a large break or caesura with the past circumstances that guided strategy. There are several points worth making about the process. The first is that without presidential support it is unlikely that any effort, no matter how creative and effective, will survive unscathed in Washington. President Bush, while generally supportive when the DPG flap occurred, was never really interested in "the vision thing" as he was wont to call it. The media attention to the DPG draft was distracting during a presidential election season and it was clear that the White House staff wanted the controversy to end as quickly as possible. The "pragmatism" of Bush, Baker, and Scowcroft disinclined them to put much stock in "big ideas"; they had minimal interest in the debate over a new strategy. This is reflected by the lack of attention to the subject in their respective memoirs.

Second, the bureaucratic process is the enemy of grand strategy. Peter Rodman has argued that our national security decision-making system has become more complicated because of the balkanized nature of the process and the expanding number of bureaucratic actors. The sheer size of those bureaucracies makes it extremely difficult for the president to get good strategic advice or enforce his policy objectives. The stove-piped system makes it particularly difficult to integrate different domains and the nature of the bureaucratic process tends to turn major strategy documents into well-intentioned "to do lists." Any document that must go through the bureaucratic maw ends up being dumbed down to the lowest common denominator. It is instructive, in that regard, to compare the DPG with NSC-68. As Nicholas Thompson notes in his recent book, NSC-68 was drafted by a small group around Paul Nitze, just as the DPG was drafted by a small group around Cheney and Wolfowitz. The difference between the two instances is that the bureaucracy was smaller in 1950 and the document went to President Harry S. Truman with relatively little fanfare. Contemporary Washington's bloated bureaucracy and the ubiquitous intrusion of the press into the process through leaked and planted stories make the elaboration of strategy in contemporary America extraordinarily difficult.[27]

Third, the importance of ideas in strategy and national policy, despite the difficulties raised above, is crucial. As several scholars have pointed out, the domestic changes in the Soviet Union led Western (and particularly U.S. leaders) to conclude that the Cold War had ended. That clearly was the case with the drafters of the DPG. Their understanding of the internal dynamics of the Soviet regime is what led them to conclude that it was possible to transform U.S. defense and national strategy. They reconfigured U.S. strategy to highlight the importance of U.S. primacy, leadership of alliances, and willingness to contemplate unilateral action (if necessitated by circumstance). They focused on forestalling the dangers of WMD proliferation, emphasized missile defense, and stressed the necessity of maintaining and, if possible, extending America's technological advantage (based on the revolution in military affairs). Their views were tacitly accepted by most practitioners of U.S. national security policy despite the lack of presidential interest, as noted above, and despite the manufactured controversy in the press.[28]

Why was that the outcome? Historians will have to examine the first Bush presidency in greater detail to provide a definitive answer, but the absence of a sufficiently compelling alternate set of ideas about the maintenance and use of American power are a large part of the explanation. The sociology of knowledge about the spread of strategic ideas is extremely inexact. That being said, the notion of maintaining U.S. primacy, expanding the zone of democratic peace, and focusing on emerging regional threats—all key elements of the DPG—became powerful ideas that successfully underpinned U.S. foreign policy for the sixteen years after the DPG was drafted. Whether they will continue to guide the Obama administration remains to be seen.

Finally, whether or not strategy is an illusion, presidents will be called upon by law and circumstance to articulate a grand strategy for the nation. As they seek to regain "strategic competence" in the face of enormous national security challenges, they should note that our country has been well served by presidents who maintained "a preponderance of power" and exercised U.S. primacy to accomplish the ends outlined by Samuel Huntington: preservation of world order; support for open societies, free markets, and democracy; and maintenance of the global commons. Historical antecedents such as NSC-68 and the Solarium project will certainly serve as examples, but policymakers and scholars would do well to examine the strange career of the 1992 DPG now that it is possible to do so on the basis of the actual documents rather than on the superficial accounts in the press or the fevered speculation of the blogosphere. There are still valuable lessons to be learned.[29]

5

A CRISIS OF OPPORTUNITY

The Clinton Administration and Russia

Walter B. Slocombe

For the Clinton administration, the great unexpected—or, more precisely, unprecedented—international event it faced was the "radically transformed security environment" that had emerged over the last few years before it took office.[1] As a consequence of this massive change in the world, Bill Clinton expected to be the first U.S. president since Herbert Hoover who would not need to be preoccupied with foreign and security problems. After a campaign whose central theme was "It's the economy, stupid," he, and most of the team that joined his administration, expected foreign policy to be a far less dominating factor than it had been for his predecessors. Of course, foreign problems would need to be attended to, but international economic questions would be the major area of foreign worries, if only because of the interaction of domestic and international economic events and policy. The traditional security issues of the sort that had engaged presidents since the 1940s, would, the new team hoped, be secondary.

In many respects, that prospect seemed reasonable. Unexpected events—the implosion, first, of Soviet control over Central Europe and, then, of the Soviet Union itself—had removed what had been for nearly two generations the central focus of international politics and the overwhelmingly most pressing U.S. national security priority—the worldwide confrontation between communist East and democratic (or at any rate, noncommunist) West. Even apart from the disappearance of the conflict with the Soviet Union, the world looked remarkably benign in January 1993. Germany, the center of so much of the geopolitics of the twentieth century, had been reunified peacefully and its partners in the European Union were moving toward economic integration with political integration a long-term, but now less implausible, prospect. The former Warsaw Pact satellites were on the way to stable democracy and market prosperity. North and South Korea had agreed on a process of denuclearization. China seemed absorbed in its internal development, having cast off revolutionary zeal in exchange for growth (and continued regime control) under market principles.[2]

Nor was the new and promising landscape limited to the old East-West confrontation line: Iraq was humbled by recent defeat in the Gulf War and under pervasive international surveillance and supervision. Apartheid was ending in South Africa, and peacefully so. Most of Latin America was emerging from rule by juntas and coups to democratic order. Taiwan and South Korea had cast off authoritarian regimes while remaining strong friends of the United States. Even in the Middle East, the Madrid agreements appeared to open the path to resolution of the Israel-Palestine problem.

To be sure, there were still outliers—Iran, Haiti, the wreckage of Yugoslavia, the seemingly endless tragedy of Africa exemplified by the chaos in Somalia, and even Northern Ireland, as well as nontraditional security challenges ranging from environmental degradation to terrorism. But, on the whole, to the new team assembling in Washington the age in which the electorate had given them responsibility seemed, if not the "end of history," a time when there was a real prospect of a world that would be broadly stable, peaceful, just, democratic and—if only the economic issues could be addressed correctly—prosperous. In short, the new administration expected to have a reasonable chance to operate in a genuinely new world order—however unwilling its spokesmen would have been to accept that particular phrase, so ridiculed when used by Clinton's predecessor.

Russia: An Opportunity Recognized

Clinton and his advisers, however, did have a strategic vision for U.S. foreign policy: to reinforce the positive trends that seemed so pervasive, based on the judgment that "for all its dangers, this new world presents an immense opportunity . . . [to] help provide security and increase economic growth for American and the world."[3] To be sure, Clinton and his team, for all their desire to concentrate on domestic issues from health care to the environment and to build a better world on a new foundation, recognized, as Clinton wrote in his memoirs, that "the 'new world order' President Bush had proclaimed . . . was rife with chaos and big, unresolved questions."[4] The new team, as I recall it from my middle-level vantage point, like their chief, believed they had an opportunity to help shape that order—as well as an unavoidable need to address the lingering problems of the past.

Nowhere was this more the case than in regard to Russia. The administration wanted to encourage the economic and political development of Russia as a key part of its overall strategy of "engagement and enlargement" toward an overall goal of "an integrated democratic Europe cooperating with the U.S. to keep the peace and promote prosperity."[5] And so it is appropriate to focus on the Russia case in this attempt to look back at the policy making and strategic planning of the Clinton administration in the fundamentally new conditions it faced.

The Russia case was in many ways unusual. Normally, the unexpected events considered most difficult for governments to deal with are thought to be the "3 a.m. phone calls," that is, the sudden attack, the sudden challenge, of which the 9/11 attacks are the paradigm example. For the Clinton administration, however, the Russia question was not an unexpected event in anything like the way the 2001 terrorist attacks were for its successor. Of course, even "3 a.m." crises usually have antecedents that are clear, at least in retrospect; certainly, that is the case regarding terrorist attacks in general, if not the particular form they took in September 2001. But "3 a.m." crises do involve tactical, if seldom strategic, surprise. And there was nothing of that sort about the Russia question in 1993. The ultimate implosion of the Soviet system was a long time coming, and was an accomplished reality in 1993.

Thus, from the point of view of considering how governments deal with unexpected events, Clinton's Russia/Yeltsin project provides a striking case—*not* primarily because it arose in an environment that was an unexpected, surprising event. Rather, the Clinton administration's Russia effort serves as an example of the challenge to government of facing unfamiliar events and circumstances that do not present threats but opportunities.

Russia in 1993 presented an unprecedented phenomenon. Seldom, if ever in history, has a major power confrontation ended leaving one party undefeated militarily, facing the challenge of shaping its future course while profoundly weakened and fragmented. The end of the Soviet era therefore posed, not the familiar problem of averting or containing or reversing a threatening development, but of how to make use of an opportunity. For the collapse of the USSR was not—unlike most crises tactical or strategic—a matter of an increased danger. Indeed, its immediate—and even today its long-term—effect was to drastically reduce the traditional military and political threats to the United States, its friends, and its interests.

A Strategy, a Plan, and a Commitment

The new administration understood that Russia presented an opportunity and chose to seize that opportunity.[6] President Clinton had a clear sense that the objective was a Russia that would be internally democratic and economically successful, and therefore likely to be internationally constructive and integrated into global structures. Shortly before the inauguration Clinton told Strobe Talbott, his long-time friend and chief adviser on Russia, that he wanted to do "good stuff with Russia and really take advantage of what's new in a positive sense over there, even if initially the task was to 'avert disaster.'"[7]

To achieve his goal, the new administration decided, as Talbott advised Clinton in a March 1993 memorandum, to seek "a strategic alliance with Russian reform," aiming "not just to prevent the worst, but also to nurture the best that might happen in the former Soviet Union."[8] More specifically, Clinton and Talbott saw Boris Yeltsin, as the best—perhaps the only—hope for a Russian leadership committed to the policy that Russia must make such a transition. Throughout his two terms, no foreign policy project or problem had a higher priority for Clinton than supporting Yeltsin as the most direct path toward the emergence of the reformed Russia that Clinton hoped to help create. Clinton's view was that "Yeltsin was up to his ears in alligators, and I wanted to help him."[9]

Clinton recognized that his goal—and his means—comported with the policy the prior administration had embraced in its final year or so.[10] For example, a policy document issued on the very last day of the Bush administration declared that "it is critical to US interests in Europe . . . that we assist the new democracies in Eastern Europe to consolidate their democratic institutions, establish free market economies and safeguard their national independence."[11] Clinton accepted this view, as he did the advice of Richard M. Nixon, the disgraced former president, who told Clinton, through Talbott, that "[Yeltsin] may be a drunk, but he's also the best we're likely to get in that screwed up country. . . . We've got to keep him from becoming our enemy, or from being replaced by someone who wants to be our enemy."[12]

Clinton and Talbott had few illusions about either the challenges Yeltsin faced or, indeed, the Russian president's own personal and political limitations. And those challenges were great. Yeltsin's personal problems apart, he and the reformers with whom he had initially surrounded himself faced unrelenting opposition from ultranationalists, Communists, entrenched old bureaucrats, and others. The economy inherited from the Soviet Union was a shambles and was being looted by those who soon would become the "oligarchs"; inflation was skyrocketing; crime and corruption were rampant; and the meager social safety net enjoyed by former citizens of the Soviet Union was collapsing. Simultaneously, the relationships between Russia and the fourteen other ex-Soviet republics, now independent states, and between the government in Moscow and many non-Russian ethnic groups within the Russian Federation were contentious, and often portentous.

Implementing the Strategy

To implement his strategy, Clinton moved quickly to build a personal relationship with Yeltsin, thereby hoping to shore up the Russian president's position and his ability to reform his country. Reflecting Clinton's view that the core of Russia's and Yeltsin's problems was economic, and that economic reform, open markets, and expanding trade were critical to Russia's internal political reform and its constructive international role, Clinton won congressional approval for a substantial increase in U.S. direct economic assistance to Russia.[13] He also pressed other countries and international financial institutions to offer assistance to Yeltsin. President Clinton directed U.S. agencies to develop assistance programs in a broad range of areas, including for humanitarian relief, energy, housing, agriculture, small businesses, civil society, pensions, and currency stabilization. He especially wanted to help the Russians secure their nuclear weapons and dismantle them. Furthermore, during the 1997 financial crisis, his Treasury team worked to secure a multibillion dollar IMF bailout on terms Russia could live with.

In the belief that Yeltsin's status would be enhanced inside Russia and that he would be more willing to cooperate outside Russia if he were treated as a major player in international affairs, Clinton labored on behalf of Yeltsin's admission to the inner "club" of world leaders. He persuaded other members of the G-7, which had been designed as a gathering of the leaders of successful market democracies to address financial and economic issues, to admit Russia and become the G-8. He also shifted the group to a more political and strategic agenda, on which Russia could more plausibly speak as an equal.

Believing it was helpful for Yeltsin to make U.S. assistance look less like charity and more the work of equal partners, Clinton sponsored the creation of a U.S.-Russia "Commission," cochaired by Vice President Al Gore, whose task was to work with the successive Russian prime ministers and drive forward the broad cooperation agenda.

Clinton—a highly successful and very personal politician—regarded himself as having far more insight and empathy than his "experts" for another politician's domestic problems. He repeatedly told aides that he thought Yeltsin's political problems were much greater than his own, and he believed the chances for reform were strongly linked to Yeltsin's personal political fortunes. Clinton sought to urge Yeltsin to be a more effective democratic politician and—at least in his own view—tried to be extraordinarily patient and tolerant of Yeltsin's periodic outbursts that included last-minute public repudiations of deals Clinton thought had been agreed upon.[14] More important, when Yeltsin faced internal opposition, Clinton backed him unreservedly—when Yeltsin battled in various elections, parliamentary debates, and referenda, when he drew criticism for undemocratic and extralegal actions, when he suspended the Russian parliament in late 1993, and, even more controversially, when he used military force to suppress a Duma-centered nationalist rebellion. Most challenging of all to Clinton's proclaimed humanitarian values and legal principles, Clinton insisted on restraint in official U.S. criticism when Yeltsin ordered a massive military repression in Chechnya.

Nonetheless, the internal "red" and "brown" oppositions in Russia gathered strength as economic and political progress faltered. Yeltsin did not build a solid political base—whether from failure to try, distrust of his "liberal" allies, or—as Clinton seems to have believed—unwillingness to compromise in the way Clinton, as a skilled practitioner of small-d democratic politics, believed was the key to success. Russia's economic problems proved greater than even the grim prognosis of 1993, and were exacerbated by the financial crisis of 1997. Internal disorder—from corruption to Chechnya—that Yeltsin could not control undermined his political position and restricted his ability to work closely with the United States.

The reformers who served Yeltsin in the early years proved unable either to build a viable domestic base by political steps or fortify their positions by economic or governance success. Yeltsin gradually replaced them with figures from the past, from the security services, and from the new elite. The ultimate replacement of reformers was Yeltsin's selection of Vladimir Putin as his successor. These new figures were committed not to democratic and market reform, but to shoring up their own position—and, to be fair, to restoring social order, bringing focus to the chaotic and irresolute Yeltsin regime, and reviving prestige and self-confidence in Russia as a nation.

A Conflict of Priorities

Single-priority strategies are seldom workable. Clinton's priority of working with Russia because of its long-term strategic importance promptly collided with other, more immediate, if arguably less crucial, priorities that he could not ignore or afford to sacrifice. The Russia question was not the only unexpected and unprecedented challenge and opportunity for American interests in Europe that followed from the collapse of the Soviet system. The dramatic challenges flowing from that collapse included the outbreak of open warfare in the Balkans, the quest of the newly independent states of Central and Eastern Europe for security assurances, and doubts about the future role, if any, of the NATO alliance.

From the first days of the administration, the most pressing, if not the most important, foreign policy issue was the Balkans. In particular, the United States was drawn into the ongoing ethnic fighting in Bosnia that UNPROFOR, the UN-commanded peacekeeping force in the country, had proved utterly unable to stop. Clinton had campaigned on the promise to find a solution, but he could not have ignored events in Bosnia as someone else's problem. Almost daily reports of new horrors, mostly attributable to the Bosnian Serbs backed by their compatriots in Belgrade and unconstrained by the ineffectual UN-organized international response, made the issue unavoidable.

Russia, however, was highly reluctant to agree to Clinton's efforts to put stronger international pressure on Belgrade and its clients in Bosnia, particularly in the form of military action. This reluctance grew partly out of a view (perhaps more faithfully held in Belgrade than in Moscow) that Serbia was a traditional ally of Russia, partly out of opposition to any international involvement in what could be portrayed as an internal ethnic conflict, and partly out of distaste for any diminution of the UN role, over which Russia held a veto as a permanent UN Security Council member.

In the Bosnia saga, Russian reluctance initially was only a marginal irritant to Clinton's hopes to partner with Yeltsin. In practice, Russia was not the chief obstacle to the administration's efforts to increase pressure on Belgrade by the threat of military action. Ambitious U.S. ideas about air strikes and arms aid for the Bosnian Muslims were unacceptable to the European allies, whose troops, unlike those of the United States, were on the ground and at risk. With time, however, continued Serb outrages and provocations exposed the European forces to humiliation and built support in European governments and publics to break free of UN constraints. In mid-1995, the British and French finally came to agreement with the United States on a combination of military strikes, diplomatic initiatives, and pressure on all factions to compromise.

At that point, although Russia was critical of U.S. efforts in public, it gave tacit agreement. Indeed, Russian diplomats had been included in the "Contact Group" that had earlier tried to negotiate a settlement, albeit more as a way of dampening Russian opposition than helping the Serbs. The Russians also participated in the Dayton talks that led to agreement on the terms to end the fighting in Bosnia. The accords also set up clumsy, but adequate, governmental arrangements for the country.

Russia was even persuaded to send military units as part of the Implementation Force (IFOR) established with UN authorization, but free of the strictures of UN command, to enforce the Dayton settlement. Russian participation was the product of the administration's decision that it was essential to include Russia in the process. This was not because the Russian military contribution would be significant in itself or even that Russia would help win Serbian acceptance of the settlement. Instead, the United States wanted Moscow involved as a symbol of American commitment to the proposition that Russia had a legitimate role to play in any major security enterprise in which its perceived interests were engaged. Finding a way to secure Russian participation in the force became a test of the degree to which the United States would work to acknowledge that role.

In the implementation of this policy, Defense Secretary William Perry, one of the strongest administration advocates of integrating Russia into a constructive international order, played a leading part in dealing with a thorny problem. Russia took the position that its forces could not be under NATO command, as was the case with the other IFOR contingents, including those from non-NATO members. Potential Russian participation in IFOR thus produced a collision not only with U.S. insistence on the principle of the unity of military command but also with the broader political need that IFOR be a NATO-run operation. The administration wanted Russian troops as part of IFOR. On both military and political grounds, however, the United States was unwilling either to have the Russian contingent under wholly independent, unilateral Russian command or to have IFOR, as a whole, be under a UN command. Perry—with the active participation of Talbott and the support of the president—worked tirelessly on the issue in unlikely association with Russian military officers who could hardly have been more different than he in personality and background. With the enthusiastic help of General George Joulwan, the U.S. Army officer who was the NATO Supreme Allied Commander at the time (and also a strikingly different personality from Perry), the defense secretary succeeded in working out a command arrangement acceptable both to the United States and its NATO allies and to the Russian government and military. That arrangement required a good deal of flexibility from both Russian and American military officers. It turned on exploiting the "coincidence" inherent in the historic arrangement whereby the NATO military commander in Europe, reporting to the Western alliance, was always the American officer who served concurrently as the commander of U.S. military forces in Europe, in which role he reported directly up the U.S. chain of command, bypassing NATO. Perry midwifed a deal whereby the Russian unit commander would report to the same individual officer as the rest of IFOR, but the Russian would deal with that general in his American, not his NATO, capacity. In practice, this convenient fiction worked surprisingly well, in part because Moscow may not have been eager to cause trouble for an arrangement that kept Russia's hand in the Balkan game, in part because both American and Russian officers in the field were not that much concerned with the niceties of higher level political arrangements, and in part because the authority of IFOR (and its Stabilization Force, or SFOR, successor) never faced a serious challenge on the ground in Bosnia, so command arrangements were never tested by combat.

The fact that Russia was prepared to have its forces formally under U.S., but not under NATO, command served to underscore that the Soviet collapse presented the Clinton administration with another, equally unprecedented issue besides the future of Russia itself—the future shape and role of NATO. Among the many questions the alliance faced in the aftermath of the disappearance of the Soviet military threat was whether its membership should expand to the east.[15] The end to Communist rule in the Soviet Union's satellite countries brought with it the collapse of the Warsaw Pact and the withdrawal of Soviet troops and bases. The newly independent nations of Central Europe were not, however, content to remain indefinitely in a "neutral" no-man's-land between the old NATO members to the west and Russia to the east, even with Russia shorn of its associated republics and with its military in a state of deep debility. To avert this outcome, they began almost at once to press for admission to NATO, as a symbol that they would in the future be linked to the rest of Europe and, more concretely, as assurance that their security would be backed by a military guarantee from the United States.

The Russian position was essentially the exact opposite to that of its former satellites: NATO was, and always had been, an anti-Russian alliance. With the fall of Communism, the dissolution of the Warsaw Pact, and Russian military withdrawal from Central and Eastern Europe—not to mention its commitment to internal reform and international cooperation—the need for NATO had disappeared. If NATO was not prepared—as it should have been—to follow the Warsaw Pact into oblivion, it certainly must not advance its frontiers eastward across Europe by bringing into its membership former Pact members, much less former Soviet republics. European security could be taken care of by direct dealings between Russia and the United States, and to a lesser extent, the original NATO allies.

Many, if not most, of the European NATO allies were far from enthusiastic about adding to NATO's membership. In part, this reluctance grew out of a conviction that there was not now and would not ever again be any external military threat from a shrunken (and hopefully a reformed) Russia, partly from a deep disinclination to become embroiled in whatever security problems there might be in distant, and on the whole, alien countries east and south of Germany, and partly out of realization that any enlargement would deeply complicate their own relations with Russia and potentially compromise the hopes—which they held as strongly as the Clinton team—for favorable internal development in Russia.

For the Clinton administration, the desire of the Central European countries for NATO membership was made all the more complicated because, unlike almost all other foreign policy issues (except Israel and trade policy), it had aroused interest in significant domestic political constituencies with little or no general interest in foreign affairs.[16] The aspirations of the former Warsaw Pact countries for NATO membership were enthusiastically backed by the organized voices of Americans who traced their ancestry to those countries. Historically, these ethnic groups had provided strong support for the Democratic Party, but that affinity had eroded in recent elections. Administration support for bringing these groups' former homelands into NATO could help sustain their links to the Democratic Party; conversely, opposition or even prolonged delay could hasten the erosion of their allegiance, for the Republican opposition could be counted on to press the case for rapid enlargement. (On the whole, commentators—including many Republicans—were distinctly divided on the enlargement issue, but elite views had much less potential direct electoral impact.)

This relatively unusual domestic political angle complicated an already difficult decision for the new administration. The core problem, however, was that the diametrically opposed desires of Russia and the prospective candidates for NATO membership presented a strategic dilemma for the administration that was far more complicated than any domestic side-effect. Inevitably—and correctly—the administration made a strategic decision that it could not choose cleanly between engagement with Russia and security guarantees to the aspirant NATO members. As the question of expanded NATO membership was emerging, Deputy Secretary of State Talbott argued to his superiors that "our strategic goal . . . was to integrate both Central Europe and the former Soviet Union into the major institutions of the Euro-Atlantic community."[17]

To be sure, this policy of balanced support for both goals had much merit. A Central Europe uncertain of its security would be a source of instability and trouble—as the Balkans seemed to confirm. A Russia that thought itself excluded from its legitimate international role would hardly be likely to be a constructive force in Europe or elsewhere. From the U.S. point of view, Russian security would be enhanced by the stability and confidence in Central Europe that NATO membership would bring, while a Russia reformed internally and included internationally would have no potential or desire to threaten the security of its neighbors. This line of argument, with its implicit message of gradualism and acknowledgement of the Russian perspective, was eventually accepted by the existing NATO allies, but found little resonance in Central Europe. The U.S. claim that NATO expansion was actually good for Russian security was even less convincing to most Russians.

The administration recognized that its dual policy was inconsistent with either a headlong rush to expand the alliance or with indefinite deferral. Rather, it required early actions that reassured the candidate countries of eventual membership, while offering some countervailing advantages to Russia. The administration, to meet this latter goal, sought to create a means for Russia to have, as the standard slogan had it, "a voice, not a veto" in NATO decisions that impacted Russian interests. The arrangements adopted to fulfill these ends included the Partnership for Peace. It was designed both to provide candidates with some reassurance during a transitional period through a commitment to consult on security challenges as well as to establish a mechanism for eventual membership. It also provided a rationale to defer an actual decision on membership until Russia could be persuaded to acquiesce to, if not support, the American initiative. The administration made persistent yet futile efforts to convince Russian officials that NATO enlargement was no threat. At the same time, along with other initiatives, it worked to set up a partnership between Russia and NATO. These efforts resulted in the establishment, shortly before the first new allies joined the Alliance, of the NATO-Russia Permanent Joint Council (PJC). In theory, Russia and NATO would consult as equals in the PJC. In practice, it proved of minimal utility, even as a forum, but it did serve its principal purpose of giving something to Russia without diminishing NATO's autonomy.

There was (and is) a solid case for the strategy that the Clinton administration adopted of pursuing both NATO enlargement and cooperation with Russia. But the logic of the strategy did not negate the fact that there were inherent tensions between those two aims. Russians, even those who had no interest in a return to the past, were convinced that whether or not NATO was a threat to Russia, its enlargement added to Yeltsin's political problems. (Interestingly enough, Yeltsin himself was among the Russians least suspicious of NATO enlargement. Periodically, he departed from the standard Russian line and suggested that if countries, such as Poland, wanted to join an unnecessary and outdated club, it was no great concern to Russia.) At the same time, most Central Europeans were (and remain) deeply skeptical of Russia's long-term capacity to be a benign neighbor, and were scornful of American and Western European theories on that score.

To some degree, the administration's efforts suffered from an unrealistic hope that the inherent tension could be resolved. For example, in response to Russian arguments that NATO was an innately anti-Russian institution, U.S. officials sometimes maintained that Russia itself might someday join the alliance. That proposition served to reinforce Russian suspicions that the Americans were not being serious, and accentuated Central European suspicions that they were not being realistic.

The Kosovo crisis of 1998–99 further exposed the limits on Russian-American cooperation in the security field. If Russia was unenthusiastic about helping the United States in Bosnia in 1993–95, it was even more so when Milošević stepped up his repression in Kosovo a few years later. By then, Yeltsin's position was weaker, and nationalist forces were stronger. And substantively, Russia found even more reason to oppose international intervention against Serbian action in what all conceded was Serbian territory: it feared, or purported to fear, that the logic of stopping Belgrade's actions in its Kosovo province and support for the ambitions of Kosovo's Muslim ethnic majority for autonomy and even independence could be turned to justify international intervention in Russia's own restive Muslim-majority regions, notably Chechnya. Moreover, Kosovo was a direct challenge to Russia's claim to oversee international military action by virtue of its Security Council status. Although the United States maintained that NATO's military action in Bosnia was justified under UN Security Council resolutions, Russia—and not only Russia—maintained that the NATO operation in Kosovo was illegal because it lacked explicit UN Security Council authorization.

Russian support for Milošević in the Kosovo conflict, however, was half-hearted. Despite some initial fiery rhetoric, Russia was skillfully—and not unwillingly—maneuvered by diplomacy into confronting Milošević with the reality that Russia would not protect him against NATO's military effort. But it was a frighteningly close encounter. The anti-NATO and anti-U.S. view of some Russian military and civilian leaders—even more worrying, the weakness of Yeltsin's hold over those elements—was exposed by a direct and potentially violent confrontation between Russian and NATO soldiers when Russian units from Bosnia moved into Kosovo in advance of NATO forces. Last-minute extraordinary diplomatic efforts defused the confrontation and even succeeded in gaining Russian agreement to participate in the NATO-led occupation of Kosovo, under essentially the same command arrangements that had been worked out for Bosnia. At a minimum, the affair deepened Russian suspicion of NATO and the United States. And since it appeared that the Russian unit's move into Kosovo was ordered by elements in the Russian military, U.S. worries grew that Yeltsin's power had eroded to the point where he was either unwilling to stop a dangerous challenge to the West, or, perhaps worse, was unable to do so.

Hopes Disappointed

Clinton's foreign policy had some important successes—stopping the Balkan wars, enlarging NATO, building a generally constructive relationship with China while standing by Taiwan, and brokering peace in Northern Ireland. Even the Russia effort was not without positive results—Russian withdrawal of troops from the Baltic countries; consensual elimination of the nuclear weapons left behind in Ukraine, Belarus, and Kazakhstan; cooperation on dismantling and securing Russian nuclear weapons; Russian collaboration, however grudging, in the Bosnia and Kosovo settlements; and acquiescence in NATO enlargement. But measured by the goals initially set, the outcome was not a success given the overall strategy of fostering a stable Russian market democracy as the foundation for international partnership.

At the end of Clinton's term, not only had Russian internal reform gone into retreat but Russia was a less constructive international player than at the beginning. That direct conflict over Kosovo had been avoided and that Russia ultimately lent its weight to the diplomacy that produced Milošević's capitulation was a real accomplishment, but, measured against the hopes of 1993, it was a limited one. Russia was never more than a difficult and reluctant—if periodically essential—partner in the Balkans, Clinton's chief short-term European policy challenge. The newly freed nations of Central Europe were—and remain—deeply (and understandably) suspicious of Russia. Likewise, many Russians who were by no means unremitting oppositionists were as deeply, if less justifiably, suspicious of NATO and of U.S. efforts to foster the independence and security of the former satellites. And there were other issues. Russia was generally unhelpful in enforcing sanctions against Iraq and vociferously denounced the periodic air strikes against Saddam for violating UN resolutions. For both commercial and strategic reasons, Russia was also unwilling to limit the export of military (including nuclear) technology to Iran and others, a reluctance that undermined U.S. nonproliferation efforts and called into question Russia's partnership in global concerns. The culmination of this failure to build a mutually beneficial relationship with Russia was the inability to get Putin, Yeltsin's chosen successor, to modify the ABM Treaty to permit a defense of the United States, subject to limits that would ensure the viability of the Russian deterrent.

The Clinton administration was even less successful in promoting internal reform. The Russia that existed when Clinton left office—and even more the Russia that exists today—is a Russia very different from the hopeful initial vision of Clinton's Russia policy. Putin's Russia is not Stalin's by any means; it is not even Leonid Brezhnev's, though it bears some resemblance to what Yuri Andropov may have thought he was going to create. The 1990s produced not the gradual maturing of a democratic, pluralistic political system, but internal disorder and political extremism contained only by reversion to a highly authoritarian system. Russian electoral democracy has become a sham, and the failure of political development has not just been on the level of formal political structure and process. State control of the mass media seems—perhaps predictably—to be the forerunner of a broader suppression of independent institutions and personal expression. Centralized control from Moscow by a handful of officials drawn mainly from the security organs has supplanted hopes for a democratic federal system.

The economic collapse that seemed on the Russian horizon in the 1990s has been averted, though more because of the high prices of commodities, especially oil, than from any fundamental transformation of the economy. Economic power appears to be passing back to the state, or the favorites of the state. That may be preferable to having it rest with robber baron oligarchs, but it is wholly inconsistent with the development of a real market system. It is not clear that either political authoritarianism or economic statism has meant better lives or even better services for the ordinary Russian.

Of course, for the United States, the most worrisome disappointment is in the realm of Russia's external policies regarding its "near abroad" and its attitude toward sanctions against Iran. The hope, so much a feature of the early 1990s, that Russia would become a reliable partner in a new international order has simply not been realized.

This failure arose not from the inability to recognize an opportunity, not from ignorance of U.S. interests, and not from an aversion to define goals. Clinton's plans for dealing with Russia were an integral part of his administration's broader vision of a more cooperative and more stable world built on expanding democracy, human rights, and economic prosperity. Nor did it fail because it eschewed a meaningful strategy for achieving the Russia-specific elements of its vision or because it disregarded the search for tactics to implement its strategy.

The test of whether a statement of policy is a strategy, rather than just (possibly useful) cheerleading and rhetoric, is whether the policy statement provides a framework for making real choices among competing priorities and for allocating scarce resources. By that standard, Clinton had a Russia strategy. And, having quite consciously set a goal, the administration strategically designed means to pursue its goal by encouraging internal reform and by wholeheartedly supporting Yeltsin with assistance, engagement, and cooperation on a broad range of internal projects. Moreover, the president and his team made this support for Yeltsin a real priority.

The Clinton administration (like the Bush team beforehand) recognized that the collapse of the Soviet Union meant that there would be a fundamentally new relationship with Russia. In an important sense, the United States—under any president—could not have avoided pondering what it wanted the new Russia to be like and what, if anything, the United States should do to shape its internal development. Even a policy of total passivity would have been a decision, if only by default.

The Clinton team, of course, pursued a far more active course. Understanding that U.S. interests would be strongly affected by the character of the new Russia, it concluded that the United States should try to shape its international behavior as well as its internal development. And it worked out a clear definition of the direction that development should take: internal democracy, the rule of law, and a market economy.

Moreover, Clinton and his advisers adopted a plan to advance that goal. Resources of time, attention, political capital, and money were allocated to Russia, and other goals were subordinated or sacrificed. The president committed his own time and that of his top advisers to relations with Russia. He promoted cooperation in international affairs, granted substantial material and technical aid, advocated Russian inclusion in international institutions, and treated Russia as a major factor in world politics (well beyond what its possibly temporary weakness mandated). He also provided all-but-unconditional support for Yeltsin personally, tolerating not only his personal foibles but also seeking to advance and protect his position inside Russia even when Yeltsin did things that would have provoked strong condemnation of any other nation's leader.

What Went Wrong?

There are several explanations for the limited success of the Clinton Russia policy.

First, the U.S. government, like Yeltsin and the Russian reformers, simply underestimated the inherent difficulty of the task.

It is fashionable to say that U.S. efforts to shape the politics, economies, and societies of other countries suffer from a lack of understanding of conditions elsewhere. This is only partly true in the case of Russia. The Clinton administration did not lack knowledge about Russia. Its Russian policies benefited from the fact that during the years of the Cold War the U.S. government and the U.S. academic and think tank community had developed a good deal of expertise in Russian affairs, much of it genuinely and eagerly committed to reform when the opportunity so unexpectedly arose. Knowledge of Russia was greater than that of the Balkans, the Arab world, North Korea, or Afghanistan.

But notwithstanding all that expertise, notwithstanding the recognition of the challenges to reform, and notwithstanding the realization that building cooperation with Russia "will be the work of generations," it seems clear that the U.S. government did not really comprehend the depth of the problems Yeltsin faced.[18] The Russian economy was in far worse shape structurally than was realized. In addition, there was more, and fiercer, opposition to the vision the administration (and Yeltsin) had for Russia, and that opposition had deeper and more intractable roots than appeared at the time. The sources of the deep cultural resistance to many aspects of the reform agenda are variously found in the poisonous effects of seventy years of totalitarian Communist Party rule, in basic elements of Russian tradition and society, and in the determination of vested interests in the bureaucracy, in the security services, and in the old Soviet (and new Russian) elites to protect their privileges. But whatever the sources, their cumulative effect was to create resistance to change far more formidable than the Clinton team had expected.

Nor did the reformers recognize some of the problems that reform itself created. The Soviet system, for all its manifold failings, had some basic structure and provided minimal services. And though it was deeply corrupt in the ordinary, as well as the moral, sense, the Soviet system did maintain a certain degree of social and civil order. For many Russians, the years after the dissolution of the Soviet Union brought disorder, unemployment, inflation, and declining living standards, even below the deplorable levels that had existed in Soviet times. Fairly or not, these conditions were blamed on reform and market democracy as well as on the policies of the Yeltsin government.

A deeper and more pessimistic understanding of Russia and its problems— and of the unintended side effects of reform—might have discouraged attempts to shape the Russian future. But it is also possible that greater understanding might have encouraged a less ambitious approach. A realization that the foes of reform would exploit economic weakness and take advantage of the widespread (and perfectly reasonable) revulsion against social disorder—might have reshaped the reform agenda. It might, for example, have meant giving more attention to the risk of "nomenklatura capitalism" in which the main benefits of privatization flowed to a small group, mostly from the old elites.

Second, there was a serious overestimation of the degree to which any external efforts could shape Russian politics, economics, and society.

In part, this was a question of resources. Even the billions spent on direct aid proved insufficient to affect an economy and society so big—and so damaged by the Soviet experience. But as large as the resources were, measured against the need they were relatively small. Total U.S. direct aid to Russia in the Clinton years was probably on the order of $10 billion. Even the "massive" IMF bailout at the time of the financial crisis in 1998 was only approximately $20 billion. These were, in absolute terms, very large amounts, but compared to the scale of the economy and society they were intended to shape, they were modest. They were dramatically less than the sums spent by the United States on defense or, more recently, on averting its own financial collapse.

It may be that governments, like individuals, tend to have even more difficulty exploiting opportunities for gain than staving off threats of losses. Governments may find it easier to commit resources and to mobilize mass political support for keeping things more or less the same than for changing them in positive ways; it may be simpler to devote resources—financial, political, and emotional—to protecting what exists than to making gains. Clinton secured significant resources for supporting Yeltsin, but compared with what the Defense Department spent on hedging against a possible confrontation with a "near-peer" competitor, the amounts were modest.

More fundamentally, however, the Clinton team exaggerated the potential of the United States to persuade and influence events abroad; it is not clear that larger allocations of U.S. resources would have produced significantly different results. Clinton and his Russia advisers were realistic enough to understand that the United States could not—or at least would not—provide enough direct financial aid to realize the Russian reform agenda. In fact, aid was concentrated on a relatively few projects, like the dismantling of Soviet nuclear weapons and missiles where the United States had a strong direct interest and where the payoff was great.

The scale of direct financial assistance was not just a matter of U.S. willingness or ability to provide money. Clinton's advisers explicitly recognized that reform was going to succeed only if it had solid Russian support. Their hope was that the United States (and the rest of the outside world) would catalyze and sustain internally driven reform by promoting cooperative projects and by providing technical assistance and counsel from both governmental and nongovernmental sources. At the time, and since, there has been plenty of criticism of specific elements of these efforts. After it became clear that early privatization efforts pushed by outside economic advisers were not working, Strobe Talbott aptly summed up the criticism when he said that what Russia needed was less shock and more therapy. But the more general lesson is that—with the best of intentions—it is very hard for outsiders to shape a basic transformation in attitudes and practices in a foreign society and culture.

Third, the vision of a full-scale U.S.-Russia partnership, even in international affairs, was too optimistic and neglected real conflicting interests.

Some of Russia's professed interests were directly and irreconcilably contrary to the United States and those of its allies. Great powers will always have some differences, even quite serious ones. Clinton's advisers, however, tried to induce Russia to take a different approach to defining its interests, so that areas of conflict would be fewer and more tractable. The results were limited. In particular, Russia's view of its security needs regarding its neighbors remained so demanding that it may be fair to claim that for Russia to be secure its neighbors must be insecure.[19] In this regard, the failure of Russian reform has had the greatest impact on direct U.S. concerns.

Fourth, the Yeltsin-centric tactic was inherently a risky way to pursue the overall strategy of promoting internal reform.

It is easy to say in retrospect that Clinton made a mistake in relying too heavily on Yeltsin, and in particular on putting too much hope in a good personal relationship with "Ol' Boris." Clinton himself recognized that Yeltsin was a "thin reed" on which to invest so much hope.[20] Any reformer would have faced strong opposition and any leader, reformer or not, would have encountered Russia's inherent problems. Yeltsin's personal problems—weakness for drink, his failing health, his unruly temper—made him an unreliable and often unpredictable partner. But the problem with Yeltsin did not stem from his personality, or his addiction, or his health; it stemmed from his outlook and his concept of reform in Russia. He was, inevitably, a transitional figure—a product of the old system, however sincere his rejection of it.

Yeltsin himself may have expressed his personal failure best in his valedictory announcing his retirement in favor of Putin:

> I ask your forgiveness for the dreams we shared that never came true; for the fact that what seemed simple turned out to be torturously difficult. I ask forgiveness for not justifying the hope that we could, in one fell swoop, lead from a gray, stagnant, totalitarian past into a bright, rich, civilized future. It turned out that I was naïve about some things. The problems were more complicated than I realized. We bulled our way forward through mistakes and failures. Many people suffered a terrible shock in these hard times.[21]

6

U.S. STRATEGIC PLANNING IN 2001–02

Philip Zelikow

The two cases of adjusting to change in 1989–90 and 2001–02 were exceptional for the fluid conditions in which policies were crafted, for the high stress, and for divisions within the governing administration. Some of the same individuals turn up in both stories. Then the resemblances dwindle.

Beginning in late March of 1989 and continuing through 1990, the U.S. government chose, as its basic goal, to support change and fashion a new international system. Many accounts of the George H. W. Bush administration, carried away with stories of its initial caution and conservatism, have fundamentally misread this period. It is true that during the transition and its first couple of months in office, the new administration came in with wary instincts and was mainly reacting to events. But in the spring of 1989, the U.S. government became highly proactive in its approach and its planning, especially to roll back Soviet rule in Eastern Europe and spur a reopening of the German question.

Yet in its policy choices, precisely because the change it sought was so dramatic, the United States attempted to manage change with reassurance. Reaching out to familiar allies, the U.S. government adapted prevalent ideas and proven institutions. In different ways, Robert Zoellick and Mary Sarotte elaborate on that theme in their contributions to this book.

In 2001, before 9/11, the foreign policy agenda of the administration of the younger Bush was deliberately modest. Its two most consequential pre-9/11 initiatives for the international system actually were spillovers from the new administration's thinking about *domestic* policy. One was to tear up the conservative fiscal approach of the previous decade. The other was to start reconceiving the U.S. approach to foreign assistance.

After 9/11, the U.S. government was reacting to a shocking attack. There was no well-developed framework either of policies or of institutions to help them cope with this shock or handle the awful responsibility of judging how to avoid another. The agenda was swamped by a reactive, desperate push to mitigate the risk of another such catastrophe. It was shaped by invention and improvisation: conservative goals, radical means.

In 2001–02, the main axioms about America's role in the world were not new; they were very much those of a generation of policymakers shaped by the end of the Cold War. Improvisation on those older themes—with new partners and new or reinvented American institutions (but not international ones)—was the norm.

In 1989–90, the goals were radical. Precisely for this reason the administration of the elder Bush adopted methods to achieve them with a veneer of familiarity, designed to reassure. In 2001–02, the goals were comparatively modest. Yet, confronting novel challenges with legacy institutions, the administration of the younger Bush chose methods that were experimental and unfamiliar. At first, in 2001–02, these experiments succeeded. Those initial successes reinforced new habits of thought and action.

The "Tongue-Tied Administration"

Like the Clinton administration before it, the new administration that took office in January 2001 under George W. Bush, the eldest son of the former president, struggled to find and articulate some overarching theme to America's purposes in the world. The national security adviser to the new president, Condoleezza Rice, later looked back on a time that "we as a nation revealingly called the 'post-Cold War era.'" It was a time, she wrote, when "we knew better where we had been than where we were going."[1]

The younger Bush wanted to concentrate his attention more on problems at home. To the extent he or Republican congressional leaders spoke at all about foreign affairs, the main message was to criticize what one intellectual (a Democrat, as it happens) had already condemned in an article entitled "Foreign Policy as Social Work."[2]

As presidential candidate, Bush had struck the dominant note: "I think one way for us to end up being viewed as the ugly American is for us to go around the world saying, we do it this way, so should you." The United States should be "humble," he said, "in how we treat nations that are figuring out how to chart their course."[3]

Of course, the officials in the new administration had many opinions about particular policy issues. But, unaided by hindsight, out of the cacophony it is hard to pick out an overarching melody.[4] George Shultz and Dick Cheney had been eminent influences in the early days of the campaign. Both were correctly regarded as traditional, conservative Republicans. When Bush asked Cheney to become his vice presidential running mate, his move was regarded as a sign that the inexperienced Texas governor had taken the "least adventurous and least sensational course possible."[5]

The notion of being "more disciplined" was a theme for the new team, one of the few generalizations that can safely be offered about them. A man who had been working in or around electoral politics practically all of his adult life, Bush may have felt he understood Clinton as just the kind of person and politician Bush had decided he would *not* be. Since the late 1980s, Bush had put aside a happy-go-lucky lifestyle and made self-discipline a life credo.[6] In ways more visceral than intellectual, the new team was not going to be like Clinton.

If Clinton had been a quintessential law school product, brilliantly teasing out every question embedded in a problem, Bush reflected the business school training of his generation. There were problem sets and solutions. The challenge, as he saw it, was to cut through the murk and find the bottom line. This shared sensibility was probably part of what had long drawn Bush to Cheney.

The most visible figures on foreign policy were Colin Powell and Condoleezza Rice: Powell, a compelling mix of competence and charisma; Rice, like Bush, underscoring a tighter definition of U.S. national interests. The new group did not have a tragic view of America's history. Their formative years had been marked by some remarkably positive changes in the world. They associated these changes with America's beneficial influence and example. Entering office, they tended to believe that traditional alliances with Western Europe and Japan had been neglected, that the armed forces and intelligence establishment were run-down and ill used, and that the diffusion of weapons of mass destruction was a new kind of threat that needed particular attention. One of the only initiatives they developed before coming into office was a push to get nuclear weapons and missile defense out of a "Cold War mentality." To do this they hoped to arrange, with Russia, quick moves to allow both countries to work more on national missile defense and make large, further cuts in the old Cold War nuclear arsenals.[7]

Other issues were a jumble. The well-informed British ambassador concluded at the time that the new administration's "batting order . . . was nuclear missile defense, Russia in that context, not a lot about the Middle East."[8] The new team had thought about international debt issues and decried the collapse of efforts to start a new round of global trade negotiations during the Clinton administration's last year. Iraq was the scene for ongoing U.S. combat operations and acute, unresolved policy dilemmas, so it received constant attention. North Korea and the Israeli-Palestinian peace process were two other large challenges in the in-box.

The new administration had large domestic plans as it came into office. The two signature initiatives were tax cuts in the expectation of fiscal surplus and the education reform program that became known as "No Child Left Behind."

Lacking such a concerted program in foreign affairs, the new president had early meetings with Mexico's leaders. He went to Europe. Varied notes were struck on North Korea, the Middle East peace process, the already moribund Kyoto climate treaty, and other issues, producing excited commentary. The first important crisis was over China, when a Chinese fighter harassing a U.S. surveillance plane collided with it and crashed. The crippled U.S. plane and its crew barely survived to land on Chinese territory. The ensuing furor was skillfully defused by Secretary Powell's diplomacy. The conservative *Weekly Standard* denounced Bush for his having supposedly accepted a "profound national humiliation."[9]

Bureaucratic entrepreneurs struck out in every direction, latching onto favored ideas or controversies in a fractious administration staffed by plenty of veteran intriguers and their allies. In the elder Bush's administration, large, contrasting egos had been knitted together by the personal connections among Bush, Secretary of State James Baker, and National Security Adviser Brent Scowcroft, with Cheney very much part of the group. They were a team. The Clinton administration, when it worked, was driven more by Bill Clinton himself and those working directly with him on his projects, or through personal networks that created teamwork among some of the key subcabinet officials at the White House and State. But in the younger Bush's administration, the president's management style made him more of a chief executive officer in a large conglomerate, with the heads of the subsidiary companies seeing themselves less as part of a team and more as executives with their own responsibilities to discharge.

Bush may have understood that he was fostering factional rivalry. He might have regarded such tension as natural or even healthy (as FDR once did, presiding over administrations riven by epic quarrels). But by the summer of 2001 the NSC process led by Rice and Hadley was being derided from all sides. Reporters heard that "meetings began without direction and ended without agreement." Amid the drift and finger-pointing, none of the other major officials were regarded as effective either. A *Time* cover story called Powell the "Odd Man Out." Secretary of Defense Donald Rumsfeld was "in retreat, under fire from all sides" as the press reported the widespread view that he would be the first cabinet member pushed out the door by the new administration.[10]

The most significant aspects of Bush's foreign policy thinking in his first months in office were not predicted by anyone. They grew out of his domestic agenda.

In domestic policy, Bush pressed for tax cuts. These were defended in part as a small government instinct, then as a Republican version of fiscal Keynesianism responding to the 2001 recession. These economic policies had significant implications for the administration's foreign policies, although they were not comprehended as such.

The elder Bush and Clinton had painfully crafted a series of centrist peace treaties with both parties in Congress in order to keep deficits down and even (briefly) generate a federal surplus. Their efforts had had large ripple effects in the global economy, mainly positive. The new tax cuts would have similarly large ramifications. They signaled much greater U.S. reliance on borrowing, both public and private, to maintain economic growth. Treasury Secretary Paul O'Neill, preferring to build on the fiscal conservatism of the previous ten years, was soon embroiled in political battle with the White House, battles he mainly lost. O'Neill was forced out of the administration at the end of 2002.[11]

Imbalances in U.S. accounts with the rest of the world were on a path to grow much larger during the next years, eventually reaching enormous and unprecedented levels by 2005. These large structural imbalances would eventually be a fundamental causal factor in the devastating global financial and fiscal crises that began in 2007.

The other spillover from the domestic agenda came from Bush's beliefs about humanitarian assistance to troubled communities. Bush's other large domestic program in 2001 was education reform. The core concept in that program was its focus on decentralized action, with Washington fostering local accountability with aid bargains to reward good choices and penalize bad ones. As Bush reflected on his approach to foreign policy in the summer of 2001, he wanted to apply this same sort of thinking, which he called "compassionate conservatism," to a globalized world.

In July 2001, Bush chose a World Bank venue to start talking publicly about this. He outlined "three great goals" for America in the world. First was to strengthen a "balance of world power that favors freedom" by moving "beyond Cold War doctrines" to deal with twenty-first century threats such as cyberterror or the diffusion of weapons of mass destruction (WMD). Second, renewing the old commitment to an Open Door, Bush stressed global economic growth "through a world trading system that is dramatically more open and more free." The third great goal, Bush said, was to "remove the huge obstacles to development" and fight illiteracy, disease, and unsustainable debt. "This," Bush said, "is compassionate conservatism at an international level."[12]

Later that month, Rice prepared a draft overview for a new "National Security Strategy." Her draft started with the phenomenon of globalization, promoting an approach that would treat these changes as "a source of opportunity, not fear." A crucial premise was that in a globalized world where great power rivalries were fading, the main problems would come from states imploding from within.[13] Bill Clinton, too, had long thought that "in the aftermath of the cold war, every good thing has an explosive underbelly. . . . We're fighting a constant rearguard action between the forces of integration and disintegration."[14] To Rice, sensing the same trends, her premise meant that international policy had to concern itself with principles "affecting both relations between states *and conditions within them.*"

As with Bush's World Bank speech, Rice was pushing beyond the campaign's emphasis on a "disciplined" policy oriented tightly around great power relations and WMD defenses. The new concepts drew attention to how transnational problems such as AIDS or failing states were blurring old lines between "foreign" and "domestic" policy.

Rice's draft strategy argued that, out of the struggles of the twentieth century, a right and proven path of progress had emerged to address dangerous conditions within states. It was a path "of political and economic freedom; peaceful relations with other states; respect for human dignity and human rights; proper incentives to stimulate creativity and entrepreneurship among a population; the rule of law; and respect for ethnic differences within the multiethnic states."

It was not for America to "impose this path on others," her draft observed. Instead, America could exert beneficial influence as an outsider by encouraging others to make better choices. In most cases of misrule or impoverishment, the United States should support "the 'pearls' both large and small—states that have made the right choice."

True, there were extreme cases of "outright despotism" in places such as North Korea and Iraq. For them, Rice's draft would have the United States "*contain* the external threats they pose while working to alleviate the internal suffering of their people."

To implement this ambitious strategy, Rice's approach thought this might be done "not by acting unilaterally or imposing any sort of 'hegemony.'" Instead the United States should organize "coalitions—as broad as possible" of able and willing states, ready "to compromise on some points but to remain focused on core objectives."[15]

Yet all this was still more of a sketch than a large policy. Bush's World Bank address had not gotten much notice. Rice and others at the White House were wondering how Bush could lay out some new master script.[16] In an opinion piece published as morning dawned on September 11, 2001, a retired diplomat and top aide at Ronald Reagan's State Department sharply observed that "when it comes to foreign policy, we have a tongue-tied administration. . . . It is hard to think of another administration that has done so little to explain what it wants to do on foreign policy."[17] During the 2000 campaign Rice had criticized the Clinton administration for having failed to provide a clear policy to replace Cold War guidelines. That void, she wrote, had left "a vacuum to be filled by parochial groups and transitory pressures."[18] That critique still seemed apt as September 11 began.

9/11 and a Global War on Terrorism

On September 11, 2001, the president was in Sarasota, Florida, reading aloud to a class of second-graders, when news of the World Trade Center attacks reached him. In Washington, Cheney assumed command. He was characteristically brusque and decisive. Later reconstructions reveal, however, little but muddle. Expecting further attacks, he or Rumsfeld or both attempted to get fighter planes in position to down other hijacked airliners. None of the institutions were ready for this contingency, and it showed. The whole huge, supposedly powerful, and supposedly efficient U.S. government was revealed, on that crisp, sunny day, to be at the mercy of a handful of poorly educated, meagerly trained zealots.[19]

Though Bush's protectors wanted to keep him far away from Washington, he overrode them. By early evening he was back. He had already concluded, he said to those with him on Air Force One, "We're at war. . . . That's what we're paid for."[20]

A few days later, after a memorial service at the National Cathedral and a visit to the smoldering site in New York and talks with families of those who had been killed, Rice remembered "they'd seen a lot together before. But they hadn't seen this." Bush huddled with his top advisers over dinner. What was decided?, a journalist later asked the president. Bush shot back:

> What was decided was that this is the primary focus of this administration. What was decided is: It doesn't matter to me how long it takes, we're going to rout out terror wherever it may exist. What was decided was: The doctrine is, if you harbor them, feed them, house them, you're just as guilty, and you will be held to account. What was decided was that: . . . This war will be fought on many fronts, including the intelligence side, the financial side, the diplomatic side, as well as the military side. What was decided is, is that: We're going to hit them with all we've got in a smart way.[21]

For the next seven and a quarter years Bush never really wavered from this focus. Leaving office in January 2009, he devoted his farewell message to the American people to the theme of how to prevent another 9/11.

After 9/11, the Bush administration waged a war on terrorist groups with global reach or, in shorthand, a "global war on terror." The military naturally converted this into an acronym, GWOT (pronounced gee-watt). The phrase identified "terrorism" as America's new enemy. By saying that the United States was at war with this enemy, the phrase implied an objective of victory—conquest or suppression of terrorism. The phrase seemed to supply the master foreign policy that had eluded Bush's immediate predecessors.

And, like the avoidance of a third world war, the GWOT seemed to have broad support among Americans and, indeed, across the world. Early polls after 9/11 showed Bush with 90 percent approval at home, and public approval of his work remained extraordinarily high through the following year.

As Bush, Cheney, and their advisers considered possible options in the days following 9/11, they settled promptly on the objective of destroying Osama bin Laden's training base in Afghanistan. Unfortunately, they had no plan whatever for ground operations in Afghanistan—none. The plans against Afghanistan, bearing the blustery codename Infinite Resolve, were little different than when the Clinton White House had looked them over after the October 2000 attack on the USS *Cole*. Central Command (CENTCOM) commander Tommy Franks regarded them as hardly deserving the title "plan."[22]

CIA chief George Tenet stepped in to offer a bridge. Ever since the 1990s, officers of his clandestine service had cultivated relationships with people in Afghanistan, Pakistan, and nearby Tajikistan who opposed the rigidly Islamic Taliban regime. "Imagine," the senior CIA manager recalled, "the power conferred upon the Afghan tribal leader who sided with the United States, whose clan's needs fell from the sky within seventy-two hours."[23]

Gradually, effective tribal units coalesced and commenced to push against Taliban strongholds. After more than six weeks of constant alarms and uncertainty, the Afghan project still looked uncertain. R. W. "Johnny" Apple of the *New York Times*, a reporter used to setting the tone for what others would say, pointed to the specter of a "quagmire."[24]

In November, the Taliban regime collapsed with startling suddenness. Advances by the anti-Taliban tribes, stimulated and leveraged by CIA money and local expertise and by small teams of highly skilled military special forces, complemented by air operations similar to those in Kosovo, eventually satisfied the craving of the administration and American public to feel that some retribution had been visited on the perpetrators of the 9/11 attacks. The Taliban fled, mainly to the Baluchi region of western Pakistan and the Afghan refugee diaspora there that had originally spawned them. Bin Laden and some of his surviving followers retreated to remote mountain hideouts in Pakistan's northern frontier region. The U.S. military net was too weak to catch them in battles such as one near a stronghold called Tora Bora. Rumsfeld and Franks had preferred a relatively light commitment of U.S. forces.[25]

A larger operation was tried against another group of al Qaeda remnants in Afghanistan in March 2002 with stronger, but still limited, U.S. forces. Relying on Afghan forces, as well as units from allies from around the world, the coalition effort slowly pushed more of the al Qaeda remnants into Pakistan. Anti-Taliban tribal leaders took over in Afghanistan. Diplomats from several countries negotiated the formation of a new Afghan government under the leadership of a minor but well-educated and politically adroit tribal leader, Hamid Karzai.

For those who did not live through the 9/11 attacks, it is difficult now to conjure up the atmosphere of those times, especially as it affected the state of mind of those charged with leading the nation. As an abstraction, they understood the possibility of a catastrophic attack. But none of America's leaders had actually experienced anything close to this.

Bush noted in a diary that 9/11 was "the Pearl Harbor of the 21st Century."[26] Even Pearl Harbor, which these leaders only knew as history, had not killed so many or struck so directly at the very capitals of the nation, politically, culturally, and economically. That this could be done not by a giant fleet but by a group of lightly trained fanatics—less than a platoon in strength—forced everyone in a position of responsibility to think again about risk, and think hard about how to limit or mitigate such risk.

For many of the leaders, the experience was not abstract at all. Bush, Cheney, Rice, White House chief of staff Andrew Card, Rumsfeld, Tenet, and other officials visited the physical sites of the attacks. The sensory experience of those vast, ugly ruins—sight, sound, even the pungent smell—was overwhelming. Trying to describe it later, Bush struggled: he called it "very, very, very eerie . . . a nightmare, a living nightmare." He and the others spent hours in burn units, in morgues, talking to survivors, and trying to share some of the anguish of the affected families.

The alarms did not stop. They were not distant abstractions either. On the night of 9/11 Bush and his wife were pulled out of bed by a Secret Service agent saying, "They're coming. We're under attack." It turned out to be a false alarm. Cheney had already been evacuated to Camp David, the first of many nights he would spend away from Washington so that either he or Bush would survive a possible attack.

Cold War doomsday scenarios, long part of official training, now seemed real. In early October, reports of deadly anthrax attacks rocked the nation; government offices were evacuated. These turned out to be real, not false, alarms. (Years would pass before suspicion centered on a deranged government scientist who, facing indictment, took his life.) Days after the anthrax attacks, Cheney's daughter was told that her house with her children in it had tested positive for anthrax. This turned out to be a false alarm.[27] Later in October 2001, about two weeks after the then-unsolved anthrax attack in Washington, Cheney visited the "pile" in New York. While there, taking that in, Cheney got the news that a White House biodetector indicated he and others in a particular area of the White House had apparently been exposed to ricin, an extremely lethal toxin for which there was no antidote. He might soon be dead. Back in Washington, Rice was receiving the same grim news that she too had apparently been exposed. Some hours later, the indicator turned out to have been a false positive.[28]

Also very personal was the sense of responsibility these people felt for stopping the next attack. As bad as the 9/11 attack had been, it was excruciating to imagine what America would be like if something like it happened again. Bush began every day with up to an hour or more of nerve-jangling morning terror threat briefings, walking through the "threat matrix." This daily routine went on for years after 9/11. Doubts about whether to pass along warnings and rumors were now resolved in favor of telling the president, who became a daily action officer for them all.[29]

For them and many others, "war" was not a metaphor or a conflict being handled by distant generals and armies. It was real. The threats could come directly into their homes or other American homes. The judgment calls that might save lives were theirs alone to make. Intelligence officers and officials, right up to the president, worried constantly, and with some reason, about the danger that al Qaeda or one of its affiliates might succeed in their long-standing effort to develop usable radiological or biological weapons of mass destruction.[30] To one senior CIA analyst, "Every single day [intelligence] was the discipline around which [the Bush administration] started their day. . . . They were in fear. In fairness to them, people do not understand how goddamn dangerous we thought it was."[31]

The pressure on Bush and his senior advisers was so direct because so much of the response had to be invented and improvised. The institutions did not yet have routines for handling these problems. In the *domestic realm alone*, the issues were enormous, including huge compensation funds and federally guaranteed insurance structures to handle catastrophic losses. Emergency legislation had to be prepared and moved through Congress; programs were developed that would spend tens of billions of dollars.[32]

When a country mobilizes in an emergency, it grabs what is on the shelf and goes. Only after the initial burst of activity, after a nation pauses to catch its breath, do leaders have the luxury to contemplate what they are learning and can even develop genuinely new institutions. So the agency with lead responsibility for addressing al Qaeda before 9/11, the CIA, became the agency in charge of the fight after 9/11. CIA leaders and the White House quickly revised and strengthened draft authorities that principals had reviewed at the beginning of September. The CIA would get its first ever guided missile program, using drone aircraft, all supplied by the Air Force.

Turning the New Policy into a Global Agenda

By the second half of November 2001, the Bush administration leaders could catch their breath and start developing plans to head off other dangers. Throughout the internal debates following 9/11 there had been a running dispute as to whether the war on terrorism should be expanded to include among its targets states that had sponsored terrorism, particularly Iraq. But when British prime minister Tony Blair visited on September 20 and asked about all the talk about Iraq, Bush assured him that Iraq was not the immediate problem. Although some in his administration might have a different view, he was the one making the decisions.[33]

Bush and his team were still not yet sure where the next catastrophic danger might come from. Rumsfeld's original October guidance for the global counterterrorist campaign asked his subordinates to draft contingency plans for possible campaigns against *six* countries, starting with Afghanistan and Iraq.[34] Rice asked one outside friend, for example, to offer ideas on how to deal with five other troubling scenarios that might arise with Iran, Hezbollah/Hamas, Saudi Arabia, Egypt, and an India-Pakistan war.[35]

Given the complete breakdown of the UN-monitored truce with Iraq during 1997 and 1998 and the ongoing U.S. air combat operations against Saddam Hussein's regime, Bush took an especially hard look at Iraq. Having just seen DoD's unreadiness in the case of Afghanistan, Bush met with Rumsfeld and Franks in late November and asked them to rough out a concept for how the United States would invade Iraq, if that turned out to be necessary.

After 9/11, the overall mandate had a warlike clarity. The drumbeat of rumor and worry never stopped. But with it came the intoxicating sense of resolve and mission that wartime can bring to officialdom. There were so many decisions, large and small, and few precedents to rely on in making them. Constantly improvising and inventing amid uncertainty and dilemmas, officials consciously steeled themselves to just make the call, take the chance. This coping mechanism became a habit of thought. And the approach also seemed to be paying off in the security of the nation, in the president's political standing, and the administration's own growing self-confidence that it was up to the task.

In late 2001, and for more than a year after that, Afghanistan appeared to be a remarkable success. President Bush's popularity was sky high. Exemplifying and capturing the moment, the White House admitted America's leading celebrity photographer, Annie Leibovitz, to shoot a spread showing the war leaders at work, unsmiling and resolved, for the magazine *Vanity Fair*. Bush has his hands on his hips, showing off his Texas belt buckle, the image of confident determination.[36]

It was quite a combination, the wartime atmosphere of decisiveness and initial successes against such an evanescent and potentially catastrophic threat. It was a potent compound of anxiety mixed with a measure of growing hubris. A stimulant to action, the atmosphere also loosened inhibitions about experiments with new ideas.

Bush saw the war as a historic, even a providential, calling. He had come to office to tackle big ideas, not to play "small ball." Before 9/11 those interests had found their outlet in the domestic issues, such as education, that Bush felt he understood best. "After 9/11," his lead speechwriter recalled, the president "defined his personal mission in terms of the War on Terror. In interviews, or the State of the Union [addresses], it was clear that his emotional intensity would rise on international issues, and fall on domestic ones." Bush's judgments were intuitive, not theoretical. A "root cause" thinker, he would often ask: "What, in the long term, would solve this problem, not just mitigate it?"[37] As he wrestled with broad questions like these, Bush would often look to Rice.

During the last weeks of 2001 and first weeks of 2002, helped along by the usual drill to prepare the president's budget and his State of the Union message, the administration began settling on a concrete agenda for 2002. Many writers have seen in this agenda, mainly the determination to settle the festering Iraq problem, some major new doctrine of U.S. foreign policy. Closer analysis reveals an extraordinary series of improvisations, of varying quality, to deal with seemingly urgent problems of the moment. These inventions were then rationalized, as the U.S. government tried to explain itself to its own officials, as well as to the American people, other governments, and the world.

The personal histories and beliefs of leading officials were certainly important (and especially those of Bush, Cheney, Rice, Powell, Rumsfeld, and British prime minister Blair). Even more important in the critical months during the winter of 2001–02, was the way these individuals weighed risk as they came out of the 9/11 shock and the beliefs they had about the action capabilities of the U.S. government, strongly influenced by the ease of what seemed to be a remarkable success in Afghanistan.[38]

The new agenda that emerged in the winter of 2001–02 can be broken down into four major "lines of action"—a phrase then much in use.

First, *intensification of counterterror work*. At that time this fantastic outpouring of energy mainly coursed through the institutions for intelligence and defense. On this part of the agenda, Cheney was Bush's key agent. Bush reportedly told the Senate's intelligence committee chairman that "the vice president should be your point of contact . . . [he] has the intelligence portfolio."[39]

Second, an agenda for *homeland security*. It began with new programs. It developed into a large restructuring of the U.S. government. In late 2001, the administration drew up plans for the next budget, doubling spending on homeland security from $19 billion to $37 billion.[40] The money was allocated mainly to border control, transportation security, stockpiling vaccines and taking other steps to counter the biological terror danger, building up capabilities for emergency response at all levels of government, and better intelligence efforts to understand possible threats at home.

As the scale of these programs became apparent, Bush and his aides confronted a problem. Such a huge effort could scarcely be led, or defended to Congress, by a presidential staffer (Tom Ridge), who was not even allowed to testify in defense of the president's budget request. The White House quietly reconsidered its former opposition to calls, led on Capitol Hill by Connecticut Democratic senator Joe Lieberman, to integrate most of these programs and their home agencies in a new cabinet department of "homeland security." Beginning in March 2002, a secretive White House planning group, supervised by Card, researched and developed a detailed, ambitious proposal to create such a department, a proposal Bush unveiled in June.[41]

Third, Bush also developed an agenda to *fight global poverty and disease*. Conceptually this was a novel feature of Bush's post-9/11 agenda, yet also one of the least noticed or understood.

Before 9/11 Bush and Rice had been taken by the idea of how to apply "compassionate conservatism" on a world scale. After 9/11 Bush saw the war on terror in civilizational terms, defending free societies against corrosive, violent despair. Much more U.S. aid might illustrate, as Bush explained in his January 2002 State of the Union address, that "we seek a just and peaceful world beyond the war on terror."

In the same address, Bush described the kind of societies the United States should try to foster and defend as he carefully articulated seven "nonnegotiable demands of human dignity." Democracy was *not* one of these core elements. At this point in the administration, democracy was regarded as just one of several ways by which people could secure their essential human dignity.[42]

Converging with Bush's desire to enlarge U.S. humanitarian and development aid there was another stream of preexisting beliefs, widely held by the late 1990s. A number of experts had concluded that the old kind of foreign aid was broken. For decades, they argued, development assistance had been massively wasteful and frequently made matters worse.[43]

With the desire to act and various fresh approaches to reinvigorate foreign aid already in the air, the Bush administration moved on several fronts. Even before 9/11 it began throwing its weight behind a growing movement to clear the slates of some of the most burdened poor countries by wiping their debts off the books. This debt relief agenda advanced during 2002. By 2005 it was substantially complete for the poorest African countries. Implementing an initiative launched under Bill Clinton, the administration also opened U.S. markets to African imports.[44]

In March 2002, using the occasion of a major conference in Mexico to rally donor countries, Bush also launched a "Millennium Challenge" program. His goal was to lead a "new aid paradigm"—a "Compact for Development" between donor governments and recipient nations that would channel money only to countries that designed promising programs and agreed to reforms in governance. In return, aid would be devoted more purposefully to the development goals and it would be funded in a longer-term process less vulnerable to annual ups and downs in appropriations.[45]

Bush's "compact" model stressed local choice, accountability, and empowerment—the international application of "compassionate conservatism." Difficult to implement, the fresh approach did open up donor wallets, especially in the United States. Bush and congressional allies in both parties won a bipartisan base of support for greatly expanded foreign aid, the first such expansion in a generation.

Bush was, meanwhile, also pushing a broader U.S. commitment to doing good as a moral obligation, concentrating mainly on public health. The United States had already helped create and fund an ambitious Global Fund for HIV/AIDS and other diseases in 2001. Later in 2002, the White House developed, with advice from the National Academy of Sciences, a plan to enlarge help for AIDS sufferers. In January 2003 Bush unveiled his President's Emergency Plan for AIDS Relief. It became the largest single international health program in history. Bush added a costly malaria initiative in 2005.[46]

Taken together these were transformative initiatives. Indeed, to development professionals, Bush's proposals to increase foreign aid were "among the great surprises of his presidency." By any measure the scale of effort was historic. The volume of U.S. aid grew "faster than at any time since the Marshall Plan [1947–1948]."[47]

Yet Bush's effort to get a hearing for his message "beyond the war on terror" was drowned out from the start. Rice and speechwriter Michael Gerson expected the press reaction to the January 2002 State of the Union to focus on Bush's (and their) careful articulation of the "nonnegotiable demands of human dignity." Instead the press only wanted to talk about another phrase: "axis of evil."[48] The fourth major line of action in the emerging agenda was Iraq.

"Preemption"

All the policymakers in the Bush administration and in Congress carried in their heads some version of the long pre-9/11 history of confrontations with Saddam Hussein's Iraq. Inheriting the dire warnings that were then so frequently voiced, including by the responsible UN officials, and full of determination, the Bush administration hit the accelerator on Iraq as soon as it took office—and promptly stalled. Officials ran straight into the same dilemma that had stymied Clinton's administration in its internal debates since 1997: Was the Iraq risk serious enough to warrant a massive invasion?

In the campaign's manifesto, Rice had said that regimes such as Iraq were "living on borrowed time, so there need be no sense of panic about them"; deterrence was adequate. This view was also reflected in the draft national security strategy she developed in July 2001. There is some contemporary evidence that, before 9/11, this was also Cheney's view (though some members of his staff had a different opinion).[49] Before 9/11 it seemed to the British ambassador that, to the Bush administration, the question of Iraq was little more than a "grumbling appendix."[50]

But Defense Secretary Rumsfeld favored surgery. He privately vented his frustrations to his colleagues at the end of July 2001. He urged them to face up to the choice, as he saw it. Perhaps the United States could just "roll up its tents," in which case "within a few years the U.S. will undoubtedly have to confront a Saddam armed with nuclear weapons." Perhaps the United States could try to patch things up in direct talks with Saddam—not an appealing option. Or the United States could accept "the risks of a serious regime-change policy." Sure, that was risky. But those risks "should," he wrote, "be weighed against the certain risk of an increasingly bold and nuclear-armed Saddam in the near future."[51]

All this was before 9/11. Prime Minister Blair's chief of staff recalled Bush "telling us subsequently that he had been actually looking at a paper on smart sanctions on the day of 9/11 and thinking about Iraq in the context of what one would do in terms of containment. 9/11, I think, changed everything for the Americans."[52]

During the winter of 2001–02, Bush conducted a strategy review on Iraq. Little about it has been disclosed. Early in 2002, Bush apparently decided to grasp the nettle and somehow settle, once and for all, the problem of Iraq and its now-unmonitored WMD programs. Bush had not decided to go to war against Iraq; he had "yet to find the answers to the big questions," as one British contact reported in March.[53] But he had apparently decided to settle somehow the uncertainty about Iraqi WMD and Saddam Hussein's future.

How unique was Bush in the way he read the situation in early 2002?

Al Gore, his 2000 election opponent, had come close to being in Bush's place. He had lived through the Clinton administration's history with Iraq. We have some contemporary evidence of his considered views since, as a leader of his party, in February 2002 Gore delivered a prepared response to Bush's State of the Union message.

Gore liked the "axis of evil" phrase. It was good, he thought, to lay cards on the table and call "evil by its name." And in that category, Iraq was in "a virulent class by itself." His bottom line was that "a final reckoning with that government [of Iraq] should be on the table. To my way of thinking, the real question is not the principle of the thing, but of making sure that this time we will finish the matter on our terms." Unlike what happened in 1991, Gore said this time any resort to force "must absolutely get it right. It must be an action set up carefully and on the basis of the most realistic concepts. Failure cannot be an option, which means that we must be prepared to go to the limit."[54]

Bush's resolve visibly hardened through the first half of 2002 and, by July, he was strongly leaning toward war. Why?

Full answers to these questions are beyond the scope of this chapter. But they can be outlined briefly. I have already discussed how the *values* of the Bush administration changed sharply after 9/11, greatly affecting the way its leaders evaluated and weighed what risks they would regard as tolerable.

The *reality* judgments about Iraq, about what was going on there, did not change much. The available evidence for the top officials suggests that the long-standing WMD concerns were the principal and universal spur to action for Cheney and Rumsfeld, and even Powell.[55] Also, swirling around the core 2002 assessments about Iraq's WMD programs and suspected stockpiles of biological and chemical weapons, there was the equally long-standing belief that Saddam Hussein was probably the world's most despicable dictator and that Saddam Hussein and his government were linked to various terrorist groups aiming at Israel and, occasionally, the United States. Some analysts were even pushing an alleged linkage of Iraq to the 9/11 attack itself; according to Tenet, it was not until May 2002 that analysts at the CIA and FBI started to discredit the most incendiary part of this allegation.

Another important belief about the world at the time was more influenced by 9/11 and was articulated best by Rice (perhaps expressing Bush's view as well), that the end of the Cold War and the 9/11 attack were bookends for a transitional period in world history. Now, after the "earthquake of the magnitude of 9/11," as Rice put it, the world was in flux. "Before the clay is dry again, America and our friends and our allies must move decisively." It was, she said, "a period akin to 1945–1947, when American leadership expanded the number of free and democratic states—Japan and Germany among the great powers—to create a new balance of power that favors freedom." In this new era, power still mattered. But the issues were no longer delineated by rival power blocs. As the great powers came to share global interests, "an era unlike any other" could begin.[56]

Beyond value and reality judgments, the final ingredient in the mix was a set of beliefs about possible actions. What to do? How hard would it be? Action judgments are conjectures. Making them, officials instinctively rely on experience, lived and learned.

In early 2002, the experience with Afghanistan dominated the foreground. In the first half of 2002, indeed during all of 2002, this effort appeared to be going surprisingly well. Though the country was larger and more populous than Iraq, with even more difficult terrain, throughout 2002 U.S. interests in Afghanistan seemed to be managed adequately with a commitment of only about ten thousand U.S. troops. That was only half the number that the United States had sent five years earlier to keep the peace in relatively tiny Bosnia. The troops in Afghanistan did little but chase al Qaeda and Taliban remnants and join a small international force to secure the capital, Kabul.

The Defense Department had no interest in getting the U.S. military involved in intra-Afghan quarrels, in tackling Afghanistan's narcotics economy, or in getting involved in nation-building. DoD officials felt the Afghans would resent a foreign presence. And, as the State Department official coordinating the effort recalled, "the administration believed that the U.S. military's proper function was to fight and win the nation's wars and not to escort children to school," paraphrasing a line Rice had used in the 2000 campaign, referring derisively to activities in the Balkans.

State's diplomats had organized the creation of a new government that was off to a promising start. Blessed by the UN, the new Afghan government was the center of attention at a conference in Tokyo, showered with pledges of billions of dollars of aid.[57] The "light" approach seemed to be working fine.

As for Iraq, by early 2002 Rumsfeld and Franks had worked for months on proposed war plans.[58] The briefings for Bush overwhelmingly emphasized doable operations to defeat Iraqi forces and topple Saddam. The February 2002 plan projected that it would take 225 days to prepare and conduct the combat operations and to accomplish the mission.

There was another factor, one that remains somewhat obscure. Bush's resolve to confront Iraq must have hardened during the spring of 2002, as the United States also received frightening intelligence about a terrorist group, Ansar al-Islam, holed up in northern Iraq and making active preparations to use biological weapons, probably against the United States. (Unlike some others about Iraq, these reports later turned out to have been well founded.) The Pentagon prepared plans for an immediate limited invasion of northern Iraq.

These plans appear to have been presented to the president in June 2002. One top official recalled that the Pentagon plan "could start a war before having decided to do so."[59] Bush said no. But, having put off this limited invasion, Bush had another reason to do something more generally about Iraq.

As Bush's post-9/11 agenda came together along these various lines of action, Rice returned to the task of explaining it in a document that would become a public "National Security Strategy." Bush went over the evolving text. Some of its emerging ideas and phrases started finding their way into White House speeches.[60]

Like Rice's July 2001 sketch, the strategy was broadly conceived, including the effort to grapple with the wider challenges of a globalized world. The document was not publicly released until September 2002. Discussion of it then was quickly consumed by the blazing debate about a war against Iraq. Drawing almost all the attention was the strategy's endorsement of a doctrine of "preemption" against states the United States considered most threatening.

The initial draft of Bush's new National Security Strategy did not use the word "preemption." Rice and Hadley inserted it, but only to describe how the United States would deal with enemy terrorist groups such as al Qaeda. The part of the strategy that discussed outlaw states thought to have WMD, such as Iraq, used a different verb: "prevent."

Subsequent drafts explained the distinction quite clearly: "A preventive strategy tries to keep enemies from acquiring intolerably dangerous capabilities to harm us. A preemptive strategy, like the one described earlier in the war on terrorism, tries to spoil the assaults of enemies that are already in open hostilities against us before their attack can be launched."[61]

Prevention could be achieved through a whole spectrum of measures, including military ones. In this view, if the United States had a case for preventive military action, even a preventive war (for example, against the Iraqi nuclear program as it existed in early 1991 or the U.S. attacks on Iraqi WMD facilities in December 1998), then the United States should make the case frankly in light of the extraordinary dangers such weapons could present.[62]

In July 2002, Rice and some of her advisers, especially her lawyer, John Bellinger, became uncomfortable with saying that a possible war might be preventive. The phrase, "preventive war," had bad associations in nineteenth-century European and early 1950s Cold War history.

Also, to Rice, at the point there was no other way to head off the menace, "preemption" of a WMD threat became identical with prevention. So, to her, these terms were just semantic nuances that did not make much real difference. In a background interview at the time, she explained to a reporter that "preemption or anticipatory defense, self-defense or however you want to put it, by whatever name you want to call it . . . really means early action of some kind." It did not necessarily mean war: "For example, in the Cuban missile crisis of 1962, the Kennedy administration thought about a lot of possibilities. I think they settled on a strategy that actually was preemptive [blockading Cuba and threatening to strike the island], but didn't use military force and thereby preserved the possibility for the Soviets to back down."[63]

For Rice's lawyer, using "preemption" had little to do with grand strategy. It had everything to do with strengthening the Bush administration's case under international law. Under international law, military action was warranted in self-defense. "Preemption" required finding imminent danger that justified an "anticipatory self-defense." The lawyer assumed that all he heard from others about Iraqi WMD was true, so he wrote language that he thought would be defensible based on the facts as he understood them in the summer of 2002.

Bush's strategy statement was redrafted accordingly. "Preemption" practically dropped out of the section on al Qaeda and terrorism, its original home, as it was transplanted to the WMD section. The legal advice was not meant to lower the bar for going to war. If anything, the opposite was true. Indeed, Rice delivered an address in October 2002 to reassure the world that the standard for preemption would be very high.[64]

But using "preemption" to frame the case against Iraq had unintended consequences. It carried other terms with it, such as finding that the danger was "imminent." This turned out to be an important shift. Since 1991 Saddam Hussein's status had been quite unusual. Unique among all leaders in the world, he was an international outlaw on probation, a condition of which was his compliance with a UN disarmament regime. Since 1997–98, when Iraq finally tossed out the UN disarmament inspectors, Saddam had violated the terms of his probation. Given this defiance, the burden of proof was on him to reassure the world and avoid a renewal of the war against him that had been suspended in 1991 on the security of his now-broken promises. That was the way the Clinton administration had justified its wide-ranging attacks on Iraq in December 1998. In 2002, by introducing "preemption," the U.S. government had, somewhat inadvertently, reframed the argument and shouldered a new burden, volunteering to prove that the outlaw posed an "imminent" threat.

"Preemption" also linked the quality of the Iraq proof to more general suspicions about the significance of this supposed "doctrine." Who else might be a target of "preemption"? The evidentiary standard on Iraq would define the precedent. So, if the evidence to prove "imminent" danger should eventually seem weak or inflated, the new doctrine would be depicted even more menacingly by those who argued that the United States, dizzy with power and fear, was formulating some novel, imperious justification for wider wars.

Conclusion

Five points stand out in this essay on the critical period of strategic planning and agenda-setting between November 2001 and March 2002, during which the decisions were made that would frame Bush's presidency for his remaining seven years in office.

First, Bush and his top advisers did not enter office with an ambitious agenda for changing the world. Their most important pre-9/11 foreign policy decisions were spillovers (unintended, in the economic case) from their core beliefs about U.S. domestic policy, where Bush's opinions were better defined and more confidently held.

Second, the "GWOT" agenda post-9/11 was predominantly reactive and defensive. But because legacy national security organizations and routines were unready and unsuited to the new tasks, it also was a period of extraordinary invention and improvisation in policies and institutions. Thus, though the core mission was relatively limited in relation to world politics (in contrast to 1989–90), the policy instruments and actions felt surprising and even shocking (also in contrast to 1989–90). The disturbing feel of all this to the outer world beyond the United States was exacerbated by the U.S. failure to reassure the world with proposed innovations in the established *international* institutions (again in contrast to 1989–90).

Third, the most innovative thinking about how to use the crisis to change world politics was mainly related to the challenge of how to encourage, from afar, responsible and accountable local governance in an age of globalization. These ideas, predominantly associated with Bush and Rice, drew on axioms that had deep roots in U.S. history, such as the belief in an interdependent and open world economy and the belief that freer societies that respected elements of human dignity tended to be more resilient and better governed. For Bush and for Rice, and probably for many others, these beliefs had been strongly reinforced by their formative experiences during and after the end of the Cold War.

The views of Bush and others at the top of his administration differed conceptually, and even temperamentally, from the more hegemonic enthusiasms associated by 2000 with the so-called neoconservative intellectuals. Bush and Rice saw concepts like the "Millennium Challenge" as different, in theory and in practice, from an endorsement of expanded U.S. military intervention to make or remake unsatisfactory nations. At least from the 2000 campaign through much of 2002, Bush, Rice, and Cheney regarded such generic muscular ambitions with instinctive distaste, not enthusiasm. Rumsfeld strongly shared the distaste for U.S. nation-building, but he was alarmed about Iraq's supposed WMD potential.

Historians analyzing the later improvisations and rationalizations associated with Iraq should be careful about how much to infer backward from them.

Fourth, the origins of the famous "preemption" language itself had little to do with grand strategy. The actual story behind that bit of drafting does not come close to living up to the large inferences that have been drawn from its placement in the document.

Fifth, the rest of the National Security Strategy document of 2002 is interesting historically mainly as a snapshot of some of the worldviews and axiomatic beliefs then prevalent among several senior U.S. officials, including the president. That is important. But neither then nor later was this document a powerful or revealing guide to concrete policy choices. That is especially true for the long-simmering Iraq war that reignited in 2003. If examined closely, that story has a twisty and curious narrative all its own.

7

QUESTING FOR MONSTERS
TO DESTROY

John Mueller

The period after the fall of the Berlin Wall can be usefully compared with the early post–World War II period. In 1945 and in 1989, the prime immediate security problem for U.S. and allied policymakers was to integrate the losers of the previous conflict into the international community: Germany and Japan in one case, Russia and to a lesser extent China in the other. In both cases, this project was, in general, handled well—for the most part, it proved to be a triumph of enlightened self-interest.

However, as Warner Schilling has observed, "at the summit of foreign policy, one always finds simplicity and spook," and after 1945 and 1989 this apparently natural proclivity expressed itself in quests to identify, evaluate, and confront new threats—or monsters.[1] Massively extrapolating from limited evidence, determining to err decidedly on the safe side, dismissing contrary interpretations, and striking a responsive chord with the public, decision makers became mesmerized by perceived threats that scarcely warranted the preoccupation and effort.

Although international Communism, with its radically different worldview and its focus on violent revolution, did present a challenge after 1945, concern became much greater by 1950 when the Korean War reinforced (or created) a tendency to envision international Communism as a direct military threat rather along the Hitler model. The result was a truly massive emphasis on exquisite theorizing and on defense expenditures. All this, primarily to confront, to deter, and to make glowering and menacing faces at a threat of direct military aggression that, essentially, didn't exist. In the process, concerns about the dangers of a subversive Communist enemy within were also much inflated.

After the Cold War, a similar process of threat identification took place as problems previously considered to be of minor, or at least of secondary, concern were promoted. In particular, weapons vastly less destructive than nuclear ones were connected to them as a new category, "weapons of mass destruction," was promulgated and elaborated, and the quest to prevent the proliferation of such weapons increasingly became a supreme policy priority. As part of this process, militarily pathetic countries were seen to pose a major security threat, and a new emphasis on "rogue states" became the rage. In addition, concerns about international terrorism very substantially increased despite the fact that the amount of destruction committed by terrorists, seen in reasonable comparative context, is quite modest. The 9/11 events set these concerns into highest relief, precipitating costly antiterrorism and antiproliferation wars and massive increases in security spending as proliferation became equated with World War III and the threat presented by terrorism at home and abroad often came to be deemed "existential." In the process, policy became a quixotic quest to extinguish threats to U.S. security that, substantially, didn't exist.

Threat identification and threat inflation are clearly important processes in international affairs and deserve far more attention.[2] There are always people trying to sell fears and threats, but their extensive efforts are no guarantee that a promoted threat or fear will "take," that people and policymakers will be convinced it is notable and important, worth spending time and effort worrying about. If extensive promotion could guarantee acceptance, we would all be driving Edsels and drinking New Coke. Thus, the American public and its leaders have remained remarkably calm about the dangers of genetically modified food while becoming very wary of nuclear power. The French see it very differently. In the United States, illegal immigration from Mexico is seen to be a threat in some years, but not in others. The country was "held hostage" when Americans were kidnapped in Iran in 1979 or in Lebanon in the 1980s but not when this repeatedly happened during the Iraq War or in Colombia. Slobodan Milošević in Serbia become a monster about whom we had to do something military, but not Robert Mugabe in Zimbabwe or SLORC (State Law and Order Council, the military junta) in Burma or Pol Pot in Cambodia or, until 9/11, the Taliban in Afghanistan. In the 1930s, Japan's ventures into distant China were seen to be more threatening than the actions of Hitler in Europe. Predicting what will arouse people's apprehensions in the future is difficult at best, and anyone who could accurately and persistently do so would likely quietly move to Wall Street and in very short order become the richest person on earth.

9/2 and 11/9

At the conclusions of World War II on September 2, 1945, and the Cold War on November 9, 1989, the victors had two key concerns: securing the peace and identifying and dealing with new threats. They did much better with the first challenge.

Securing the Peace

A central and immediate policy concern after World War II focused on Germany and Japan, and the goal was to bring those defeated countries into the responsible family of nations and, of course, to keep them from repeating what they had done in World War II. Of necessity, the Japanese and the Germans were the principal charters of their own destinies, but Western efforts to guide, nudge, assist, browbeat, bribe, and encourage them deserve credit as well. In the process Germany and Japan were converted (or converted themselves) from violent and intensely destructive enemies into prosperous friends, allies, and peaceful competitors whose perspective on the world is much the same as that of the Western victors. As policies go, this might well be counted as among the greatest triumphs of enlightened self-interest, and it is probably the most important historical development in the second half of the twentieth century.

Judging from the contemporary perspectives of important participants and observers, the Cold War essentially ended by the spring of 1989, making the settlement of outstanding issues concerning arrangements in Central and Eastern Europe the first major task of the post–Cold War era.[3] This was accomplished with astonishing speed. Equally impressive is the alacrity with which the post-Communist countries in Europe, with Western support and urging, took up capitalism and democracy. The historically unprecedented transition was hardly problem free, but, compared to the gloomy predictions common at the time about minds that had been permanently warped by decades of Communist indoctrination, the shift has been a quite remarkable success.[4] Moreover, post–Cold War prophesies of international instability in East Asia have proven to be essentially empty.[5]

Identifying Threats Abroad

In addition to dealing with former enemies, policymakers after 1945 needed to size up Soviet communism, and to evaluate its potential as a threat. After the Cold War, a similar exercise in threat identification was put into action.

According to the ideology on which the Soviet regime had been founded in 1917, world history is a vast, continuing process of progressive revolution. Steadily, in country after country, the oppressed working classes will violently revolt, destroying the oppressing capitalist classes and aligning their new regimes with other like-minded countries, eventually transforming the world. But the Soviets, however dynamic and threatening their ideology, never subscribed to a Hitler-style theory of direct, Armageddon-risking conquest to move history along, and the tactical sense of regime founder Vladimir Lenin was decidedly cautious. As Josef Stalin put it in 1945, they envisioned "socialism in one country"—the USSR—where "the dictatorship of the proletariat" would be consolidated, "using it as a base for the overthrow of imperialism in all countries."[6] The notion, then, was that while holding the capitalist world at bay by defensive military preparations and ingenious political maneuvers, the Soviets would aid and inspire subversive revolutionary movements throughout the world. Aggressive, conquering Hitlerian war by the Soviets themselves would foolishly risk everything; it does not fit into this scheme at all.

Western policymakers were aware that the Soviet expansionist threat was likely to be expressed primarily in what they called "indirect aggression": subversion, diplomatic and military pressure, revolution, and armed uprising—all inspired, partly funded, and heavily influenced by Moscow. To deal with this challenge, the policy of containment was formally set in motion. In the long run, it was hoped, the Soviets, frustrated in their drive for territory and expanded authority, would become less hostile and more accommodating. The issue of direct military aggression by the Soviets, however, was more problematic. Many people, like George Kennan, one of containment's chief architects, felt its likelihood was exceedingly small.[7] But no one, of course, could be sure.

With the evaporation of the Cold War contest in 1989, a quest to identify things to worry about was launched. Thus, Central Intelligence Agency chief James Woolsey testified darkly in 1993 that "we have slain a large dragon, but we live now in a jungle filled with a bewildering variety of poisonous snakes" and he helpfully went on to enumerate the snakes, or monsters, he spied: "the proliferation of weapons of mass destruction and the ballistic missiles to carry them; ethnic and national hatreds that can metastasize across large portions of the globe; the international narcotics trade; terrorism; the dangers inherent in the West's dependence on Mideast oil; new economic and environmental challenges."[8]

Most of the "poisonous snakes" Woolsey specified were already there in full measure during the Cold War, and thus, applying his metaphor, the post–Cold War jungle had snakes whereas the Cold War jungle was inhabited not only by the snakes but by a dragon as well. Some people might consider that a notable improvement and, as jungles go, a palpable reduction in the complexities of daily life.

However, when big problems (dragons in Woolsey's characterization) go away, small problems (snakes) can be elevated in perceived importance, and, in the wake of 11/9, four of the snakes were so elevated.

Initially, new alarms were issued about those "economic and environmental challenges," and a dangerously new enemy was identified on the economic front: insidiously peaceful Japan. This concern faded in 1993 when the Japanese economy tanked, but was quickly replaced by anxiety over those metastasizing "ethnic and national hatreds," cosmically elevated by some to portend full-blown "clashes of civilizations" focusing especially on a set of civil wars that erupted in the former Yugoslavia. But this snake, too, receded by the end of the 1990s. Civil wars remained contained in relatively unimportant portions of the globe, and then declined in number.[9] And, most of them, on examination, seemed to have been the clash more nearly of predatory thugs than of "civilizations."[10]

Two of Woolsey's snakes, however, retained, or even gained, potency as the decade ended and as the new century began: proliferation and international terrorism.

Without the Soviet dragon to worry about, the acquisition of nuclear weapons by far lesser states (or snakes) was elevated in importance, focused, in particular, on Saddam Hussein's militarily pathetic Iraq. To help with this elevation of concern, the phrase "weapons of mass destruction" was increasingly taken to denote not only nuclear arms but chemical and biological ones as well—devices that are far less effective at killing.[11] With any of these kinds of weapons, it was claimed, Saddam could somehow come to "dominate" the Middle East, and damaging sanctions were accordingly slapped on his regime, a necessary cause, it appears, of hundreds of thousands of deaths in Iraq—far more than died at Hiroshima and Nagasaki combined.[12] Similar anxieties about another even more pathetic "rogue" state, North Korea, were drummed up nearly to the war level in 1994.

The impact of terrorism has often been more in the exaggerated hysteria it generates (it had mesmerized the Reagan administration in the 1980s, for example) than in its actual physical effects. Although fewer Americans had been killed by terrorists than had been killed by lightning in the preceding decade, concerns about the menace of international terrorism seem to have grown considerably during the 1990s, impelled, in particular, by an attempt to bring down New York's World Trade Center in 1993 and by explosions at two American embassies in Africa in 1998.

Importantly, promoters of these fears found the public to be receptive. By the end of the decade, in polls asking about "critical threats" facing the country, 84 percent of Americans included terrorism (up from 69 percent in 1994) and 75 percent included "unfriendly countries becoming nuclear."[13]

Identifying Threats Within

If Communists could subvert countries abroad, many after World War II increasingly worried about the danger of subversion at home, finding the small domestic Communist Party to be a potential threat. Fears rose substantially, especially when a respected former State Department official, Alger Hiss, was accused of having sent huge quantities of classified documents to the Soviets before World War II. Then a former Communist, British physicist Klaus Fuchs, admitted that he had sent atomic secrets to the Soviets. The trail from Fuchs soon led to the arrests of various co-conspirators and ultimately to the celebrated trial of two Americans, Julius and Ethel Rosenberg, who were convicted as atomic spies.

After the Cold War, there was a similar concern, though initially a less alarmed one, about terrorism within the United States. For the most part, however, the focus remained predominantly on the dangers presented by terrorists abroad.

6/25 and 9/11

In related but different ways, the Korean invasion by the Communists on June 25, 1950, and the terrorist attacks on New York and Washington on September 11, 2001, were crucial in massively escalating the threat alarm that had been built up over the previous years.

The Triggering Events as Aberrations

The events of 6/25 and 9/11 proved to be substantially counterproductive for their instigators and were more nearly aberrations than the harbingers they were taken to be at the time.

In 1950, Stalin was led to experiment with outright warfare—albeit in a seemingly safe corner of the world. In late 1949 his close ally, Kim Il Sung, the leader of Communist North Korea, insisted that, in Nikita Khrushchev's reflection, if prodded with the "point of a bayonet," an "internal explosion" in South Korea would be touched off. Although Stalin had misgivings, Kim was "absolutely certain of success," promising that South Korea would quickly fall into the Communist camp before the West even had much of a chance to react. Eventually, both Stalin and the Chinese Communists accepted the scheme.[14] What Stalin approved was a distant war of expansion not by the Soviet Union but by a faithful ally, a war that was expected to be quick, risk free, and cheap. And, in allowing Kim to proceed, he made it clear that if things went badly, Kim would have to depend on China, not on the Soviet Union, to help.[15] The venture may have been envisioned by its perpetrators as a limited probe, but it proved to be a resoundingly counterproductive fiasco with the American intervention on the side of the beleaguered South Koreans.[16]

The terrorist acts of September 11, 2001, also proved to be substantially counterproductive from the standpoint of the perpetrators. Indeed, the key result among jihadis and religious nationalists was a vehement rejection of al Qaeda's strategy and methods.[17] Moreover, no matter how much they might disagree on other issues (most notably on America's war on Iraq), there was a compelling incentive for states—including Arab and Muslim ones—to cooperate to deal with any international terrorist threat emanating from groups and individuals connected to, or sympathetic with, al Qaeda, and their diligent and aggressive efforts have led to important breakthroughs against the terrorist group.[18] This post-9/11 willingness of governments around the world to confront international terrorists was much reinforced and amplified by subsequent, if sporadic, terrorist activity in such places as Pakistan, Saudi Arabia, Turkey, Indonesia, Egypt, Spain, Britain, Morocco, and Jordan.[19]

Although much hampered in other ways, the leaders of al Qaeda retained their ability to posture and to issue threats. The record of the group's achievements, however, suggests that its threatening proclamations have mostly been flagrant efforts at deception and desperate self-promotion. Although the terrorist organization designed, equipped, and executed several large attacks before 9/11, every al Qaeda-"linked" terrorist attack since seems to have been mostly perpetrated by unaffiliated or, at best, "franchised" groups or people. And, outside of war zones, even these efforts have resulted in the deaths of at most a few hundred people a year worldwide.[20]

Massive Extrapolation

Although the attacks of 6/25 and 9/11 proved to be aberrations, not harbingers, and counterproductive to the goals of the perpetrators, the victims of the attacks insisted in placing them in the most cosmic of contexts, with extravagant and essentially dire consequences for policy and expenditure.

The Communist venture in Korea was a limited, opportunistic, and quite cautious military probe at a point of perceived vulnerability in a peripheral area. There was no evidence at the time that Stalin actually had anything broader in mind, nor has any come to light since. From the perspective of the Communists, the event was a unique opportunity and an extreme risk on its own terms. It seems unlikely, accordingly, that, even if successful, such a venture would have been attempted elsewhere much less one even more risky, such as a direct attack on Western Europe or the United States. And the American intervention must surely have much enforced that line of thought. A few people at the time advanced this interpretation—State Department counselor and Soviet specialist Charles Bohlen among them—but they were ignored even though their interpretation was plausible and could not be rejected based on the evidence available at the time (or, as it happens, since).[21]

Policymakers were correct to see expunging capitalism and Western-style democracy as the ultimate goals of the international Communist movement, but they massively extrapolated from the Korean experience to conclude that the Soviets were willing to apply direct military action to advance that goal. Almost everyone simply assumed that the war was being directed from Moscow and was part of a broad, militarized quest for "world domination." As President Harry Truman bluntly proclaimed at the time without even a hint of qualification, "The attack upon Korea makes it plain beyond all doubt that Communism has passed beyond the use of subversion to conquer independent nations and will now use armed invasion and war."[22] Defense analyst Bernard Brodie recalls that many, particularly the Joint Chiefs of Staff, "were utterly convinced that the Russians were using Korea as a feint to cause us to deploy our forces there while they prepared to launch a 'general' (total) war against the United States through a major attack on Europe."[23] A direct analogy with Hitlerian aggression in Europe was readily applied: as Truman recalled later, "If this was allowed to go unchallenged it would mean a third world war, just as similar incidents had brought on the second world war."[24] A National Security Council document darkly suspected Korea to be "the first phase of a general Soviet plan for global war," and the CIA authoritatively opined that "in the belief that their object cannot be fully attained without a general war," the "Soviet rulers may deliberately provoke such a war" before 1954.[25]

Not only did policymakers massively extrapolate from the Korean experience, but they then proceeded to spend extravagantly based on those fanciful extrapolations. Impelled by the Berlin blockade and even more by a successful atomic bomb test by the Soviet Union in the late 1940s, an alarmist National Security Council report, NSC-68, had been promulgated shortly before the Korean War urging huge increases in defense spending. President Truman's reservations about this proposal were abruptly cast aside after 6/25.[26] The American defense budget quadrupled—something that previously had been thought to be politically and economically infeasible. And to confront the imagined threat of a frontal Soviet invasion of Western Europe, NATO was rapidly transformed from a paper organization (big on symbolism, small on actual military capability) into a viable, well-equipped, centrally led multinational armed force, mostly with the enthusiastic support of the Europeans who embraced essentially the same extravagant interpretations of the Communist threat.[27]

Brodie, one of the few defense analysts of the time seriously to consider the premises of such policies, came to the Bohlenesque conclusion by 1966 that it was "difficult to discover what meaningful incentives the Russians might have for attempting to conquer Western Europe—especially incentives that are even remotely commensurate with the risks."[28] After it was all over a great amount of documentary evidence became available, but as Robert Jervis notes, a decade after the collapse of the USSR, "the Soviet archives have yet to reveal any serious plans for unprovoked aggression against Western Europe, not to mention a first strike against the United States."[29] But deterring the essentially nonexistent threat of direct military aggression became a central, even overwhelming, preoccupation. As Robert Johnson puts it, the process (which he aptly labels "nuclear metaphysics") involved "making the most pessimistic assumptions possible about Soviet intentions and capabilities" and then assuming that the capabilities (which turned out almost always to have been substantially exaggerated) would be used "to the adversary's maximum possible advantage."[30]

Similar, or even more massive, extrapolations were made after 9/11. To begin with, it was almost universally assumed in the months and then years afterward that the terrorist event was a harbinger rather than an aberration.[31] Moreover, the threat posed by al Qaeda, a fringe group of a fringe group in 2001 that was substantially discredited by the events of 9/11 and then eviscerated by the policing activities of the United States and almost all other countries in its aftermath, has been repeatedly rendered in the most extreme terms. In 2002, National Security Adviser Condoleezza Rice insisted that "after 9/11, there is no longer any doubt that today America faces an existential threat to our security—a threat as great as any we faced during the Civil War, the so-called 'Good War,' or the Cold War."[32] Following this line of thinking, it has become fashionable in some circles to denote the contest against Osama bin Laden and his miserable band as World War III or World War IV (depending on how the Cold War is classified). President George W. Bush, who came into office proposing a "humble" foreign policy, probably took such thinking to its highest pitch when he proclaimed shortly after 9/11 that the country's "responsibility to history" now was to "rid the world of evil."[33] Very much on this wavelength was the *New York Times* editorial board when it announced on April 23, 2008, that "the fight against Al Qaeda is the central battle for this generation," even as Homeland Security czar Michael Chertoff proclaimed the "struggle" against terrorism to be a "significant existential" one—carefully differentiating it, apparently, from all those insignificant existential struggles we have waged in the past.[34]

Concerns that terrorists might go atomic were much elevated by 9/11: an Internet search to discover how often variants of the term *al Qaeda* appeared within ten words of *nuclear* came up with seven hits in 1999, eleven in 2000, 1,742 in

2001, and 2,931 in 2002.[35] And fears about rogue states and proliferation were much enhanced by fancies that a nuclear rogue might one day decide suicidally to hand over some of its precious and potentially traceable arsenal to irresponsible groups it could not control. This process massively enhanced antiproliferation passions, and made politically possible an armed invasion of Iraq to remove the fully containable and fully deterrable regime of the pathetic Saddam Hussein (who so feared a coup that he supplied his troops with little or no ammunition and would not allow the army to bring heavy weapons anywhere near Baghdad) at an eventual cost of more lives than were extinguished at Hiroshima and Nagasaki combined.[36]

The Enemy Within

Both the Korean War and the 2001 terror attacks massively heightened concern about the enemy within.

In 1950, it was commonly assumed that the Soviets could not have gotten their atomic bomb without the secret plans purloined for them by domestic sources and that this possession emboldened Stalin in his plan for world conquest that had begun so ominously on a hapless peninsula in distant Northeast Asia. There was little or no effort at the time to try to refute (or even examine) these understandable, but entirely speculative, assumptions, and later research strongly suggests that neither happens to be true.[37]

Nonetheless, many now became convinced that U.S. Communists were devoted to a system dedicated not only to the revolutionary overthrow of the American government but also ultimately to a direct invasion of the country itself. Accordingly, fears about the dangers presented by "the enemy within" became greatly heightened and then fully internalized, and politicians scurried to support billions upon billions to surveil, to screen, to protect, and to spy on an ever-expanding array of individuals who had come to seem suspicious.[38] In fact, despite huge anxieties about it at the time, there seem to have been few, if any, instances in which domestic Communists engaged in anything that could be considered espionage after the Second World War. Moreover, at no time did any domestic Communist ever commit anything that could be considered violence in support of the cause—this, despite deep apprehensions at the time about that form of terrorism then dubbed "sabotage."[39]

As far as I can see, at no point during all this did anyone say in public, "many domestic Communists adhere to a foreign ideology that ultimately has as its goal the destruction of capitalism and democracy and by violence if necessary; however, they do not present much of a danger, are actually quite a pathetic bunch, and couldn't subvert their way out of a wet paper bag. Why are we expending so much time, effort, and treasure on this?" It is astounding to me, however, that that plausible, if arguable, point of view seems never to have been publicly expressed by anyone—politician, pundit, professor, editorialist—during the Cold War.

Between 11/9 and 9/11, anxieties that international terrorists would strike within the United States were not as great as those inspired by the threat of domestic Communism between 9/2 and 6/25. After 9/11, however, concern about the terrorist enemy within escalated massively.

Redirecting much of their effort from such unglamorous enterprises as dealing with organized crime and white collar embezzlement (which have actually happened since 2001), agencies such as the FBI have kept their primary focus on the terrorist threat. As with the quest to uncover the Communist enemy within, almost all of this activity has led nowhere. In 2002, official U.S. intelligence estimates held that there were as many as five thousand al Qaeda terrorists and supporters in the country.[40] In the succeeding years of intensive and well-funded questing, however, the FBI and other investigative agencies have been unable to uncover a single true al Qaeda sleeper cell or operative within the country.[41] Indeed, they have been scarcely able to unearth anyone who might even be deemed to have a "connection" to the diabolical group.

Concluding Perspectives

From this comparative exercise, I would like to lay out three perspectives. One looks backward, the other two forward.

Looking Backward: The Cold War as Farce

Throughout the Cold War, the contestants engaged in a security dilemma: each cumulated an impressive military arsenal to deter a threat of direct military aggression that didn't exist, and each took the other's buildup to be threatening, requiring them to accumulate more armaments in order to deter the nonexistent threat. Jervis characterizes the security dilemma as "tragic."[42] But surely, since it resulted primarily in frantic, if fundamentally insignificant, sound and fury, the theatrical form it most resembles in this case is farce. Because neither side had the slightest interest at any time in fighting the other militarily, there never really was much danger of a direct war between them—that is, neither actually had anything to deter. Nonetheless, each continued to pour massive resources into arms, and the absurdity of the situation is poignantly captured in an exasperated comment by President Dwight D. Eisenhower at a 1956 National Security Council meeting:

"We are piling up armaments because we do not know what else to do to provide for our security."[43]

There were also farcical elements in the policy of containment, as formulated by Kennan. He was clearly woefully wrong in his emphasis on the Soviet Union's succession dilemma—the "great uncertainty" arising from "the transfer of power from one individual or group of individuals to others."[44] However, although the process took much longer than he seems to have anticipated, he was essentially right about the disillusionment and skepticism of the Russian population, about the fundamental precariousness of Soviet economic development, and about "the dangerous congealment of political life in the higher circles of Soviet power." Kennan argued that "Soviet power, like the capitalist world of its own conception, bears within it the seeds of its own decay."[45] In the end, that proved to be right, and Nikita Khrushchev correctly framed the contest in his "kitchen debate" with Richard Nixon in 1959: "Who can produce the most goods for the people, that system is better and it will win."[46]

However, this suggests that the policy of containment was logically flawed. If the Soviet system really was as rotten and as destined to self-destruct as Kennan more or less accurately surmised, then the best policy would not have been to contain it, but to give it enough rope—to let it expand until it reached the point of terminal overstretch. Indeed, one of Kennan's favorite quotes came from Edward Gibbon: "there is nothing more contrary to nature than the attempt to hold in obedience distant provinces."[47]

As it turned out, at the international level what ultimately helped to bring about the mellowing of Soviet expansionism was not containment's success, but its failure. In 1975, three countries—Cambodia, South Vietnam, and Laos—toppled into the Communist camp. Partly out of fear of repeating the Vietnam experience, the United States went into a sort of containment funk and watched from the sidelines as the Soviet Union, in what seems in retrospect to have been remarkably like a fit of absentmindedness, opportunistically gathered a set of Third World countries into its imperial embrace: Angola in 1976, Mozambique and Ethiopia in 1977, South Yemen and Afghanistan in 1978, Grenada and Nicaragua in 1979. The Soviets at first were quite gleeful about these acquisitions—the "correlation of forces," they concluded, had decisively and most agreeably shifted in their direction.[48] However, almost all the new acquisitions soon became economic and political basket cases, fraught with dissension, financial mismanagement, and civil warfare, and the situation in neighboring Afghanistan so deteriorated that the Soviets found it necessary to send in troops, descending into a long period of enervating warfare there. Moreover, by the 1980s, the Soviets' empire in Eastern Europe had also become a severe economic drain and a psychic problem.[49] As each member of their newly expanded empire turned toward the

Soviet Union for maternal warmth and sustenance, many Soviets began to won-der if they would have been better off contained.

The "internal contradictions" the Soviets came to confront, then, were a direct result of misguided domestic and foreign policies, and these contradic-tions would have come about no matter what policy the West chose to pursue. Soviet domestic problems derived from decades of mismanagement, mindless brutality, and fundamental misconceptions about basic economic and social realities. Their defense dilemmas came from a conspiratorial ideology that cre-ated external enemies and then exaggerated the degree to which the enemies would use war to destroy them. And their foreign policy failures stemmed from a fundamentally flawed, and often highly romantic, conception of the imper-atives of history and of the degree to which foreign peoples would find the Communist worldview appealing. It took forty years but, plagued by economic and social disasters and changes, the Soviets finally were able, as Kennan had hoped, to embrace grim reality, and decisively to abandon their threatening ideology.[50]

The Western policy of containment helped keep some countries free from Communism. But Soviet communism would probably have been forced to con-front its inherent contradictions somewhat earlier if its natural propensity to expand had been tolerated rather than contained.

Looking Forward: The Limits to Massive Extrapolation

During the Cold War, massive extrapolation hit a hard ceiling, at least in one prime arena of concern, with the war in Vietnam. After that fiasco, there was a strong desire—usually called the Vietnam Syndrome—not to do that again. And, in fact, there never were other Vietnams for the United States during the Cold War. Due to fears of "another Vietnam," administrations were kept by Congress even from rather modest anticommunist militarized ventures in Africa and, to a lesser extent, in Latin America—though there was bipartisan support for aiding the anti-Soviet insurgency in Afghanistan.

A rather comparable "Iraq Syndrome" now seems likely, and there will prob-ably be notable increases in skepticism over the notion that the United States should take unilateral military action to correct situations or regimes it considers reprehensible but which present no very direct and very immediate threat to it. In particular, as the Democrats (and quite a few Republicans) strongly opposed other potential Vietnams after the American debacle there, they are likely to ques-tion any other Iraqs unless there is severe, unambiguous provocation. The rising dismay over the war in Afghanistan—a venture that once enjoyed nearly consen-sual approval—suggests the process is well under way. Under Barack Obama, the country has become more inclined to seek international cooperation, sometimes even showing perceptible, if occasional, signs of humility.

Looking Forward: Terror, Proliferation, and the Self-Licking Ice Cream Cone

The experience with international and domestic Communism suggests that once a threat becomes really internalized, the concern can linger for decades even if there is no evidence to support such a continued preoccupation. It becomes self-perpetuating, a self-licking ice cream cone. Although the most costly and destructive policies (or adventures) fabricated by creative and massive extrapolators during the Cold War lost support after Vietnam, the general concern with the perceived Communist threat continued to be supported and extravagantly financed. And something similar seems likely in the case of today's monsters: proliferation and terrorism.

However, the situation after 9/11 may be different from the one that prevailed after 6/25 in one important respect. The Communist monster could have its 11/9 and therefore, like Grendel (and his mother), it could terminally and convincingly expire as a perceived threat. Like crime, terrorism can be carried out by an individual or small group and can therefore never vanish from the human experience. The same can be said for the knowledge and technical capacity of errant states and small diabolical groups to fabricate nuclear and other "weapons of mass destruction." Other colorful monsters may arise from time to time to garner the attention and to strut and fret their hour upon the stage. But the monsters of terrorism and proliferation, and the internalized fears they have inspired, show distinct signs of being timeless.

8

THE ASSUMPTIONS DID IT

Bruce Cumings

I propose to examine how sudden events, either ones that might have been expected or had a modest probability, or those that happen utterly unexpectedly, tend to fit into existing assumptions of policymakers and scholars alike, skewing their reactions to such events and biasing future policy decisions. I will also explore theories about anticipating and predicting future events, and take particular cases—the shattered world of 1945, the fall of the Berlin Wall and the collapse of the Soviet Union, 9/11, and post–Cold War North Korea—and try to explain how statesmen and scholars sought to explain these cases, reacted to them, and evolved new policies to deal with their aftermath. Finally, I will suggest ways to understand how people form ideas, conceptions, and metaphors that may help or hinder explanations and predictions about the world we live in.

Obviously, as an historian, I bring to bear a different perspective, external to the world of policy making, and by virtue of working in Chicago, external to inside-the-Beltway debates. I have never been a policymaker, and although I have participated in Beltway debates, I don't remember winning any of them. But by reading thousands of policy papers inside of archives and out, open papers and formerly classified papers, I have learned to be humble before the agonizing task of making life-and-death decisions in conditions of imperfect knowledge. But I have also come to believe that people's basic assumptions are at least as important as the knowledge and information at their disposal, particularly when something entirely unanticipated happens.

A crystal clear example of how knowledge, events, information, intelligence, even history itself can wither in the face of rooted convictions is McGeorge

Bundy's stunning acknowledgment (unfortunately several decades after the fact) that he never took his Vietnamese enemy seriously. When asked what most surprised him about the Vietnam War, he said it was "the endurance of the enemy." He had failed to understand this, he later admitted, because "he didn't think they warranted his attention." Boston Brahmin that he was, he had no real interest in the Vietnamese and their motivations.[1]

If policy analysts couch their recommendations in classic option A-B-C form, with A and C as the extreme or flawed alternatives and B the analyst's preference, scholars seek shelter in numbers and consensual paradigms. Social scientists want to be predictive, but in my experience they rarely succeed—and perhaps never can succeed, because history, politics, economics, and sociology are not sciences. We had a remarkable demonstration of this in the fall of 2008, when very few economists anticipated a once-in-a-half-century financial collapse, could not explain it when it happened, and offered few useful predictions for how to get out of it or what the future held. Political scientists also prize their quantitative skills and, like economists, use numbers and probabilities to forecast political outcomes.[2] The romance with numbers occurs because reducing complex ideas and conceptions to numbers is seductive—like magic, it makes the complexity appear to disappear—and allows all sorts of mathematical manipulations (like lightning-fast trading of commodity fictions called derivatives or credit-default swaps). But when numbers refer to political probabilities, they are metaphors— and they are always less important than the assumptions that inform the model.

Did any social scientist using such methods predict the fall of the Berlin Wall, or the collapse of the USSR? Actually the answer to that question is yes, but somehow these predictions did not count—because they emanated from the wrong paradigm. I sat on a panel of the American Political Science Association annual meeting in 1984 and heard sociologist Immanuel Wallerstein predict that the Soviet and East European communist systems were eroding and would soon disappear; the Solidarity movement in Poland was one manifestation, but there were many others. After Communism collapsed, he said, the region would end up dependent on a unified Central European behemoth called Germany. Professor Wallerstein made this prediction in a number of publications before 1989, but it was not based on numbers or any occult Kremlinological knowledge, or even on Solidarity's strength. It was based on his theory of how the modern world works, which stated that all the Communist systems controlled state machineries within a world economy that was fundamentally capitalist, and all their attempts to overcome this fact, from the socialist world market of COMECON (Council for Mutual Economic Assistance) to North Korea's Hermit Kingdom, would fail sooner or later. His prescience existed in the depths of his own paradigm, his own assumptions, but not in any special knowledge or foresight.[3]

Likewise, George Kennan's conviction was that the USSR was an expansionist great-power empire masquerading as a global Communist menace; similarly to Tsarist Russia it expanded along its periphery, like an amoeba or capillary diffusion, but with limited global reach; an adroit blocking of its thrusts here and there (but not everywhere) would contain the problem and create the preconditions for the USSR itself to change. His limited definition of containment rested on a parsimonious theory: advanced industrial capacity was necessary for serious war making; the Soviets had one such base and the West had four (the United States, the United Kingdom, Western Europe, and Japan), and containment meant keeping things that way. The history of containment as national strategy proved to be tumultuous, but in 1991 Kennan's prescience appeared astonishing, at least to me, as the Soviet system disintegrated primarily for internal, systemic reasons.

Kennan was self-conscious enough to realize that what we call "American policy" after World War II meant something much deeper—"*politics* on a world scale," in his words. Still, Kennan's theoretical presuppositions were based in a turn-of-the-century realpolitik that had little to offer policymakers such as Dean Acheson after the Truman Doctrine established his limited strategy in 1947; for example, Acheson threw away Kennan's draft for his Press Club speech in January 1950, which suggested the best American policy for Korea would be to get out and let the Russians and the Japanese once again establish a balance of power in Northeast Asia. Again, like Wallerstein, his assumptions were operating here, and facts—like Korea's desire for postcolonial independence—made little difference. And for forty years, he was wrong about the Soviet system.

Being wrong for such a long time about the USSR, and then suddenly to be right, is also nothing new. When a grand but unexpected event occurs in history it may be a clairvoyant's orphan, but once it happens everyone has an explanation— and almost always, it is the explanation dear to their hearts (the Reagan arms buildup did it, the rot in the bureaucratic class that Trotsky and Milovan Djilas were early to diagnose did it, and so on).[4] The collapse of Western communism and the end of the Cold War occasioned a hailstorm of commentary, in which analysts found it easy to see their own assumptions, paradigms, and illusions confirmed; each doctrine (or illusion) carried its own diagnosis and prognosis, its own set of "I told you so's," and its own time-bound subjectivity: but we won't know who was right until years from now, or maybe we will never know.[5]

How Do We Know When We're Wrong?

One answer to this question was provided time and again by Mikhail Gorbachev in the 1980s: "life will teach us."[6] We try to give a direction to future events, and then history—or life—tells us whether we were right or wrong. He may have hoped for the demise of the Soviet system as it existed in the 1980s, but he certainly did not want the collapse of the USSR. Instead, he was groping toward some form of democratic socialism, and it dribbled out of his hands. The West, and particularly Americans, hailed his policies because they precipitated the collapse of both—the USSR and social democracy. But in post-Soviet Russia, particularly during the 1990s years of slash-and-burn capitalism, he was reviled: a prophet without honor. Contrast Deng Xiaoping: in 1978 he adopted, in effect, a venerable American philosophy—pragmatism. "Seek truth from facts," he said, while turning his back on the Maoist era and the huge potential for conflicts over its legacy with pithy aphorisms: "Mao was 70% right and 30% wrong." Deng launched a revolution that led to double-digit growth in the next three decades, while merely saying he was only "feeling for the stones as we cross the river." His modesty before the results were in on a watershed decision at a Central Committee plenum in December 1978 was entirely appropriate, because who knew if it would work? And it is shrewd politics: by appearing to take small steps Deng detonated a true "great leap forward"; by launching the major programs of perestroika and glasnost Gorbachev plunged into an unknown future that ultimately defeated him.

But his idea is a good one: we make predictions in the present, and life tells us whether we are right or wrong. The bipartisan Washington consensus through three Bush and two Clinton administrations was that post-1989 North Korea was on the verge of collapse. The CIA told Congress year in and year out that, in Director John Deutsch's words in 1995, it was not a question of whether the North would collapse, but when. Within forty-eight hours of this statement the top military commander of the Democratic People's Republic of Korea (DPRK) said it was no longer a question of whether another Korean War will break out, but when. More than two decades after the Berlin Wall fell, North Korea is still standing. Give it ten more years, and it will have existed as long as the entire run of the Soviet Union. Life should have taught the bipartisan Washington consensus that something is wrong with their grasp of North Korean affairs. Why they do not accept this judgment is something I will come to later.

Hegel's "cunning of history" is another way to tell when we are wrong—history coils up and bites us, or slaps us in the face when we least expect it. From my point of view this is what happened when five people on the Supreme Court (five "Republicans" in Dick Cheney's argot) decided in December 2000 that George W. Bush had won the presidency despite losing the popular vote by half a million votes, and perhaps also the Electoral College (pending a full recounting of Florida's contested votes). Four years later some fifty-five million

American voters said they were right to have done so. For a person who voted against Bush, this was a worse comeuppance.

But any honest person of the Left has to admit that the past two decades have been full of utterly unanticipated events, beginning with the fall of the Berlin Wall and culminating in the unimaginable collapse of the Soviet Union. The cunning of history left us without a single socialist system that could be recommended to anyone else, if there ever was one; the remains of the day were varieties of meliorist American liberal democracy and European social democracy that ultimately had to answer to the market. Whether that is a good or a bad thing is not the point: the point is this was hardly the pot of gold at the end of the socialist rainbow. Meanwhile, a decade after 1989, the tribunes of neoliberalism had to watch as an entire continent (South America) said no to their nostrums, and elected to bring one variety of would-be socialist (Chavez) or social democrat (Lula) to power. The cunning of history is an equal-opportunity avenger and a relentless reminder of human fallibility.

A third method of finding out we are wrong is to have history prove it to us, and then sail ahead undaunted. I think many people on the left explicitly or implicitly did this in 1989. All you do is redefine the issue: the Communist countries of Eastern Europe and (in 1991) the Soviet Union were not really socialist; they were for a long time Stalinist, and when reform came (Dubček in 1968) they repressed it with force. The uprisings of 1968 meant many things in the West, but in the East they meant that whenever democracy finally arrived in the region, it would not be socialist. This might be called the "New Left" position, because from the 1961 Port Huron Statement onward the New Left announced a plague on both houses—the USSR and the United States.

Oddly, they were moving on well-trod ground without knowing it. A more sophisticated version of this argument began in the 1940s with Michel Foucault. To say this name is enough to make some people terminate a conversation, but he first made his mark at a time when concerns about "the end of History" gripped a generation of young French intellectuals, and, moreover, at a time that made it all seem plausible: 1945. The defeat of fascism, the collapse of European empires, the spread of communism, and the substitution of American for British global leadership appeared to signal the end of the prehistory of the modern: but then the modern took two forms, liberal America and the communist Soviet Union, each providing a stark alternative to the other, and thus an occasion for philosophers such as Foucault, Jean-Paul Sartre, Maurice Merleau-Ponty, and Raymond Aron to mount the deepest inquiry into the meaning of the bipolar rivalry that came to dominate the postwar world.[7] To this debate Foucault eventually provided a radical alternative, a highly sophisticated body of thought that was nonetheless consonant with the global emergence of a "New Left": the United States and the

USSR were two sides of the same modern coin; for each their pretensions to new forms of freedom were less important than their joint acceptance of the modern project to discipline, mold, and punish their citizens.

Neither the Old nor the New Left, however, has had an answer to the proposition whether socialism or communism, as it had been conceived since 1848, could be made to work without the free operation of market signals. Perhaps there exists no better statement of the negative side of this position than Karl Polanyi's *Great Transformation*. Whatever one says about that great book, it is a consistent polemic against the workings of the market. But modern history, as we apprehend it today, seems to have penned a conclusion to this discourse: the more or less regulated market is the essential structure of economic activity, however meliorist or boring that may seem to intellectuals, radicals, and would-be tribunes of the people.

The point: history, or "life" (in Gorbachev's sense), can show us we are wrong and, even so, we sail along with our basic assumptions intact because they are constituent to our worldview, and thereby embody our own life experiences, our character, and even our soul. Assumptions are like the sand in the bottom of a plastic dummy: you can push the dummy over time and again, but the ballast at the bottom brings it back upright. So, we can be proved wrong to anyone else's satisfaction, but rarely (if ever) to our own.

Life has a solution to this human failing, too, which is to bring to the fore new generations who do not know what we are talking about—and usually don't care. There are many examples, but one is a friend of mine who lost many relatives in the Holocaust, and will not visit Germany or buy a German car. His son drives a BMW and loves present-day Berlin. This is, again, the cunning of human history. Another is a graduate student from Beijing who walked through my door a few years ago, nearly native in his English, funny and relaxed, his body language and interests undistinguishable from American students. Graduate students from the People's Republic of China like him did not exist in 1979 or even 1989, but he is par for the course today. He owes a great deal to a vastly experienced leader who in the 1920s showed Ho Chi Minh where to get the best croissants in Paris: Deng Xiaoping. But I doubt that he thinks much about that.

Back to the Future: Forecasting World Order in 1945

Now let us have a look at statesmen who had to make decisions in the middle of Foucault's cataclysmic "end of history." As World War II came to an end, a host of daunting problems and contingencies emerged that appeared overwhelming:

THE ASSUMPTIONS DID IT

the destruction of industry across the United Kingdom, France, Germany, and Japan; the dominance of the Soviet army in the Eurasian heartland; the rise of anticolonial movements in what came to be known as the Third World. If there is one statesman who embodied the decisions of the era it was Dean Acheson. And as it happened, he had plans for what to do about the postwar world that he had articulated many years earlier.

Acheson embodied the fullness of American ambition and expressed it concisely in a speech delivered shortly after Germany invaded Poland in September 1939, entitled "An American Attitude toward Foreign Affairs." As he later put it in reflecting back on this speech, he had really sought at the time to "begin work on a new postwar world system."[8] "Our vital interests," Acheson said in this speech at Yale, "do not permit us to be indifferent to the outcome" of the wars that had broken out in Europe and Asia; nor was it possible for Americans to remain isolated from them—unless they wished a kind of eternal "internment on this continent" (only an Anglophile such as Acheson would liken North America to a concentration camp). He located the causes of the war and the global depression that preceded it in "the failure of some mechanisms of the Nineteenth Century world economy" that had led to "this break-up of the world into exclusive areas for armed exploitation administered along oriental [sic] lines."

In its time, "the economic and political system of the Nineteenth Century . . . produced an amazing increase in the production of wealth," but for many years it had been in an "obvious process of decline." Reconstruction of the foundations of peace would require new mechanisms: ways to make capital available for industrial production, the removal of tariffs, "a broader market for goods made under decent standards," "a stable international monetary system," and the removal of "exclusive or preferential trade arrangements." Here, of course, is a succinct summary of the steps later taken at Bretton Woods. The world economy was his main emphasis, as usual for him, but he also called for the immediate creation of "a navy and air force adequate to secure us in both oceans simultaneously and with striking power sufficient to reach to the other side of each of them." Acheson later had the opportunity to implement these ideas, first at Bretton Woods, then with the Marshall Plan and the Truman Doctrine, and finally with NSC-68. He is the person who comes closest to being the singular architect of American global strategy from 1944 to 1953.

The fundamental assumption of Acheson and his allies in the years immediately after the war was that reconstruction of the world economy came first, reorienting the relations between former enemies came second, and containing Communist power came third (in these priorities we see a certain commonality with Wallerstein's theory). The postwar order took shape through positive policy and through the establishment of distinct outer limits, the transgression of which was rare or even inconceivable, provoking immediate crisis—the orientation of West Berlin toward the Soviet bloc, for example. The typical experience of this hegemony, however, was a mundane, benign, and mostly unremarked daily life of subtle constraint, in which the United States kept allied states on defense, resource, and, for many years, financial dependencies. This penetration of allied nations was clearest in the frontline semisovereign states such as Japan, West Germany, and South Korea, and it was conceived by people such as Acheson and Kennan as an indirect, outer-limit control on the worst outcome, namely, orientation to the other side.[9] The unprecedented stationing of bases and troops on allied soil is sixty-five years old by now, and I doubt that anyone could have imagined this outcome in 1945; it was a cumulative reaction to world events. But that mostly unremarked structure of military power—"hidden in plain sight"—solved the problem of what to do about the formidable Japanese and German militaries.

The third great problem—what to do about the vastly expanded Soviet sphere in the world—was dimly perceived in 1945 but acted upon in 1947–51, with Kennan's parsimonious strategy dominant until 1950. After that, the Acheson–Paul Nitze strategy of a global response to Communist expansion was dominant. We all have our common or disparate understandings of what happened in that period. But for our purposes it is more important to ask how those "present at the creation" picked up their shovels and hammers and went about constructing a new world order. How did a coherent, functioning, and ultimately successful system emerge?

In Robert Latham's terms, structure, contingency, and agency interacted in the making and remaking of the postwar order.[10] The structure was the global order-in-the-making. Contingency was the historicity of a unique world crisis, namely the Depression and the world war, but also the potency and essential indeterminacy of its lingering effects. Acheson, Kennan, and the others were the agents. They had ideas, of course, and the most prominent idea was to create institutions that would avoid the disasters of the 1930s, both international and domestic (isolationism), especially ones that could remedy the imbalances and worst tendencies of the unregulated market. The old rules didn't work and the new ones hadn't been invented: what to do? In retrospect, Bretton Woods appears to be the answer, but in fact the IMF and the World Bank failed to solve the economic problems of the late 1940s and one Bretton Woods institution, the International Trade Organization, never got off the ground (or perhaps did not until the 1990s—and thus the World Trade Organization). The Bretton Woods agreements can reasonably be seen as a planned, logical outcome of internationalist presuppositions, a follow-on to Acheson's 1939 speech: they just didn't work to resuscitate the industrial economies, so something else had to be done (the Marshall Plan, the "reverse course" in Japan). But another critical part of the subsequent global order was unplanned, illogical, and it *did* work. This would be the global archipelago of military bases, advisory groups, and aid programs. Here the conjuncture of agency and contingency brought about an enduring structure, and the utterly unanticipated consequence of a far-flung and theoretically unlimited militarized global space, necessitating unprecedented expenditures to service it, and leading to a national security state and a large standing army for the first time in American history.

The internationalist presuppositions molded into the bones of Franklin D. Roosevelt, Acheson, Robert Lovett, Henry Stimson, and many others by the experience of the 1930s explain how a new world economy came into being after World War II. And so the world of the 1990s was the anticipated consequence, the unfolding of an internationalist telos yielding a liberal, one-world order. But this order also had a completely unanticipated history that ran through bloody and disastrous wars in Korea and Vietnam, the ongoing reorientation of revolutionary China, and the collapse of the Soviet bloc—all experiences that would have flabbergasted a statesman seeking to chart the postwar order in 1945, should a mystic have conjured them in a crystal ball. Here we encounter a human agency the Achesons and Kennans (not to mention McGeorge Bundy) never imagined: the fierce energy of aroused colonial or semicolonial peoples in the 1940s, collectivities for whom imperialism and a recent feudal past were hated realities, and the promises of liberal world order an utter chimera. These aroused peoples were also the "agents" of unimaginable "contingencies" that built the postwar "structure."

But that was then and this is now; all that is over and done with. Instead the post-11/9 world ushered in a true long peace among the advanced industrial states. When the "Other" disappeared in 1989–91, the structure continued in place and, in the 1990s, achieved the full one-world florescence that its planners had imagined in the 1940s.[11] That is, the "New World Order" that George H. W. Bush and many others cast about for after 1989 was both the same old order and the ongoing fulfillment of the structures built in the late 1940s. Unified Germany does not dominate Europe, Japan has not gone nuclear, China discovered the market, France has a world-historical predicament of national identity, and American hegemony remains largely unchallenged by any power of sufficient weight to imagine replacing it.

This is the arena of the largest scope and the most importance: relations between the advanced industrial states—and it is hard to argue that things have not gone well since 1989 (in many ways the trade disputes of the 1980s were much worse than anything since). Here, in brief, is also the answer to why various people hoping to be the "Mr. X" of the post–Cold War era got it wrong, including Samuel Huntington ("clash of civilizations"), John Mearsheimer ("Back to the Future"), and Frances Fukuyama ("the end of history"): realpolitik does not govern the contemporary actions of the big powers, regional clashes of older civilizations in places such as the former Yugoslavia and South Asia mask the burgeoning triumph of modern civilization (to which they are also—and ineffectively—reactive); and the triumph of the liberal program does not mean "the end of history" because modern liberalism is itself a heterogeneous, contested, and deeply unfinished business.

Another way to explain the continuity and lack of big-power conflict since 1989 is less interesting, but perhaps more important in history: simple inertia. The collapse of Western communism and China's turn outward had little effect on the solid and functional underpinnings of the global system formed and developed over decades since 1945, except to expand the scope of the world economy to include hundreds of millions of new participants from the former Soviet bloc and China. Likewise, the world-historical inertia generated automatically in the Pentagon prevailed over early 1990s demands to convert many of its assets and budgets to peaceful uses, just as more than seven hundred U.S. bases around the world soldier on in spite of losing their primary adversary ("I'm running out of enemies," Colin Powell said after the Gulf War; "I'm down to Castro and Kim Il Sung").

In the absence of serious alternatives—of any serious alternative ideology that is also modern—and any insurgent power with the capability to say no and make it stick, and with the continuing inertial, even atavistic, mechanism of the Pentagon's far-flung bases and its hold on one-third of the federal budget, the "one world" that Roosevelt hoped would appear after 1945 materialized after 1989 and continues apace (although it is a world much more militarized than he would have wanted). In my view that is the largest meaning of 11/9.

September 11: A Date That Will Live in Infamy?

I remember . . . remarking on the criminal futility of the whole thing, doctrine, action, mentality; and on the contemptible aspect of the half-crazy pose as of a brazen cheat exploiting the poignant miseries and passionate credulities of a mankind always so tragically eager for self-destruction . . . a blood-stained inanity of so fatuous a kind that it was impossible to fathom its origin by any reasonable or even unreasonable process of thought.[12]

In this manner Joseph Conrad rendered his first impressions on hearing the news in 1894 that a lone anarchist had killed himself in a failed attempt to blow up London's Greenwich Observatory. It was to this old novel, *The Secret Agent*, that I first turned after the attacks that toppled the World Trade Center on September 11, 2001. Conrad's first impression then became my conviction: nothing in our adult lives prepared us for such a contemptible fusion of willful mass terrorism, bloodstained earthly tragedy, and passionate, ardent conviction—the adolescent fantasy that one big bang will change the world and usher in a global "jihad," a new epoch of "Crusades," or the final solution to eight decades of history that have passed since the Ottoman Empire collapsed, or perhaps the centuries of history since the Moors ruled Spain (all are bin Laden's historical analogies).

In its utter recklessness and indifference to consequences, its craven anonymity, and its lack of any discernible "program" save for inchoate revenge, 9/11 was an apolitical act. What programmatic direction issues forth from the collapse of the twin towers and the attack on the Pentagon? Throwing the moneylenders from the temple? But the banks remained open and stable, and the stock market reopened in a week. A curse on globalization, by attacking its skyscraping symbols? Peaceful protesters and agitators had done much more in the years since Seattle to draw attention to the pretensions and inequalities of globalization than either the anarchist saboteurs in their midst, or the foolish wreckers of a pristine September day in New York. What is their next step, what is their program, what is their strategy, how will the chief terrorists know when they have achieved their goals? What would a "peace negotiation" look like with such criminals? The perpetrators are dead—that is not a starting point, but the end; they accomplished a terrible but ultimately futile and self-defeating act, because they brought into being the very forces that may well put an end to two decades of mindless terrorism.

For these reasons, history and social science can have little to say about September 11, it seems to me. We can all tally the grievances of Muslims and Arabs going back eight decades (or eight centuries for that matter), just as we can tote up the very long list of errors, misguided ventures, mass violence, and criminal acts that can be laid at the door of the United States. In the aftermath of 9/11 many on the Left, in my view, made the fundamental error of framing the terrorist attacks against the sorrier aspects of the American record abroad, when in fact nothing that has ever happened since the United States was founded could sensibly justify such wild, wanton, and inhuman recklessness. It is as if I were to get upset about the war in Vietnam, which happened forty years ago, and decide to commandeer a Mack truck, load it with explosives, and run it headlong into the Sears Tower.

In other words, the act bears comparison to the sick individuals with some sort of grievance who have shot up schools and malls or blew up the Federal Building in Oklahoma City, and who are later shown not to have taken their daily dose of Thorazine or to be stupid enough to have a getaway car without a license plate. Others say, look at how the Muslims hate America: Do they not have legitimate grievances? The answer is twofold: yes, they do have legitimate grievances, and one of them is the continuing mutual terror of the Israeli-Palestinian conflict. And no, they had no particular grievances in 2001 that were different than their grievances in the past sixty years; at any point since the creation of the state of Israel it was child's play for any demagogue to stoke popular Muslim anger against the United States.

For these and other reasons, I still ask myself if 9/11 was a beginning—"the first war of the 21st century" in CNN-speak—or an ending. We have had three decades of global terrorism, roughly dating from the Iranian Revolution. How much longer will it last, given that its stated goals (such as the erasure of Israel) are no more likely today than in 1980? Certainly, one country after another on a belt running from Indonesia to Algeria produces desperate young men by the tens of thousands, unemployable in their economies; Egypt is said to graduate twenty thousand lawyers a year of whom perhaps 10 percent get jobs commensurate with their degrees. Clearly, this reflects a colossal failure of development in critically important countries such as Pakistan and Egypt, but that is hardly anything new. But think of the consequences flowing from 9/11: dozens of U.S. military bases in Iraq, where the civil war detonated by Bush's 2003 invasion is either over or in suspension; dozens more in Afghanistan, South Asia, and the former Soviet Union, as a result of the war in Afghanistan. No one knows how either war will turn out, but if postwar history is a guide, American military power will be permanently stationed in critical regions where it did not exist before 9/11.

Many analysts have leapt forward with historical analogies to 9/11, but as the reader may have guessed, I cannot think of any. Comparisons with the Cold War are truly absurd: whatever one may think about Stalin's Soviet Union, it competed head to toe against the United States and offered a top-to-bottom alternative system that was at the same time modern; both powers were complete believers in material progress and both were committed to a global competition between two different kinds of modernism. As Americans we witness this commonality of aspirations in a clip from CNN's 1997 Cold War documentary: the first human to descend from outer space, Yuri Gagarin, parades through Moscow in 1961 in a Zil four-door convertible with huge chrome bumpers, soaring tailfins, and wide whitewalls setting off the metallic green paint of a car that mimicked the last American four-door convertibles, still being made then by Lincoln.

We cannot imagine bin Laden and his Taliban friends in such a scene; these might be the only people on earth who regret that the wheel was invented. (They give new meaning to the word *antediluvian*.) The USSR was rational and could be deterred. It had no wish for suicide, and carefully stayed out of going to the brink with the United States—in Iran in 1946, Berlin in 1948, Korea in 1950, and

Berlin again in 1961. The exception was the Cuban missile crisis, but a strong and wise American strategy of confrontation and negotiation ended that episode to the detriment of Moscow. And had it been bin Laden in 1962, he would joyfully have tugged on his end of the knotted rope that Khrushchev so memorably (and eloquently) spoke of. In short, bin Laden and his followers have not the slightest thing in common with our old enemies, whether the Communists such as Stalin or the national liberation figures such as Ho Chi Minh. Nor do they resemble Arab leaders such as Saddam Hussein: his aggression in 1990 was of the common, old world Bismarckian variety—and it did not work.

Philosophers in the just war tradition have long argued that self-defense is the only legitimate reason to kill other human beings, a judgment carrying the corollary that an aggressor bears an unconscionably heavy burden because he cannot know the consequences of his aggression. History is littered with testimony to this truth. Consider a common analogy to September 11, Pearl Harbor: a rash and reckless attack, but one that eventually brought upon the heads of the perpetrators the gravest consequences for the Japanese nation—for the first time in its long history, it was occupied by enemies. Pearl Harbor was aggression of a kind the Old World had seen many times but no more than that, and it had a usually unremarked military efficiency: total American casualties in the Pearl Harbor raid were 2,335 naval, army, and Marine personnel dead, and 1,143 wounded. Total civilians killed: sixty-eight (almost the exact opposite of bin Laden's attacks).[13] But if you drive north on I-94 in downtown Chicago, you will still see a gigantic sign saying "December 7, 1941; September 11, 2001; Never Forget!"

The Limits of American Power

The one important and determining lesson history has taught since 9/11, it seems to me, is that the ubiquitous nature of the terrorist threat has vastly compounded the venerable problem of a relatively provincial America reacting to a threatening world. During the Cold War the Communists, who were so visible abroad and so invisible at home (thus the necessity to *look* for them), frightened average Americans because most had never encountered a real Communist. Now we have an inchoate enemy who might be here, there, and everywhere: in Yemen or Kyrgyzstan or at your corner convenience store. If Americans had trouble fathoming the historical roots of successful Communist movements, how much less could they understand an operator like Osama bin Laden (if they could find him)? "There is always an imbalance between the nationalist outcry and the reality of the threat which it meets," Louis Hartz wrote, but after a thousand treason trials and congressional investigations, "the Martian remains"—and through his invisibility "he keeps coming closer all the time." Today, the Martian is a nihilistic terrorist, he's closer all the time, and in one important sense he knows what he is doing: "All we have to do," bin Laden said in 2004, "is to send two mujahedeen to the farthest point east to raise a piece of cloth on which is written Al Qaeda, in order to make the generals race there to cause America to suffer human, economic, and political losses."[14] This critical imbalance poses a dire threat to the free institutions of this country because everybody and everything can be a suspect in somebody's tableau—and meanwhile American power stretches across the globe to the breaking point.

A couple of examples will have to suffice: in 2002 the Pentagon announced a new commitment to lay down "a long-term footprint in Central Asia," as reporters put it: an air base near Bishkek, the capital of Kyrgyzstan, that would hold up to three thousand troops; massive upgrading of existing military bases and facilities in Uzbekistan (e.g., the former Soviet base at Khanabad) and Pakistan (where several bases now secretly house American forces); creation of new bases and expansion of remnant Soviet military bases in Afghanistan; and the replacement of Marine expeditionary forces sent into Afghanistan after 9/11 with Army regulars settling in for the long haul ("Army units tend to establish more permanent bases," reporters said with considerable understatement). The spokesman for the U.S. Central Command told reporters that in the future the United States will find great value "in continuing to build airfields in a variety of locations on the perimeter of Afghanistan that over time can do a variety of functions, like combat operations, medical evacuation and delivering humanitarian assistance."[15]

Other press reports detailed American plans to send some six hundred troops to help combat Islamic guerrillas in the Philippines and to work together with the Indonesian military (which ruled the country for thirty years until Suharto was overthrown in 1998) in antiterrorism operations, which may inevitably embroil the United States in trying to maintain the precarious integrity of this far-flung island nation.[16] Meanwhile, the most obvious example, the war in Iraq, created hundreds of new U.S. bases. The Obama administration says the troops will all come home from Iraq in 2011, but if the past is prelude, American forces may remain in these places for decades.

There are good social science reasons for the American inability to extricate itself from wartime entanglements, however much those commitments depart radically from anything the United States experienced up until 1945. Vital interests are asserted where none existed before, temporary expedients become institutional commitments, military and bureaucratic interests proliferate, the Pentagon bean counters take over, every new appropriations season in Congress becomes an occasion for defending this or that outpost (new or old, vital or marginal)—and American power is mired in works of its own doing. Among the services, the U.S. Army finds its permanent mission in garrisoning various highly developed bases around the world; there officers confront real enemies (as in Korea) or command important posts (in Japan or Germany), and thus gain experience essential to promotion.

World War II was the clearest kind of military victory, yet American troops remain on the territory of their defeated enemies, Japan and Germany, and exercise a lingering constraint on their autonomy; however many justifications come and go for that remarkable and unprecedented situation (in that the leading global power stations its forces on the territory of the second and third largest economies), the fact remains that it has persisted since 1945 and shows no signs of ending. Meanwhile, the war in Afghanistan grinds on and gives a huge boost to an American presence in Central Asia that never existed before, where the United States had never asserted strategic interests, but where the interests of four nuclear powers intersect: Pakistan, India, Russia, and China.

History by the Numbers versus Rules of Thumb

Another method of letting history tell us whether we are right or wrong is to assign numbers and probabilities to current affairs, assuming that there is an identity between the number and the thing described, and that by collating and manipulating these numbers and probabilities, the future can be foretold. History by the numbers we can call it. A well-known practitioner of this method is Bruce Bueno de Mesquita, a political scientist who was given a big spread in the *New York Times Magazine*. It said he was so good at forecasting future events that the CIA employed him time and again to assess various futures around the world.[17]

People who inhabit different disciplines in academe get along by not sticking their noses into other academic fields. But when it came out in 1988 I read Buena de Mesquita's book on Hong Kong and, knowing nothing about his equations, I knew he was wrong to argue that Hong Kong would be quickly communized when it went back to mainland control.[18] I did not do any investigation: my assumptions told me that China would not kill this goose that had been laying golden eggs for it since 1949, and that if that somehow were not true, the implications of communizing Hong Kong for the people of Taiwan would be enough to get them to stick to "one country, two systems." So far I have been right and he has been wrong.

His method is mathematical probabilities; mine is what James Scott calls *mètis:* the rules of thumb that accumulate as a career progresses, and virtually scream out to you "this will not happen." A mechanic will tell you that you cannot find a pre-1990s Jaguar with reliable electronics; if you do, it is a fluke. An historian will tell you that if North Korea had collapsed in 1989, like Romania did, he should have gone into another line of work—auto mechanics, perhaps—because his whole understanding of that place would have been proved wrong. It is not so much a matter of knowing *what* will happen as ruling out various alternative scenarios that appear to be highly unlikely.

The "coming collapse" of North Korea is as old as the post–Cold War era. If "know your enemy" is the sine qua non of effective warfare and diplomacy, the United States has been badly served by those who claim expertise on North Korea in Washington. The mantra that the DPRK would soon collapse began with Bush I and lasted all through Clinton and Bush II. Deputy Secretary of Defense Paul Wolfowitz journeyed to Seoul in the aftermath of the apparent American victory over Saddam to say (in June 2003) that "North Korea is teetering on the brink of collapse." In intervening years we heard Gen. Gary Luck, commander of U.S. forces in Korea, say (in 1997) that "North Korea will disintegrate, possibly in very short order"; the only question was whether it would implode or explode.[19] In this, he was merely plagiarizing another of our commanders in Korea, Gen. Robert Riscassi, who never tired of saying Pyongyang would soon "implode or explode" (Riscassi retired in 1992). Even the American pledge to build two light-water reactors to replace the Yongbyon plutonium complex in the 1994 freeze agreement was premised on collapse: since they would not come onstream for a decade, by then they would belong to the Republic of Korea (ROK). When does the statute of limitations run out on being systematically wrong? But I know from experience that any attempt by outsiders to break through this Beltway groupthink merely results in polite silence and discrete headshaking. North Korea's coming collapse is still the dominant opinion today.[20]

The leading Washington pundit on North Korea is Nicholas Eberstadt, who has been predicting the impending collapse of North Korea since at least June 1990, but his views are best sampled in his 1999 book, *The End of North Korea.*[21] (When a *New York Times* reporter asked John Bolton what the Bush administration's policy was on the DPRK, he strode to his bookshelf and handed him Eberstadt's book: that's our policy, he said.) Eberstadt's error is fundamental; once again it is at the level of assumptions and not evidence, because he sees the DPRK entirely through the lenses of Soviet and East European communism and therefore cannot grasp the regime's very different history, the pragmatic shrewdness of its post-Soviet foreign policy, the desperate and cruel survival strategies it is willing to undertake, let alone the anticolonial and revolutionary nationalist origins of this regime (and those in Vietnam and China, yielding no break since 1989 in Asian communism, except for the one true Soviet satellite: Mongolia).

In 1997, the CIA invited Eberstadt and other outside experts to join a panel of government officials, which concluded that North Korea was likely to collapse within five years. Robert A. Wampler, who obtained this report under the Freedom of Information Act, quoted senior Foreign Service officer David Straub's observation that one expert after another came through the Tokyo Embassy in the 1990s, "pontificating on their prognoses for the inevitable collapse of the North Korean regime, giving odds that allowed Pyongyang anywhere from a few months to perhaps two years before falling."[22] Kim Jong Il, the assembled CIA experts thought, was likely to have just "a brief window of time" to cope with all his difficulties before suffering a probable "hard landing." Without major reform, some "catalyst" would come along "that will lead to collapse." The majority of the group doubted that Kim's regime could persist "beyond five years," yielding a "political implosion." Yet many of them expressed surprise that in spite of the degraded economy and the beginnings of a famine that would soon grow much worse, somehow the "delusionary" (their term) Kim Jong Il "remained firmly in control." Among those outsiders whom the CIA invited to this exercise besides Eberstadt were academics Kenneth Lieberthal and Robert Ross and Daryl Plunk and James Przystup from the Heritage Foundation. No academic experts on North Korea were there (Lieberthal and Ross are China experts), but, more surprisingly, neither was anyone from Brookings or the Carnegie Endowment—the liberal anchors of the (may I say narrow?) spectrum of Beltway opinion. Here was the CIA under the Clinton administration reaching out to the Right for guidance on "North Korea's coming collapse."

The Endurance of the Enemy

Successive administrations and Beltway pundits get North Korea wrong because they know next to nothing about its origins, view it through the lenses of Soviet behavior, and cannot come up with any North Korean interests that they deem worthy of respect. For many, it is an outrage that the regime continues to exist at all (this was the dominant opinion in the second Bush administration). But in the end, what difference does this make? Is the DPRK going to erase itself because the American Enterprise Institute thinks it should? Eberstadt eventually got tired of predicting the DPRK's collapse and decided to do something about it: in 2004 he argued that America and its allies should waltz in and, in his Reaganesque flourish, "tear down this tyranny."[23] At the time he had excellent backing for such views in Vice President Dick Cheney's entourage. With the demise of the Bush vision, if one can call it that, enthusiasm for such a course has waned. But it was the preferred policy of hard-liners for several years, amid the internal civil war that shaped Bush's policies toward North Korea—where most meetings on North Korea turned into raging shouting matches.[24]

Our media takes it as given that the North Koreans are irrational. What about us? Since the Berlin Wall fell a Beltway consensus embracing leaders of both parties has adhered to four core axioms: (1) North Korea stands for nothing, has no support from its people, and will soon collapse; (2) American pressure on this regime will either hasten this process (Republicans) or change its behavior (Democrats); (3) if engagement works to get rid of their nukes, fine, but the end goal here, too, is a "velvet" form of regime change; (4) if it doesn't, resort to military force is justified to stop the North from becoming a nuclear power weapons state. All of these assumptions are false and, in the light of recent history, irrational. What is to be done? A sincere inquiry into the history of U.S. relations with North Korea since 1945 would be the place to begin. But if you don't believe the North had the capability of independent action—at least not until 1991—then why would anyone do this? If you are not interested enough in your enemy to learn something about its motivations—in other words if you are like McGeorge Bundy—how can you account for his persistence against all odds? How can you hope to triumph over him? So we return to the terrain of assumptions, presuppositions, and metaphors—impervious to history.

Conclusion: Round Up the Usual Metaphors

Shortly before he died Michel Foucault said he was really just a student and interpreter of the work of Friedrich Nietzsche. Nietzsche sowed the seeds of poststructural and postmodern thought, but more particularly for my purposes here he developed an understanding of our human relationship to the world that is quite close to the dilemma I have sought to develop in this chapter, of how we humans acknowledge and overcome our tendency to act like plastic dummies with a ballast of sand in the bottom. The answer, to extend this trite metaphor, is to plunge into the sand oneself—to be what Dean Acheson called a "reexaminationist," one who doesn't prune back the errors of policy but pulls the plant out of the ground and turns the roots upside down. We need to examine our assumptions, interrogate our presuppositions, and ask whether we have learned the lessons that life has tried to teach us.

Nietzsche was first of all a psychologist, plumbing his own psyche as perhaps no one else before him had done, to reveal truths about human nature. He believed that all human knowledge involves metaphor (the Greek word means to *carry over, carry across,* or *transfer*) because it is the means by which humans bridge the gap between subject and object. And he asked:

What then is truth? a movable host of metaphors, metonymies, and anthropomorphisms: in short, a sum of human relations which have been poetically and rhetorically intensified, transferred, and embellished, and which, after long usage, seem to a people to be fixed, canonical, and binding. Truths are illusions we have forgotten are illusions; they are metaphors that have become worn out and have been drained of sensuous force, coins which have lost their embossing and are now considered as metal and no longer as coins.[25]

What Nietzsche means is that we construct a second human nature for ourselves through language, concept, metaphor and experience, and this is what distinguishes us from animals. Language *is* rhetoric, of all kinds, including the presumably objective formulations of natural science, the perfect abstract order of mathematics, and the probabilities of economists. Language does not connote "things in themselves" of the real world; there is no such thing as the thing in itself, apart from our words, conceptions, and metaphors. Metaphors transfer meaning; synechdoches take the part for the whole; metastasis involves the shift from one subject to another—good generalizations shifting to good truths, for example.

New ideas appear, Nietzsche thought, out of nowhere; an idea appears when *it* wants to, not when you want it to. This kind of thinking cannot be reduced to a method, but can be called implicit or tacit knowing, as an extension of the self, *mêtis* or the "feeling for" the subject of study that good scientists and scholars have, an intimate awareness of the objects they study, whether lemons, neutrinos—or the postwar order, the collapse of Western communism, the persistence of North Korea, and the essential meaning of nihilistic terrorism.

9

FAULTY LEARNING AND FLAWED POLICIES IN AFGHANISTAN AND IRAQ

Odd Arne Westad

We all try to draw lessons from history. In our work, we attempt to improve what we do by understanding why things went wrong (or right) in the past. All world religions teach that we can become better men and women by learning from our mistakes, and most of political theory does the same. Liberalism is particularly insistent on both the obligation and the need to perfect the present in light of past errors—the concept of progress that is built into all kinds of liberal political systems assumes that the future is perfectible if we can draw on history as a reservoir of lessons for why bad things happen. And the twentieth century has left us with so much going wrong in human affairs that it does not take much convincing to believe in the need for improvement, even among those who are more skeptical of the ineluctability of progress than are most liberals.

As a rule, today's historians are worried about putting too much emphasis on the need to learn from history. Deeply aware, as we should be, that one person's positive lesson may be another's deterrent example, historians try to avoid the impression that the history they write can provide a guide to future choices. This approach is right both in the sense that simple historical parallelism is rarely useful, and in the sense that historians are no better than other people in providing guidance about today's affairs. But, still, each person's study of history through reading or through research can provide insights that will be valuable for his or her choices, especially on the bigger issues in life (what is sometimes called strategy). Besides, we do have a need to understand why and how lessons of history have a place in history, so to speak. Although I am rather an agnostic on the matter of whether we are capable of learning from history, I do believe that we are primed to attempt such self-instruction.[1]

This essay is about possible lessons of the Cold War for the U.S.-led interventions in Afghanistan and Iraq in the 2000s. It is primarily about how perceived lessons from earlier decades influenced decisions that U.S. policymakers made over the past decade. But it also reflects my own view of how the history of the Cold War, and especially the way it ended, can be used to construct much less interventionist forms of engagement with the outside world than those that ruled American foreign affairs between 2001 and 2008. The invasions of Afghanistan and Iraq were calamitous events, with very few advantages for the countries in which they took place, for their regions, or for U.S. foreign policy.[2] They came out of a deep preoccupation with changing the world in order to make America safer. But because the statesmen who directed them misinterpreted the societies into which they intervened and overestimated the U.S. capacity for forcing change, these interventions became examples neither of U.S. power nor will, but rather of the increasing inability of all great powers to use military interventions to their advantage.

The Argument: Why These Interventions Failed

The United States was the victim of a large terrorist attack on September 11, 2001, and any country that is attacked has the right to defend itself. The administration of George W. Bush chose, sensibly, to do so by attacking the government that had given shelter to the terrorists who inflicted such damage on the United States and thereby attempted to crush the networks that the terrorist organizations had built up. While the administration struggled to figure out what kind of conflict it was in (producing the unfortunate "war on terror" metaphor in the process), its military effort in 2001 was rightly concentrated on Afghanistan. By working with the domestic enemies of the Afghan Taliban regime and deterring assistance by its foreign friends (first and foremost Pakistan), the United States succeeded in overthrowing the government of Afghanistan after a few weeks of fighting with the involvement mainly of U.S. Special Operations units and a minimal loss of American lives. By mid-December 2001 the fighting in Afghanistan was over and the Taliban's power as a political and military organization was broken.

In the wake of the military victory of U.S.-supported forces in Afghanistan, the Bush administration made two major mistakes that undermined the positive effects of that victory for the United States and for the Afghans. First, it let the remnants of the political leadership of the Taliban and their al Qaeda allies escape into Pakistani territory without forcing the military dictatorship in Islamabad to accept a U.S.-led offensive against them. In early 2002, with international support for the U.S. hunt for Osama bin Laden at its peak and with the Pakistani military's alliance with Islamist extremists increasingly unpopular within its own country, it would have been possible to create conditions under which President Pervez Musharraf, or another Pakistani leader, would have had no choice but to accept the rooting out of the Islamist camps in the north, in the tribal areas, and in Baluchistan. But the alliance with Musharraf and the Pakistani military was in itself deemed too important to the United States for such a demand to be made absolute.[3]

Second, instead of concentrating almost exclusively on aiding Hamid Karzai's regime and the northern warlords, the United States and its Western allies should have offered far more civilian assistance to the Afghan regions, especially in the Pashtun-dominated south and east, in the crucial two years after the victory over the Taliban. The aim should have been to form agreements between the donors and local leaders, and then reduce the foreign military presence gradually, intending to end it no later than 2005. Such a strategy—aid and gradual withdrawal from the provinces, with the rival political factions left to squabble over power in Kabul—would have been a more realistic approach to the chronic political instability of the Afghan state and the need to prevent a return of Islamist extremist organizations among the Pashtun.

As for Iraq, the invasion there not only took attention away from the need to destroy al Qaeda in Pakistan and from the programs of rebuilding in Afghanistan, but it also failed to improve the security of the United States and its key ally in the region, Israel; it augmented the power and influence of Iran (at least temporarily); it increased Islamist extremism within Iraq; and it has so far cost the lives of almost five thousand U.S. and coalition soldiers and at least one hundred thousand Iraqis (if one counts indirect casualties of the war among Iraqis the number is at lest five times higher).[4] The invasion set off an Iraqi civil war that is still smoldering, even though by now the Shias have clearly won the contest for power, something that has led to a sharp reduction in the overall level of violence. And the power and prestige of the United States was diminished worldwide, both among its enemies and its friends, because of the demonstrable lack of the original *casus belli* and the chaos that followed in the wake of the invasion.

My argument here is that some (though not all) of the reasons for the mistakes made in Afghanistan and Iraq derive from misinterpretations of American successes during the Cold War.[5] I will discuss a few of these misinterpretations on the following pages: the overreliance on technology; the instrumentality of regime change; the predilection for moral absolutes; the failure to detect blowback; and the belief in the utility of speedy change and falling dominoes.

Technology

The way the Cold War ended created a very strong belief among many that it was the superiority of U.S. technology that had won the day. By the 1980s, the United States possessed advanced military technology that the Soviet Union could not match, especially in terms of targeting, command and control systems, intelligence, and aviation technology. It also had, through private enterprise, developed a consumer technology that could be used to create a more attractive society, at least in the eyes of those who did not possess its products or lacked the means to acquire them. By the mid-1980s, the United States had taken the first steps toward what would become, as the Cold War ended, a worldwide information technology network, joining ever-increasing computing power and telecommunications together to create a web that integrated finance and trade. The Soviets had built a state and a society that could not equal any of these developments, and it is clear that the realization that the Soviet economy could not compete in terms of these forms of innovative output was a major reason for the reforms of Mikhail Gorbachev and for his policy of cooperating with rather than confronting the United States. The technological advances of the United States helped defeat the Soviet Union internationally and forced Gorbachev's hand.

By the late 1990s, however, it was clear that even if U.S. technology had stemmed Soviet ambition and led to a revolution in finance and military affairs worldwide, it could not easily be employed against terrorists and insurgents in distant parts of the world. Already in Somalia, where President George H. W. Bush had sent U.S. troops to assist UN relief missions during an increasingly vicious civil war in 1992, the U.S. dependence on high-tech military operations began running into trouble. The loosely organized militia of Mohamed Farrah Aidid not only held its own in street fighting against U.S. troops in Mogadishu, killing eighteen U.S. army Special Operations soldiers, but it also pushed President Bill Clinton into withdrawing all U.S. troops from Somalia in October 1993. In Bosnia, the reliance on high-tech forms of warfare was among the factors that prevented an American decision to intervene, and while U.S. airpower proved perfectly capable of destroying the Serbian military's ability to operate in Kosovo in 1999, many military experts worried about the efficacy of U.S. ground troops in combat against irregular forces in the former Yugoslavia.

In Afghanistan and Iraq, the military and the military doctrines that came out of the lessons of the Cold War were up against their toughest tests yet. Although U.S. forces easily defeated the regular army of the Saddam Hussein regime and provided crucial assistance to its Afghan allies through the use of airpower in the overthrow of the Taliban, they were much less able to cope with controlling territory against insurgents or protecting civilian operations. While operating on the ground, in regions with multiple power holders and an unclear military and strategic situation, and with targets difficult to identify, the emphasis that had been put on technology over training became very evident. For Afghanistan, for instance, the draft official history of the campaign notes that the al Qaeda "set of targets, and the preparations that had been made to strike them, were the only 'plans' available . . . on the morning of 11 September 2001."[6] As for Iraq, the job was regarded as straightforward at the time. Max Boot, an early advocate of the war, summed it up in 2003:

> Spurred by dramatic advances in information technology, the U.S. military has adopted a new style of warfare that eschews the bloody slogging matches of old. It seeks a quick victory with minimal casualties on both sides. Its hallmarks are speed, maneuver, flexibility, and surprise. It is heavily reliant upon precision firepower, special forces, and psychological operations. And it strives to integrate naval, air, and land power into a seamless whole. This approach was put powerfully on display in the recent invasion of Iraq, and its implications for the future of American war fighting are profound.[7]

One of the key lessons of the Cold War should have been that symmetrical wars can be won by superior technology, whereas asymmetrical wars cannot. U.S. defense planning from 1992 up to the mid-2000s instead emphasized the technological advantages of the United States, which, while able to secure aims in interstate wars, have done little good in wars against loosely organized enemies who are not themselves dependent on high-tech weapons, or—for that matter—on holding territory or defending civilians. Although it is undoubtedly true that U.S. technological superiority helped defeat the Soviet Union on a number of different levels of competition, it mostly failed to deliver results in Third World conflicts, just as it failed to produce results after the military victory in Iraq and is failing to produce results in Afghanistan.

Regime Change

U.S. policy during the Cold War was, at least to some extent, about a form of what is now called "regime change." The containment of the Soviet bloc was intended to create the conditions of its downfall, fully expecting that downfall to come from within. During the war in Korea, the U.S. aim was to overthrow the regime of Kim Il Sung and replace it with a government friendly to the United States. By the 1980s, however, as the Cold War was being won, the idea of using the U.S. military to attack other countries and force regime change started to work its way into the American vocabulary. With the bipolar international system gone, the United States was much freer to use force in order to replace a regime abroad with one more friendly to Washington. President Ronald Reagan's instructions with regard to Libya in 1986 used the term, and during the Clinton administration it became a stated U.S. aim with regard to Iraq.[8]

Although there has always been much discussion about what regime change means in each case in terms of U.S. policy and commitments, the Cold War linked it inextricably to concepts such as state-building and even nation-building. One contemporary and later critique of the U.S. war in Vietnam rested on the per- ceived lack of willingness to use massive force and of being afraid of cross-border operations. The George W. Bush administration believed it had learnt these les- sons with regard to both Afghanistan and Iraq. But instead the focus on destroy- ing the military power of conventional opponents in both places deflected from a focus on what would happen *after* the enemy regime was toppled. In Afghanistan, the administration stumbled into a position that is remarkably similar to that held by the Soviets, charged with upholding an increasingly unpopular regime in Kabul that is not able to defend itself. In Iraq, the unpreparedness for working within the evolving political situation meant that U.S. forces found themselves caught in a civil war on which they had very limited influence.

In a triple irony, the insistence on learning from Cold War lessons from Third World interventions led to situations that over time proved remarkably similar to the U.S. tragedy in Vietnam: although massive force was used successfully against conventional enemies in both of the 2000s interventions, how to use it and who to use it against after the first victory had been won remained unclear. And some of those who had deplored U.S. unwillingness to extend U.S. ground operations into North Vietnam were themselves unwilling to deploy cross-border strategies against a nominal ally (Pakistan) or against an opponent (Iran) who had ben- efitted from the fall of Saddam and who worked with some of the same political and religious leaders on whom the Americans depended for their state-building effort in Iraq.

Imposing a new form of government on an unwilling population in the 2000s was as difficult as it had been during the Cold War, even though achiev- ing military victory may have become easier. When major military operations ended, the supporters of the Taliban and Saddam regimes were just two fac- tions within complex mosaics of political, ethnic, and religious groups, most of which opposed a foreign military presence. Although some Bush advisers thought that "when we act, we create our own reality," the reality created on the ground in Iraq and Afghanistan turned out to be composite, consisting of the aims and aspirations of many actors, of which the United States was only one.[9] The main problem with creating social change abroad is that it takes an extraordinary degree of commitment and willingness to sacrifice on behalf of the outside power, and even then success is in no way likely unless one has strong local allies whose aims are broadly similar to one's own. Neither of these two conditions existed in Afghanistan and Iraq, and, as a result, the attempts at state-building (not to mention "nation-building") largely failed. The way the Cold War ended seems to have moved the United States toward a belief in its own ability to change forms of government abroad through decisive action. It is a faulty lesson, not only because most change at the end of the Cold War came from within—as assumed by George Kennan and other proponents of containment—but also because many of the difficulties in imposing societal change abroad remained unchanged after the Cold War was over.

Moral Absolutes and National Values

Although the term "American triumphalism" may be of use in critiquing the approach of some U.S.-based historians to the outcome of the Cold War, it makes little sense applied to policymakers of the 1990s and 2000s. The United States won the Cold War, and its victory gave rise to different forms of assertive nationalism that are not unlike those found in other nations that have succeeded in a great enterprise. The neoconservatives represent one such trend, but at the Republican end of the political spectrum the neocons are mostly the mouthpieces for other assertive nationalists who want the United States to pursue its Cold War victory by creating a world that is more amenable to U.S. interests, ideologically, politically, and economically. In the Bush administration it was nationalists such as Vice President Dick Cheney, Secretary of Defense Donald Rumsfeld, and National Security Adviser/Secretary of State Condoleezza Rice who dominated policy making and who set the standards for achievement, while Deputy Secretary of Defense Paul Wolfowitz and other neocons were charged with presenting the framework for U.S. policy to the world. This hierarchically based division of labor often overshadowed distinct differences in opinion between the two groups, but on key issues of definition that came out of the Cold War they were very much in agreement.

One such definition is that American national values are good (for everyone, not just Americans) and that the Cold War had therefore been, in its essence, a battle of good versus evil. Projected into the post–Cold War era, there is a teleological aspect to these beliefs: the United States won the Cold War largely because it was on the side of good against the evil Soviet Union, and the policies of good continue after victory has been won. Listen to Paul Wolfowitz in 2002:

I think our interests are defined by our values in a way that makes them much more consistent with other people's interests. So it's not a matter of . . . saying that we can dominate the world or have the world run our way. It's rather I think a matter of saying that if people . . . are really liberated to run their countries the way they want to we will have a world that will be very congenial for American interests.[10]

The main critique of the Clinton administration was that it had not been clear enough on these issues. As a report produced by Republican conservatives before the 2000 election put it: "Global leadership is not something exercised at our leisure, when the mood strikes us or when our core national security interests are directly threatened; then it is already too late. Rather, it is a choice whether or not to maintain American military preeminence, to secure American geopolitical leadership, and to preserve the American peace."[11]

In both Afghanistan and Iraq, the U.S. conviction that it represents values that are both moral absolutes and are common to all of humanity clashed with local notions of rights, of religion, and ultimately of one's own worth. Time and again, U.S. policies collided with concepts of such rights (to territory, to water, to religious manifestations) that locals were willing to defend, often with their lives. In both countries the U.S. position was further complicated by there being different sets of local ideologies and beliefs, often in conflict with each other, and, of course, by the existence of extremist Islamist groups, whose total ideology for many locals resembled the demands put on them by American moral absolutes. Even though the Islamist groups killed a lot more people, Americans naturally got blamed for what they termed collateral damage, that is, civilian losses during military operations. In Afghanistan, especially, air force operations against suspected opponents of the Karzai regime killed civilians who may or may not have been opposition supporters. These operations undermined American claims to stand for good against evil: it is very hard, when one's territory is being bombed from the air, to see much moral good represented by the bombing.[12]

The claims to represent the forces of good are of course particularly hard-pressed to win local adherents when made by people who represent another country and another religion. Although many Americans believed that the processes of globalization that took place around the end of the Cold War made the world smaller in the sense that people's values everywhere began to veer toward those held in the United States, this is not very obvious when seen from areas in which the benign effects of globalization are only visible in a very thin layer of the population. Instead, as often happened during the Cold War, outside forces are seen as occupiers and enemies, even when they in their own opinion are doing good. This key problem with intervention was overlooked in terms of strategy both in Afghanistan and Iraq, because some people thought that the way the Cold War ended had changed global perceptions enough for the United States to make a believable case for its own moral authority even in places such as Kandahar or Karbala.[13]

Blowback

One main reason why the authority of the United States in Afghanistan and Iraq has been challenged by large groups of the population is what some intelligence experts began calling blowback, meaning unintended negative consequences of past U.S. covert operations. In Afghanistan, the United States supported extreme Islamist groups against the Soviet-backed Afghan government between 1979 and 1991. It also supported military regimes in Pakistan, which organized and trained Islamist groups for operations in Afghanistan and against India. In the case of Afghanistan, there is little doubt that without this support radical Islamism would have been a negligible force in the country. As a result, many Afghans blame the United States and the Pakistanis for their current predicament, making it very hard to convince the non-Islamist majority about the current good intentions of the U.S. administration.

In Iraq, there is a similar story, although with a twist. In order to contain the Shia Islamists in Iran, the United States supported Saddam Hussein's regime after he attacked Iran in 1980. In spite of the many human rights violations of the Saddam regime and in spite of his country being the obvious aggressor, the Reagan administration supplied Baghdad with economic aid, intelligence, and weapons. Donald Rumsfeld's visit to Baghdad as a presidential envoy in December 1983 ended with the conclusion that it "marked [a] positive milestone in [the] development of US-Iraqi relations and will prove to be of wider benefit to [the] US posture in the region."[14] Reagan's National Security Decision Directive 139, issued in April 1984, found that preventing the collapse of the Iraqi regime was in the U.S. interest. An NSC staffer dealing with the region in the Reagan White House, Howard Teicher, later explained:

> The United States actively supported the Iraqi war effort by supplying the Iraqis with billions of dollars of credits, by providing U.S. military intelligence and advice to the Iraqis, and by closely monitoring third country arms sales to Iraq to make sure that Iraq had the military weaponry required. The United States also provided strategic operational advice to the Iraqis to better use their assets in combat. . . . The CIA,

including both Director Casey and Deputy Director Gates, knew of, approved of, and assisted in the sale of non-U.S. origin military weapons, ammunition and vehicles to Iraq.[15]

The most devastating result of blowback from the 1980s for the 2000s wars was the enduring U.S. relationship with the military regime in Pakistan. Instead of supporting the secular civilian opposition forces in that country, the United States—to a large part because of ties that had existed in the past—continued to give its support to the regime of General Musharraf, even if it knew that both the Taliban and the al Qaeda leaderships were to be found in Pakistan, where they had been evacuated by elements of the Pakistani military in 2001 and 2002. U.S. policy on Pakistan helped set that country on the road to disaster and made certain that its own enemies in Afghanistan survived to fight another day. As the material situation on the ground deteriorated in southern Afghanistan in 2004 and 2005, in part because of the U.S. refocus on Iraq, the Taliban made a comeback in the Pushtun regions, leading to the renewed war from 2006 on, a war that will be very difficult for the present Kabul government to win.

Blowback is a difficult term to use, because it often serves as cover for various conspiracy theories with no basis in reality. What should concern us here are the political and military effects of blowback, as they come up against the perceived lessons learned from the end of the Cold War. Although U.S. policymakers of the Reagan administration remained proud of the alliances they had created in order to fight the Soviet Union more effectively than previous administrations had, they were not prepared for the kind of blowback in terms of popular perceptions from these alliances. As Wolfowitz professed in April 2003, "I happen to love history. I think, in fact, it's very important in approaching any country to understand its history. I also think that people who live in the past will never make progress. . . . We have to get past the past. The past is fascinating, it's rich, it's important to understand it, but the future is much more promising than the past."[16] What Wolfowitz did not see was how one's own history in some cases may return to bite the tail of the best-laid plans for the future.

Speed and Dominoes

One of the most impressive aspects of U.S. diplomacy in the period when the Cold War came to an end was its willingness to help speed up processes of change. This approach was first and foremost seen in the Reagan administration's readiness to work with Mikhail Gorbachev in 1986–87, when the Soviet leader was feeling his way toward a new form of cooperative diplomacy, and in the George H. W. Bush administration's promptness to accept rapid German reunification when all key European leaders were skeptical. In both cases, the United States decided that a speedy reorientation of past policies was needed and, as a consequence, helped achieve remarkable results.[17]

The way communism collapsed in Eastern Europe and in the Soviet Union fastened the belief that when change first began in one major country within a region (in this case Poland), then other states would be profoundly affected as well. In Cold War terms, the astonishing turnovers of power in 1989–91 from Vilnius to Sofia and Moscow looked like a set of reverse dominoes, and made some U.S. policymakers believe that the same spread of speedy change could be achievable elsewhere. The collapse of a failed dictatorship in a major country could serve as inspiration for the peoples of countries related by ethnicity, religion, or shared experience to carry out the same kind of revolutions themselves. And, of course, the distinct support for U.S. models of development and U.S. policies in Eastern Europe after the fall of Communism confirmed the sense that a massive and sudden breakdown, a revolutionary break with the past, may be in the U.S. interest elsewhere as well.

The problem with the transfer of the Soviet bloc experience to the Middle East and South Asia is that the countries of these two regions have extremely different historical experiences from those in Eastern and Central Europe. Instead of growing gradually into a reasonably stable relationship with another part of their own continent that was successful and affluent, as Eastern Europe did from 1975 to 1989, Iraq and Afghanistan lacked any stable, prosperous neighbors. In fact, they had both been at war with many of their neighbors quite recently. The United States had a close alliance relationship with Afghanistan's most important neighbor, Pakistan, but that U.S. ally was not just in economic freefall, it also had a vested interest in preventing the emergence of a successful Afghan regime. In Iraq, the state with which the largest population group wanted closer relations was Iran, a theocratic state with proven anti-U.S. credentials. Unlike most nations in Eastern Europe in 1989, the two states in which the United States intervened in the 2000s had no history of democracy, no tradition of functioning capitalist economies, and no national leaders who could overcome ethnic and religious divisions.

Most important, of course, change in Afghanistan and Iraq was not helped along by U.S. diplomacy, but brought in by the force of American guns. The United States therefore took responsibility for the revolutions that had to follow and would be blamed for the upheaval they produced. Instead of assisting a gradual process from the outside, the United States had to carry out a rapid operation of state-building from the inside, within the two countries in their regions where such a procedure had the least chance for rapid success. With do-

mestic support for increased aid and troop levels flagging, with local governments beset by factionalism and regionalism, and levels of violence high in Iraq
and rising in Afghanistan, there was no way in which the U.S.-induced processes
of change could be seen as inspiration for other peoples in these regions. The
idea of a domino-like spread of democratic change in the Middle East after the
invasion of Iraq was therefore a chimera. Instead, the chaos and civil war that followed the U.S. invasion has in some places become an argument *against* further
democratization.[18]

Conclusion

Based on the very limited evidence we have today, there is reason to believe
that unsuccessful attempts to learn from the Cold War played an important
role in the renewed U.S. interventionism of the 2000s. Whereas the Clinton
administration had believed the U.S. Cold War triumph to have beaten the way
for history's march toward greater international cooperation based on common
economic interests in American-style progress, the Bush administration instead
saw tasks not completed and obstacles uncleared, especially after the 9/11 attacks. Instead of letting history amble along at its own pace, as Clinton was seen
to have done, the new administration wanted to help steer its course, like Ronald Reagan in the 1980s. Even before 9/11, waiting for the intentions of others to
be tested by their own actions was not an alternative. In the 1970s, détente had
produced an upswing in Soviet global power. In the 1990s, Clinton's inaction
had helped encourage America's enemies. The Bush administration wanted to
win, and in the lessons outlined above it saw some of the tools it needed.

But while there is no doubt that the Cold War, as the last international system in existence, played a particular role in providing lessons from the past, the
2000s interventions stand in a much longer trajectory of U.S. interventionism. As
I have discussed elsewhere, U.S. foreign policy has been built on interventionist
principles since the nineteenth century.[19] Part of this interventionism is based on
a firm conviction that one's own society is the pinnacle of human achievement.
The English historian E. H. Carr, when criticizing leaders who saw their own
values as comprising the public good, disapprovingly quoted Woodrow Wilson's
dream from 1914, that as "the world knows more and more of America it . . . will
turn to America for those moral inspirations which lie at the basis of all freedom, . . . and that America will come into the full light of day when all shall know
that she puts human rights above all other rights, and that her flag is the flag
not only of America, but of humanity."[20] The linking of American values with
American interests, and both with the values of the world, are as strong in U.S.

foreign policy today as they were a hundred years ago. In this sense, the end of the Cold War changed little in terms of the central agendas of U.S. foreign policy or the ideology that guides it.

What will remain, I believe, of the present critique of the Bush administration's failures after a generation or so has passed is not so much the immediate response to 9/11, the mishandling of alliances, the scant attention to civil liberties, or the invasion of Iraq. It will be that the administration chose the worst possible places to attempt the spread of democracy, and thereby set the cause of pluralism and political participation worldwide back by many years. Through the way it acted, it helped convince people elsewhere that democracy equals chaos and leaders elsewhere that they can act unilaterally if their interests are at stake. If, as is likely, the rivalry with China for influence in Asia will be the central agenda for U.S. foreign policy over the next generation, these lessons will be exactly the ones that the United States least wants others to learn.[21]

10

10

HOW DID THE EXPERTS DO?

William C. Wohlforth

When contemplating policy responses to dramatic and unexpected developments, should policymakers heed nongovernmental experts' advice? If so, then
U.S. strategic choices after the fall of the Berlin Wall and 9/11 present something
of a puzzle. For if we reduce the complex and varied U.S. policy responses to
four discrete decisions—the two immediate responses (unification of Germany
within NATO, intervention in Afghanistan), and the two most salient follow-on
decisions (NATO enlargement to Central Europe, the invasion of Iraq)—what
stands out is expert opposition. Only the invasion of Afghanistan reflected a
rough consensus between the government and the relevant nongovernmental
expert community. Expert majorities counseled against the other three policy
responses.

A large and influential scholarly literature holds that an expert consensus
against a policy is a powerful signal that the policy is ill advised. This suggests
that U.S. strategic planning in these key cases was presumptively flawed, and the
country likely would be more secure today had the government taken its cue
from the experts. The recommendation that would follow is the need for enhanced channels for interaction between the government's strategic planners and
the independent expert community.

In this chapter I argue that the 11/9 and 9/11 cases actually imply a more quali-
fied role for outside experts in strategic planning. The conventional view fails to
distinguish between normal levels of uncertainty and the extreme levels that decision makers had to confront in the kind of paradigm-shifting events considered
in this book. There are good reasons—backed up by the most comprehensive

research on expert judgment—to suspect that scholarly experts will be at a comparative disadvantage when confronting such events. Not every expert consensus is probative for policymakers, who may have good reasons to discount even fervently expressed and nearly unanimous majority expert advice. The trick is to know when such a consensus actually conveys a strong signal that a contemplated policy rests on weak foundations.

This chapter is a necessarily preliminary effort to identify the properties of a probative expert consensus. I begin by unpacking the scholarship on expert evaluation and then assess the experts, with a focus on the scholarly consensuses that formed against U.S. policies on Germany, NATO, and Iraq.

Expert Assessments and Policy Choice

Most scholars believe that policymakers should heed the advice of nongovernmental experts when confronting major, paradigm-shifting events. Nongovernmental experts, they argue, can exploit years of dispassionate scholarship and hard-won knowledge to subject the government's reasoning or evidence to critical scrutiny. Experts can bring new arguments and evidence to bear, puncture comfortable governmental "groupthink," and face fewer incentives than governmental experts to please powerful higher-level officials by telling them what they think they want to hear. These arguments have a long pedigree but have recently been restated forcefully in important studies by scholars of international relations showing that when decisions are exposed to review and critique in an unfettered "marketplace of ideas," poor policies will tend to get winnowed out.[1] The implication is that when the normally squabbling community of outside experts begins to converge on a recommendation against a proposed policy, it is a strong signal that the policy is ill advised.

But the scholarship underlying this recommendation makes no distinction between policymaking under normal times as opposed to abnormally high levels of uncertainty that unexpected, paradigm-shattering events leave in their wake. For two reasons, scholars may be at a particular disadvantage under those unusual circumstances. First, officials' information advantage might assume unusual importance in an especially fast-moving situation. A policy's success, at least in the short term, often hinges on reactions by other governments, and officials are likely to have much better information on that score than nongovernmental experts. Without direct access to other governments' thinking, experts tend to use methods of inference—reading local media, interacting with their expert counterparts, applying general theories or empirical findings concerning similar cases, and so forth—that may lag substantially behind or misestimate operational assessments in the halls of power.

Second, and most important, the very style of reasoning that lends experts such apparent analytical power both in normal times and in hindsight may hamper their ability to update quickly when the underpinnings of a long established strategic equilibrium come unhinged. Scholarly experts bring many unique advantages to the table, but two intellectual assets stand out: theory and systematic empirical research. Compared to governmental experts and officials, scholars invest much more intellectual capital in the articulation and defense of explicit theories and elaborate efforts to test general propositions about international affairs. Theories may be informal and historical or formal and mathematical. Empirical research may reflect case studies or large-N statistical analyses. But as much variation as there is within the scholarly community, the contrast between academic experts as a group and government experts and officials is greater.

In normal times, theory and systematic research give academic experts a potent comparative advantage in policy evaluation. Whereas scholars rarely can match an insider's immersion in issue specifics and knowledge of the policy process, few insiders can long stand toe-to-toe with a good academic expert when it comes to unpacking and evaluating the general assumptions about causality that underlie any policy recommendation. But theory and cumulative empirical research inevitably reflect some induction from a relatively stable equilibrium. When producing a theory relevant to some phenomenon—such as the potential for revolution, or peaceful change, or the nature of likely security threats—a scholar will naturally make sure that the theory is consistent with existing information about how the world works. To get off the ground, the theory has to explain or predict (or "postdict") relevant events up to the present. Thus, induction from recent experience informs the theory, even if it is presented as universal and deductive. The same goes for empirical research: statistical models are routinely fitted to known observations, and case studies are conducted in knowledge of hindsight.[2] The result is confidence that regularities can be known and even forecast, which feeds strong confidence in criticizing policy proposals that seem to run afoul of such regularities.

If a seminal event is propelled by changes exogenous to accumulated theory and research, the scholar's comparative advantage is undermined. The problem is not just that such events may occur at the thin low-probability tails of a normal bell-shaped statistical distribution of political probabilities. Rather, it is that in such times the entire curve takes on hitherto unimaginable forms, unmooring even the most careful, probabilistic mental models fitted to the old curve. To be sure, a scholar will still have the relative independence, the freedom, and the hard-won knowledge that mark academe. But unless the scholar is nimble enough intellectually to abandon painstakingly gained theory and research, those assets will come to naught. Major lines of research in cognitive psychology and the philosophy of science warn of an inverse relationship between intellectual investment in a given theory or empirical explanation and the willingness to abandon it in light of discrepant evidence.[3]

Psychologist Philip Tetlock put this conjecture to a compelling test.[4] He and his collaborators surveyed experts over an extended period of time, eliciting forecasts of events in their fields of expertise, as well as their reactions to predictive failures. Overall, the results are depressing. Experts are terrible forecasters, and governments would do as well by throwing a dart or tossing a coin as they would by relying on a randomly selected expert. But the news is not all bad. Tetlock's research suggests that some kinds of experts do better than others. Drawing on Isaiah Berlin's famous essay, Tetlock separates "hedgehogs," who make their intellectual investments in "one big thing" and seek to apply it to cover new cases, from "foxes," who have a more balanced portfolio of intellectual assets, knowing "many little things" out of which they improvise contingent forecasts for novel cases.[5] Experts with cognitive styles resembling Berlin's fox systematically outperform expert hedgehogs.

The implication is that an expert consensus that embraces both foxes and hedgehogs ought to be probative. But as I seek to show below, paradigm-shattering events seem to accentuate the hedgehog in many scholars. If scholarly experts are more prone to hedgehogism than government officials and if seminal events tend to bring out the hedgehog in normally foxlike experts, then a logrolled "hedgehog consensus" may emerge of which governments would be well advised to be skeptical.

1989–1990: Asymmetrical Conservatisms

The Bush administration's response to the collapse of Communism in Central Europe is well documented.[6] It followed roughly four phases: (1) a strategic reassessment that entailed a pause in the rapidly ripening entente with Moscow initiated by President Reagan and General Secretary Gorbachev; (2) a diplomatically competitive phase premised on the continuance of the bipolar Cold War framework in which Washington sought to regain the initiative under the slogan "a Europe whole and free"; (3) a brief effort to bolster the two-bloc status quo as the GDR's position unraveled in the summer and fall and fears of instability mounted; and (4) the late fall decision to back Helmut Kohl's unification drive, with united Germany's membership in NATO as the *conditio sine qua non*.

It is easy to forget how radical this final decision was. In the words of two participants, the diplomacy of German reunification involved the United States and the Federal Republic of Germany forcing the Soviet Union to face "a reversal of fortunes not unlike a catastrophic defeat in a war."[7] Yet it also contained a powerful conservative strain: that the signature Cold War institution of NATO would be maintained and adapted to the radically new circumstances that were clearly emerging.

With some allowance for oversimplification, it is fair to characterize the contemporary assessments of scholarly experts as resisting both elements of the government's response in turn. They were generally much, much slower to part with the status quo. Most supported a far more robust version of the administration's phase 3 policy of bolstering the two-bloc status quo, which in practice meant propping up the GDR and the Soviet position in Central Europe. Most were initially highly critical of the administration's bold departure in supporting Kohl's unification drive. With time, however, the roles of conservative and revisionist switched, as the government's insistence on the continued centrality of NATO in the new post–Cold War setting struck scholars as dangerously destabilizing.

What were the sources of the experts' initial conservatism? A key judgment underlying the government's policy was that Moscow would acquiesce on the issue, and thus that the transition could be managed peacefully. In public, Bush was extremely careful to say nothing to humiliate Gorbachev. But privately the president and his aides believed the United States had won the Cold War. As Bush told Kohl at the Camp David summit in February, "the Soviets are not in a position to dictate Germany's relationship with NATO. What worries me is talk that Germany must not stay in NATO. To hell with that! We prevailed, they didn't. We can't let the Soviets clutch victory from the jaws of defeat."[8] Some officials in the National Security Council and the State Department were even more bullish about the U.S. position and even less concerned about a potential Soviet backlash, and they argued for an even tougher line.[9] Meanwhile, intelligence analysts in the CIA produced reports concluding that economic necessity would compel Moscow to make concessions whether or not Gorbachev remained in power.[10]

Scholars were far slower to reach this assessment, arguably partly owing to their information disadvantage. Data about the depth of the economic crisis of the Comecon (Council for Mutual Economic Assistance) in general and the GDR in particular began to cascade into government circles in late October, when East German planning minister Gerhard Schürer produced a devastating report on the dire state of the country's economy whose findings were quickly conveyed to Gorbachev.[11] U.S. officials and their Bonn counterparts learned of this situation and, critically, of Gorbachev's response—a steadfast refusal to use force or even to contemplate policies that risked the use of force, and an increased desire for Western aid and credits—long before scholars got wind of it. Thus, the Bonn-Washington team had what we now know was a more accurate gauge of their own strong bargaining hand and on the probability of a limited Soviet response to the unraveling of Moscow's position in Central Europe—and thus on the likely near-term success of a push for rapid unification in NATO—than outside experts did.

But scholarly fears of a too rapid move away from the Cold War two-bloc system had much deeper intellectual roots. These are clearest in John J. Mearsheimer's sensational "Back to the Future" article, in which he argued that bipolarity was the guarantor of peace in Europe and a return of multipolarity would raise the specter of war. It followed that "the West has an interest in maintaining the Cold War order, and hence has an interest in maintaining the Cold War confrontation," meaning, of course, that Western powers should support "the continued existence of a powerful Soviet Union with substantial military forces in Eastern Europe."[12] Needless to say, policymakers did not heed this advice, proffered around the time the 2+4 negotiations were getting under way.

But one did not have to be a neorealist to have a hard time accepting the proposition that a nuclear-armed superpower would acquiesce gracefully in such a dramatic retraction of its power. Reading carefully the pre-1989 theoretical literature on change in world politics, as well as the more speculative writings of international relations scholars and Sovietologists about the prospects of near-term change, it becomes clear that the primary reason both scholarly camps failed to grasp the potential for a bold conclusion to the Cold War on Western terms is implicit or explicit association between rapid, politically consequential change and large-scale violence.[13]

Most theories of international politics that addressed the issue of large-scale change associated such transitions with war. Most international relations scholars, realist and nonrealist alike, followed E. H. Carr in regarding peaceful change as the fundamental problem of international relations.[14] Significant territorial change among the major powers, and rapid, substantial shifts in the status and security of great powers, were generally linked theoretically to large-scale violence. Social theory in general and international relations theory in particular had constructed numerous and ramified functional explanations for war. They elucidated many mutually supporting reasons why war and change were associated. Indeed, war and change were so closely linked in the minds of scholars that they often equated "stability" with "peace."[15]

Most analysts shared this basic assumption that major violence was a likely accompaniment of any fundamental change, and precisely for that reason believed that change needed to be slowed in the near term. They assumed, at first, that the relevant political actors themselves would be constrained by the association of war and change. Fearing that radical change would raise the specter of war, the key political actors would endeavor to moderate their behavior in a rational cost-benefit calculation. So when talk of German unity began to circulate and, especially, when Kohl started pushing the issue, the expert reaction was alarm: decision makers seemed to be taking huge risks for near-term political gains.

For experts steeped in scholarship, prudence made perfect sense. After all, the association between war and change appeared to hold. Historical and quantitative studies suggested that while not all change is accompanied by war, the more rapidly change occurs, the more it bears on the security, status, and capabilities of the major powers, and the more it involves the basic hierarchy or structure of their relations, the more likely it is to be associated with war.[16] Indeed, the U.S.-Soviet Cold War is the only enduring rivalry between great powers that ended without war or the appearance of a new threat from a third state. As for experts on Soviet and Russian politics and history, few disputed Paul Kennedy's assertion in 1987 that "there is nothing in the character or the tradition of the Russian state to suggest that it could ever accept imperial decline gracefully."[17]

Scholars of East European politics, Germany, and the German question tended to share this concern about moving away from the status quo.[18] Indeed, by the 1980s scholarship had entered a new phase highlighting the legitimacy and staying power of Soviet-type regimes. Scholars rejected what they regarded as simplistic and dangerous insistence on rhetorical support for German unification, which became associated with right-wing and cold-warrior politics. Experts who mastered the Talmudic intricacies of the Cold War German Question were hyperaware of all the dangers that lurked. When the wellsprings of stability were called into question by upheavals in the Soviet bloc, the policy recommendation that emerged from this scholarship was a robust and explicit endorsement of Bush's brief flirtation with bolstering the status quo: Western recognition of the GDR and a negotiated two-state solution. As one analyst put it in the 1989–90 issue of *Foreign Affairs:*

> Recognition [of the GDR] would be a political masterstroke, slicing through the Gordian knot of East European and East German change, European stability and German power. As European policy, it would be a structural guarantee promising a much needed measure of certainty and predictability, thereby freeing the F.R.G., and perhaps ultimately the G.D.R., to lead the way in forging a permanent East-West détente and rebuilding Europe from the inside out. As inner-German policy, it would immediately create the conditions necessary for major economic and political reform in the G.D.R., beginning with freedom of travel and ultimately leading to political freedom and economic prosperity for all Germans in both states.[19]

It is difficult to avoid the conclusion that scholars were much slower to update their analytical models of the strategic situation than policymakers—at least, those in Washington, Bonn, and Moscow. For intellectuals steeped in the seemingly immutable realities of the post-1945 bipolar world, the prospect that Germany could be reunified entirely on Western terms with virtually no bloodshed and against the stated security interests of a nuclear-armed superpower appeared remote almost until the day it happened. And one important reason why experts failed to grasp the potential for change was their incorrect belief that the U.S. government's insistence on unity-in-NATO would have disastrous near-term consequences.

1994–1999: NATO Enlargement

A second key assumption underlay the U.S. response to 1989–90: that NATO was a necessary condition of the U.S. presence in Europe, which itself was a necessary condition of European peace and stability. Despite their basic confidence in their country's overall power and prospects as well as its deep cultural and historical ties to Europe, officials believed that America's position in Europe hung precariously by the NATO thread. If NATO were somehow sidelined or replaced by other security institutions, the U.S. commitment could not be sustained, American troops would have to come home, and Europe would plunge into an uncertain and dangerous multipolar world. Hence, U.S. officials portrayed their insistence on expanding NATO to a united Germany as a fundamental prerequisite of regional and global security.[20]

This assumption, coupled with confidence that Moscow was weak and would cave, lay behind the consistent U.S. effort to quash all talk (whether it came from Berlin, Moscow, or Paris) of creating a new security order in Europe based on an inclusive architecture.[21] The rapid pace of events, the fact that the world's strongest power and the strongest European power both wanted unity in NATO, and the fact that the second strongest power would not or could not back an all-Europe alternative with resolve and capabilities—all pulled the legs from under proponents of alternative visions. Sarotte's comment about policymakers ("there was not much time for perfecting plans and ideas") applied in spades to scholars.[22] Those who did manage to get ideas in print in the period after the GDR's weakness became clear, but before the 2+4 settlement was reached, tended to favor a symmetrical solution involving the dismantling of both NATO and the Warsaw Pact, with eventual reunification proceeding within the context of a new all-European security architecture.[23] A critical mass of experts was thus never happy with the government's core assumption that NATO had to remain the basic security institution linking the United States and Europe.

Once German unity in NATO was an accomplished fact, this assumption became the fulcrum of a major and prolonged divergence in the assessments of the U.S. government among a strong majority of scholarly experts. Many scholars agreed with Scowcroft that U.S. involvement and some institutional structure were necessary conditions of peace in Europe, but they parted company on the suitability of NATO for this role. Most shared the view expressed by George Kennan in November 1989 that NATO was a creature of the Cold War that could not be adapted to the new setting, which "implies the necessity of an alternative framework of security for the entire continent."[24]

Percolating within the Washington bureaucracy was a different view: that NATO could and should be adapted to the post–Cold War world, that its expansion to Central Europe and beyond would consolidate peace and democracy in the region while linking U.S. and European security, and that Russia's sensibilities could be managed. Ultimately, this became the official policy of the Clinton administration.[25] All the varied sources of expert concern over the direction of post–Cold War U.S. strategy converged into an intense opposition to any further expansion of NATO. The Clinton administration's consideration of extending membership to Poland, the Czech Republic, and Hungary exposed "a significant gap ... between those who make grand strategy and those who reflect on it," John Lewis Gaddis observed. "Official and accumulated wisdom are pointing in very different directions." Indeed, he noted, "I can recall no other moment in my own experience as a practicing historian in which there was less support, within the community of historians, for an announced policy position."[26] Kennan insisted that it "would be the most fateful error of American policy in the entire post–Cold-War era."[27] Most international security experts from political science, realist and liberal alike, agreed with their counterparts in history departments.[28]

In this case, scholarly experts had years to evaluate a policy under active contemplation in Washington. By the mid-1990s, their reasons for opposition were complex and well developed. Common to most assessments was the argument that enlargement was unnecessary: the three Central European countries would add few capabilities to the alliance, and membership was unnecessary for their security, prosperity, or democratic consolidation. But scholars could see the political (and, by their lights) emotional appeal of the policy, so they had to forecast not just low benefits but high costs, which they projected along three dimensions.

First was the threat of Russian counterbalancing. Although not always expressed in theoretical terms, this forecast emerged straight from realist balance of power theory.[29] As Gaddis put it, "If country A feels threatened by country B, it is apt to align itself with country C." Country C in this case was China, which was "less likely even than Russia to see its interests as compatible with ours."[30]

And counterbalancing was not just a matter of great-power alliance formation. Russia would also seek to counter the United States in Europe, Eurasia, and other theaters, as well as engage in "internal balancing" by revamping domestic sources of military power. As Kennan put it, "I think it is the beginning of a new cold war."[31]

The second projected cost was the sheer economic and military burden of extending NATO's defense commitment to states so close to the Russian bear. As Paul Kennedy titled an opinion piece, "Let's See the Pentagon's Plan for Defending Poland."[32] The United States would not only generate a strategic opponent in Russia, it would be assuming a defense burden far beyond its capacity. "We have signed up to protect a whole series of countries, even though we have neither the resources nor the intention to do so in any serious way," worried Kennan.[33] In Gaddis's view, this violated the core strategic principle of "providing the means to accomplish selected ends."[34]

The third major expected cost was democracy in Russia. Specialists on international relations, the spread of democracy, and Russian politics and history converged on the forecast that NATO expansion would be a major blow to hopes of Russian democrats and serve as a mobilizing spur to nationalist and authoritarian forces.[35]

A final important forecast was less about expected costs than unrealized potential gains. For most scholars, at stake was a durable and effective post–Cold War settlement. They wanted a 1945- or 1815-style settlement, not the 1919 version that excluded and alienated a great power. To be sure, this forecast overlapped with the others: failure to include Russia as an equal partner in the new global security architecture would make Moscow into a dissatisfied, revisionist, authoritarian power whose counterbalancing would impose unsustainable costs on the United States. But the vision included major gains in great-power cooperation on a range of issues, from proliferation to the Middle East to counterterrorism, all of which could be expected to progress far more successfully in the context of a great power concert including Russia.

How well did the forecasts built in to the expert consensus against NATO fare? A truly satisfying answer is impossible, for it would require endless counterfactual analysis. Not expanding NATO, and, especially, including Russia fully in a new regional or global security regime to replace or sideline NATO, also entailed risks. For every gain a critic can imagine, a corresponding loss can be conjured up by a defender. No fully persuasive method exists for weighing the gains scholars envisioned for their preferred post–Cold War settlement against the risks policymakers anticipated from abandoning a tried-and-true alliance. And establishing the presence or absence of links between NATO expansion and the fate of democracy in Russia is, at the very least, an intricate task far beyond a chapter of this scope.

But we do have some leverage on the more tractable expert forecasts. It is clear that scholars radically overestimated the costs of potential Russian counterbalancing. The expected alliance formation in response to NATO expansion simply did not occur. Instead, a far more modest Sino-Russian alignment took shape, one that had very little to do with countering NATO.[36] There was little measurable Russian internal balancing. It would be very hard to substantiate the argument that NATO enlargement had much bearing on Russia's fitful and largely unsuccessful efforts to reform its military and defense industry. After defeat in Chechnya, any government in Moscow would have wanted to reform the military regardless of what NATO did. Russia's efforts to consolidate its position in the former Soviet space were under way before NATO expanded, and there is little evidence that NATO expansion had more than a marginal effect on Moscow's desire for a hegemonic role in the region or the inclination of other states in the region to bandwagon with Russia.

Vladimir Putin–era Russia's efforts to counter U.S. influence globally are a pale shadow of the visions conjured by scholarly opponents of NATO expansion, and, in any case, they follow a major effort by Putin to establish a close partnership with the United States after 9/11. The Putin-Bush rapprochement, involving substantial Russian concessions on issues of long-standing concern such as the ABM treaty, occurred only two years after the first round of NATO expansion and the alliance's first major use of force against Russia's ally Serbia. Surely, the explanation for current U.S.-Russian travails lies more clearly in what happened after this rapprochement than before it.

Similarly, there is scant evidence of the imperial burden scholars expected to come with the expansion of NATO. Indeed, the balancing and imperial overstretch forecasts have their roots in intellectual processes similar to those at work in 1989–90: slow updating of information and the hold on expert minds of theories developed in radically different international settings. Underneath the dispute between the "official and accumulated wisdom" in the mid-1990s was a debate about Russian power. Experts criticized the government for underrating Russian power, which they saw as diminished but clearly still rating "great power" designation. But Russia's fall was far more dramatic than scholars realized; indeed, the country's relative capabilities were in freefall throughout the 1990s as the NATO debate raged. Official representations about Russia's real capacities hold up far better in retrospect.

Thinking of Russia as a great power, scholars applied the relevant mental models and historical analogies: balance of power theory and Versailles. But the international system was not multipolar or bipolar, so the standard precepts of balance of power theory simply did not apply and the set of feasible policy options for Russia were quite different from those of interwar Germany.[37] Scholars were right that Russia did have choices, but they were wrong to equate them with the choices a great power has under multipolarity. Real balancing that would have the kind of systemic effects scholars warned of was simply not a feasible option for Russia.

The debate over NATO expansion has not ended and will not end any time soon. Nor can it be settled in some universal sense. But if you read the debate of the 1990s, you will be struck by the size, intellectual cohesion, and stridency of the expert opposition. Many of their arguments cannot be evaluated now, and history may well come to favor them. But their near-term forecasts of costs—precisely the arguments of most relevance to pragmatic policymakers—were wildly off the mark, and for reasons intertwined with the comparatively hedgehog-like cognitive style that marked the expert consensus.

From 9/11 to Iraq

The United States' major initial response to the terrorist attacks on 9/11 was to demand that the Taliban regime in Afghanistan turn over the perpetrators and to prepare to use force in the likely event Mullah Omar refused. A bombing campaign in Afghanistan soon got under way. The published record leaves little evidence of strong contemporary opposition to this response among international relations scholars focused on security affairs. Security scholars and noted regional experts—including many who would later become furious critics of the march to war in Iraq—broadly supported the thrust of the policy, even as they forwarded constructive criticisms about tactics and implementation.[38]

It was the follow-on decision to threaten Iraq with invasion and regime change if it did not disarm that generated strong opposition.[39] One indicator is that after the U.S. invasion of Iraq, the "support Afghanistan/oppose Iraq" position was endorsed by over eight hundred security scholars in an open letter claiming that the invasion was the "most misguided policy since Vietnam."[40] As Robert Keohane remarked, "I think it is telling that so many specialists on international relations, who rarely agree on anything, are unified in their position on the high costs that the U.S. is incurring from this war."[41] That opposition embraced not just security scholars but also regional experts, international lawyers, and scholarly experts from many other fields.

As substantial as it was, scholarly opposition prior to the invasion was not as broad and vocal as it became afterward. Several well-known international relations scholars supported the war option and engaged the opponents in print.[42] Indeed, it is easier to find supporters of the Iraq War than supporters of NATO expansion among prominent security scholars. And the window for analyzing the potential use of force to resolve the Iraq issue was relatively short—approximately six months. Security experts who supported the threat of force but not regime change may have found little to criticize in the Bush policy until quite late in the game. The same goes for scholars who were inclined to support force if sanctioned by the UN Security Council: before the endgame, the government was acting in ways consistent with their recommendations.

Hence, the most salient expert opponents before the fact were those who strongly favored the pre-2002 policy of containment, deterrence, and sanctions. Relying on the published record, what stands out from the debate during the buildup to war are the following propositions, advanced by regional experts, terrorism scholars, and, perhaps most prominently by international security scholars John Mearsheimer and Stephen Walt.[43]

First, a policy of deterrence and containment would work. Saddam Hussein was detestable but deterrable. Establishing this argument took up the bulk of realist scholars' policy criticisms prior to the invasion in 2003. Walt and Mearsheimer clearly thought that the lynchpin of the government's argument was that Saddam Hussein could not be deterred. They carefully sifted the circumstantial evidence surrounding Saddam Hussein's behavior since taking power, examining each use of force and each response to threats to his regime. The conclusion: Hussein was sensitive to relative costs and benefits and could be "kept in a box" indefinitely. Even if he acquired nuclear weapons, he could not use them without inviting self-destruction at the hands of the United States or Israel. Even if he perceived an interest in handing nuclear or other mass-destruction weapons to al Qaeda, he could be deterred from doing so.

Even if Hussein's Iraq could be deterred and contained, such a policy would entail substantial costs, which were fresh on Washington's official mind. Hence a second forecast was crucial to the opponents' argument: war would be costly in blood and treasure, and would likely spread instability in the region, ultimately harming U.S. interests. Although security scholars all forecast a U.S. victory, some, at least, were concerned at the potential costs of urban fighting or of countering Iraq's likely use of chemical or biological weapons, or Iraqi attacks on oilfields in Saudi Arabia and Kuwait, which would increase oil prices and harm the global economy.

Third, critics argued that even if initial victory were assured, there was no exit strategy. Both the Kurdish and the Shia vs. Sunni problems were seen as potentially explosive, raising risks of regional involvement in an Iraqi civil war, the prevention of which would require a prolonged and costly U.S. occupation.

Fourth, war with Iraq would jeopardize the campaign against the real enemy—al Qaeda—by diverting material resources and attention and inflaming anti-Americanism in precisely the region where intelligence and other forms of cooperation were most needed. Indeed, many scholars warned that invading and occupying an Arab country would only increase the threat of terror via increased anger and recruitment.

As in the case of NATO expansion, evaluating the core forecast underlying the experts' policy analysis—that a policy of deterrence and containment would have generated a better outcome for the United States than invasion and occupation—will forever remain a matter of informed conjecture. In evaluating the specific shorter-term forecasts underlying security experts' analyses, however, four noteworthy generalizations emerge.

First, many of the forecast costs did not eventuate. The war did not spread regionally, and Hussein did not inflict heavy casualties on coalition forces with weapons of mass destruction or urban warfare, nor did he lash out against oil fields in Iraq or its neighbors.

Second, many criticisms that scholars would make retrospectively were absent from their prewar arguments. Most notable is the problem of intelligence failure regarding Iraq's suspected weapons programs. The entire debate in the lead-up to the Iraq War was carried out on the assumption that Iraq maintained serious commitments to WMD development. To date, I have been unable to find any evidence of any international relations scholar who questioned this assumption. Many scholars have since focused on allegations of a deliberate campaign of threat exaggeration by the Bush administration. In a careful analysis, however, Robert Jervis makes a strong case that the core reason for intelligence failure was the collective failure to identify a compelling explanation for Saddam Hussein's deceptive behavior other than that he had something to hide.[44] As far as we know, this applied also to governments and intelligence services that opposed the rush to war. Remarkably, even scholars steeped in deterrence theory and the cognitive psychology of decision making, and who were opposed to war and thus motivated to question assumptions underlying the government's view, did not explore alternative explanations for Saddam's deceptive behavior, such as deterrence of the United States and/or Iran. On that issue, scholars proved no more prescient than government officials.

Third, the prospects for a potent Sunni insurgency did not figure as prominently in prewar assessments as they did in retrospective critiques. To be sure, security scholars highlighted Iraq's fractious domestic politics. They argued that Iraq was a poor prospect for "nation-building," and forecast that a prolonged and costly occupation would likely be required to hold the state together. But the specific problem of a Sunni insurgency that would cause the greatest U.S. and civilian casualties and consume the attention and resources of the U.S. govern-ment did not foreground prewar scholarly assessments.

Yet, there is no question that scholarly experts' opposition to the impending U.S. invasion of Iraq holds up better in hindsight than the earlier majority analy-ses that undergirded expert criticism of rapid German unification and NATO expansion. After all, the postwar evidence appears to show that Hussein *was* de-terred before the war. Even though no one guessed at the thought process that appears to have supported his decision to resist his disarmament obligations, the logic is nonetheless far more consistent with realist scholars' reading of his risk propensities and rough "rationality" than the war supporters' portrayal of an un-deterrable cost-insensitive rogue. And though the extreme costs and challenges of fighting a major counterinsurgency did not headline opposition arguments, critical experts' forecast of a prolonged and costly occupation was dead on.

And this provisionally positive reading brings up the fourth generalization: the contrast in cognitive style between the scholarly consensus in this case as opposed to the cases of German unification and NATO expansion. Even though the most prominent war opponents among international relations scholars were self-described realists, their published analyses were remarkably foxlike. To be sure, the expectation that state leaders tend to be rational is consistent with realist theory. But they deployed their realist theory with so light a touch that it is hardly detectable. What stands out is the extraordinarily detailed case-specific analysis. Indeed, political scientists Mearsheimer and Walt—poster children for hedgeho-gism in 1990—relied far less on reference to timeless generalizations, theoretical propositions, and broad strategic principles than historian Gaddis had in his equally prominent opposition to NATO expansion five years before.

Conclusion

These initial case studies of expert analysis under unusually high levels of un-certainty do not provide a warrant for sweeping conclusions. Humility is further dictated by the intrinsic difficulty of the task: identifying experts' cognitive styles is a matter of contestable judgment and rating predictive accuracy is contingent and potentially controversial. And in no case can we assess confidently the crit-ics' most important prediction: that U.S. interests would be better served today if their policy alternatives had been adopted.

Nonetheless, scholarly experts were undeniably slow to update in the Berlin and NATO expansion cases, and the headline predictions associated with their policy evaluations were quite wide of the mark. In both cases, I made at least a circumstantial case that scholars' comparatively hedgehog-like cognitive style played a role in their analytical and predictive performance. In the Iraq case, scholars did not do as well before the fact as they claimed afterward. Some of the scholarly wisdom we now see on display concerning the obvious calamity that awaited the United States in Iraq is an artifact of hindsight. Yet a clear-eyed appraisal of pre-war scholarly analysis puts it in a comparatively favorable light. For the uncertain and complex realm of international politics, the predictive performance in this case is outstanding. And the cognitive style that informed it does appear to match up much more with Berlin's fox than with his hedgehog.

To be sure, we do not know precisely *why* cognitive styles varied between the Germany and NATO cases and the run-up to Iraq. The events discussed here lend credence to the argument that especially sudden, large-scale changes bring out the hedgehog in many scholarly experts. The issues under debate in the lead-up to Iraq were shrouded in uncertainty, but the underlying dynamics concerning the potential success of invasion and regime change vs. containment and deterrence may not have been in as dramatic flux as were the underpinnings of the Cold War order in Europe after 1989.

Strategic planners should certainly make use of outside academic expertise. Nothing in the foregoing analysis undermines the common view that exposure to nongovernmental review and critique is good for policymakers. But majority expert opposition does not necessarily impugn a policy. After major, unexpected events upset a previously stable geopolitical equilibrium, the government's information advantage is especially important and the scholarly assets of theory and systematic empirical research may be devalued. And that suggests a word of warning to scholarly evaluators of the performance of governments operating under unusually profound uncertainty: look in the mirror. We do not perform brilliantly ourselves under the best of circumstances, and dramatic, paradigm-altering events may bring forth the very cognitive styles most likely to lead us astray.

Conclusion

STRATEGY IN A MURKY WORLD

Melvyn P. Leffler and Jeffrey W. Legro

Making national strategy is a byzantine business in the best of times. When dramatic events happen, when the international arena is complex and changing, when threats and opportunities are uncertain, leaders struggle to understand and react effectively. The fall of the Berlin Wall and the attacks of 9/11 opened vistas that were unfamiliar and complicated. How did U.S. leaders manage those transitions?

In this conclusion, we aim both to clarify and analyze what the United States did and how it fared during the momentous years that followed the end of the Cold War. First, we sketch the evolution of strategy from the fall of the Berlin Wall to the onset of the Obama presidency. We then attempt to identify the accomplishments and failures of U.S. planning under uncertainty. Finally, we explore some of the key impediments to effective strategy-making in times of uncertainty and outline what we might learn from the record so that we can do better in the future.

Recovering the trail of U.S. strategy is no simple task. In the aftermath of the Cold War, the complexity and uncertainty of the international landscape confounds our retrospective view. We cannot fully re-create the cognitive and emotional mind-sets of U.S. officials. Judgments rest on counterfactuals ("things could have been different") that presume a grasp of alternative outcomes that are unknowable. So we move forward aware of our own limitations and recognizing that we benefit from hindsight. We summarize in broad thematic strokes and attempt to glean what we can from the mix of insider information and scholarly analysis.

Reviewing U.S. Strategy

Despite their limited visibility, U.S. leaders struggled to come to grips with the challenges and opportunities created by the collapse of the Wall and the attacks on 9/11. What is notable is that the focal point of U.S. strategy did change dramatically from the end of the Cold War to the onset of the Obama administration: failed states and internal governance eclipsed the fears of great powers. As dangers and opportunities were reassessed, U.S. officials also reappraised their ideas about power and their attitudes toward prevailing international institutions. They developed a growing appreciation of the threats that might accompany the march of globalization and open borders.

It has not been easy for U.S. policymakers to think about strategic challenges in nontraditional ways. From the time Washington assumed a major role in the international arena after World War II, the main threat had been another state (the Soviet Union), its lethal capabilities (nuclear weapons), and its hostile communist ideology ("we will bury you"). The crux of American strategy was to contain or roll back the Soviet Union, co-opt and integrate former foes (Germany and Japan), and win friends among newly emerging nations in Africa, Asia, and the Middle East. In a world that was undergoing dynamic change as a result of decolonization and revolutionary nationalism, in a world that had few rules and that was infused with ideological conflict, Soviet capabilities seemed like the greatest danger to the United States.

America's hope during the Cold War was that growing economic interdependence, the attractions of a marketplace economy, and the spread of human rights and democracy would win adherents to the American way of life and create a more stable international order along liberal and capitalist lines. To the extent the free movement of goods, money, ideas, and people could be encouraged, there was an opportunity to foster a different kind of world. The postwar development of Germany and Japan provided a comforting precedent; so did the growth of Western European integration and the dynamic advances of South Korea, Taiwan, and other Asian tigers, as they were once called. U.S. officials hoped that one day perhaps even the Soviet Union or China would follow this same path.

The American view in the Cold War was binary: threats emanated from the ideological-political-military realm of the major Communist powers; opportunities stemmed from the productivity of the American economy, the strength and reach of U.S. military forces, the latent appeal of open trade, the impact of the communications revolution, and the lure of consumer capitalism. After 11/9 and 9/11, policymakers again hoped to capitalize on these opportunities; they wanted to persuade other powers to embrace an American vision for the international order. Yet they had to grapple with the dangers stemming from the globalization of trade, capital, people, and ideas.

1989

The immediate challenge facing the United States after the fall of the Berlin Wall was familiar to U.S. leaders: they needed to achieve a political settlement in Germany (and Eastern Europe), one that would satisfy the major powers in Europe and win approval from their citizens. It was a formidable task, and the U.S. response to "1989" represents one of the most notable tactical success stories in the history of U.S. diplomacy. Mary Sarotte says it was a "punctuational moment," a time when rapid change takes place and the decisions made shape events—in ways intended and unintended—for years afterwards. Robert Zoellick incisively recounts how, notwithstanding the pressures of rapidly moving events and the demands of constituencies across many countries, the United States was able to achieve an outcome unimaginable even one year before: a united Germany within NATO. In his chapter, William Wohlforth highlights the magnitude of the accomplishment. Most nongovernmental experts, he notes, were critical of the policy because they expected that rapid change favoring one side's preferences would produce conflict, but it did not occur.[1]

Who was responsible for this victory? Paul Wolfowitz argues that Ronald Reagan was the prime agent. He established the conditions that made rapid progress possible "when the Cold War ice cracked." Wolfowitz also praises the team of George H. W. Bush and James Baker for skillfully handling the inter-allied diplomacy, ensuring that the Cold War ended in peaceful and advantageous ways for the United States. But success depended on initiatives that went well beyond the agreements over the future of Germany and the accords on strategic and conventional armaments. Zoellick usefully underscores these other dimensions of U.S. foreign policy—specifically foreign economic policy. Major progress was made to promote the free flow of goods and capital—setting the parameters that would lead to NAFTA and the Asia-Pacific Economic Cooperation (APEC) group. These efforts, Zoellick asserts, nurtured domestic support for international engagement and encouraged liberalization of the international economy. Although this trajectory had long been characteristic of U.S. policy, officials responded to the new uncertainties in the world arena after the Wall came down by accelerating their efforts to promote economic interdependence and to spur the pace of globalization.

But it is not clear that foreign economic policy was integrated in a purposeful way with either the security architecture of Europe or a post–Cold War military strategy. Zoellick rightly emphasizes the consensus among U.S. officials on the desirability of economic integration. They believed that integration would foster economic growth, stability, and democracy (as it had in Western Europe). Policymakers in the Pentagon, such as Wolfowitz and Eric Edelman, shared these views. But security and economic planning after 1989 nonetheless moved on two different tracks in response to different pressures and events.

Officials also faced a clash between long-term opportunities and immediate demands and risks. U.S. decision makers after 11/9 passed on opportunities to create new international institutions that proponents thought would be better suited to deal with the evolving nature of international politics. They did so because they believed that prevailing institutions such as NATO could help absorb and anchor a united Germany, preserve America's role in Europe, reassure allies, and allow the United States to manage the immediate aftermath of 11/9. Although this orientation seemed wise in 1989 and 1990, it appeared less so with the passage of time. After 1991, reforming and enlarging NATO mostly exacerbated relations with Russia, a formidable former enemy whose partnership was now desirable in order to build a Europe whole and free as well as to manage other problem areas such as the Middle East and Central Asia.

John Ikenberry, a well-known political scientist, has argued that after major victories and in times of flux it is in the interest of the United States to remake existing institutions.[2] Stephen Brooks and William Wohlforth have asserted that the United States could and should have used its position of primacy to be more activist in creating and shaping international rules.[3] These views echo the words of Douglas Hurd (foreign secretary of Great Britain from 1989 to 1995) who noted that after 1991 the United States forfeited an ideal opportunity to "remake the world, update everything, the UN, everything."[4]

In chapter 1, Mary Sarotte reiterates this viewpoint. She points out that the United States made a conscious choice to preserve existing Cold War institutions rather than create new ones, as leaders had done after 1945. The United States might have tried to integrate the Soviet Union into the West, perhaps through a collective European security architecture. Failure to do so, Sarotte maintains, had serious consequences. Citing the *9/11 Commission Report*, she identifies the rigidity of Cold War institutions and thinking as one of the causes of U.S. vulnerability to the terrorist attacks in 2001.

Of course, at the time, the advantages of alternative approaches were not self-evident. Zoellick notes that new institutions—especially "third way" ones—might not have been popular or efficacious in the rapidly evolving international landscape after 1989. Yugoslavia began to unravel, and vicious ethnic conflict threatened to destabilize Europe. And at the same time, Iraq invaded Kuwait. Suddenly, the attention of Bush 41 officials gravitated to questions of internal governance in failing states and to regional stability. They had to decide whether to assume the burdens of nation-building in the Balkans and the Middle East, whether to use their counterattack to defeat Saddam's army, march to Baghdad, and tackle the problems of an ethnically and religiously divided Iraq. Bush and his advisers hesitated to do so. They were not ready to reshape societies they knew little about or abandon the tried-and-true mechanisms like NATO that had served the United States so well for so long.

The Aftershock of 1991

The repercussions of the Persian Gulf War and the collapse of the Soviet Union in 1991 revealed an ill-defined U.S. architecture for global affairs. The American people clamored for cuts in the military budget and for relief from the onerous obligations of the Cold War. Improvising as he went along, Bush 41 heralded a "new world order" and tried to act collaboratively with other countries. In thwarting Saddam Hussein, he opted to go to the United Nations for approval for the war, worked closely with the Soviet Union, put together a huge coalition including major Arab nations, and decided not to seize Baghdad or seek total victory. He was trying to foster principles such as multilateral cooperation, partnership with the Soviet Union, and great power self-restraint.[5]

The main strategic planning effort that occurred after 1991 was the crafting of the Defense Planning Guidance (DPG). As Eric Edelman and Paul Wolfowitz recount, this was an attempt to anticipate the emerging post–Cold War world and adjust to it. Their final report, "Defense Strategy for the 1990s: The Regional Defense Strategy," delineated the many requirements to meet the new enemy—President Bush called it "unpredictability."[6] The authors of the DPG emphasized the need to safeguard U.S. primacy in international affairs and the importance of configuring forces to meet uncertain but inevitable crises that would erupt in regions of the globe deemed vital to U.S. interests. They also stressed the significance of integrating former Communist countries into a community of democracies, the benefits of free trade, and the salience of a U.S. "forward presence" to thwart the possibility of nationalism and militarism reemerging in Germany and Japan.[7]

Although Wolfowitz and Edelman vigorously and insightfully rebut many of the clichés that have surfaced about the DPG, the planning exercise highlighted a dilemma that confronts leaders in time of uncertainty: how to deal with well-known threats from the past and at the same time identify new ones lurking in the unfamiliar international landscape. In fact, after the collapse of the Soviet Union, new threats in the altered strategic environment were not identified, especially the dangers emanating from failed states and nonstate actors. Planners focused on state threats—especially from countries with significant power potential in regions of vital importance—and worried about the eventual reconstitution of Russian power. In writing the DPG, they displayed more concern with states that had power, even if they had good intentions and were U.S. allies (Germany and Japan), than with nongovernmental actors who wanted to harm the United States. Wolfowitz and Edelman, in fact, make an important contribution to our understanding of the DPG when they stress that U.S. planners believed that sustained defense spending was needed in part to dissuade Japan and Germany from remilitarizing. Nonetheless, Edelman acknowledges that "the document can be faulted for not sufficiently anticipating the danger of Islamic extremism, state failure, and terrorism."[8] The same can be said about their Democratic successors.

U.S. policymakers not only had to deal with a rapidly changing international landscape, but also with a volatile domestic political scene. The salience of domestic politics was highlighted when James Baker resigned from his position as secretary of state and became White House chief of staff in August 1992 in order to manage George H. W. Bush's presidential reelection campaign. Zoellick describes how Baker tried to forge a campaign plan that "linked America's foreign engagement with domestic interests."[9] He failed: voters focused on the domestic economy and Bush 41 was defeated.

The end of the Cold War sundered whatever bipartisan consensus still remained on foreign policy.[10] Thereafter, vicious partisan conflict hindered the ability to plan coherent national strategy. The opportunity to forge new global principles, treaties, and organizations compatible both with American traditions and new global realities was lost.

Democrats in Charge, 1993–2000

For the incoming Clinton team, "the world looked remarkably benign in January 1993."[11] But in an era marked by unipolarity and globalization, the international environment presented enticing possibilities as well as formidable challenges. The new administration decided to assign priority to encouraging democracy in Russia. In his chapter, Walter Slocombe recounts how the linchpin of Clinton's strategy—America's relationship with Russia—was really an effort to shape its internal political character. The goal was to encourage Russia to become a market democracy that would be a congenial and reliable international partner.

This objective, however, clashed with another U.S. priority, one that was also related to internal governance and geopolitics: the enlargement of NATO and the democratization of Eastern Europe. Many Russian leaders deeply resented the extension of NATO membership to former Warsaw Pact countries. They saw it as a violation of agreements signed at the end of the Cold War—a claim that was not inscribed in any legal document, but that was understandable in view of the conversations that had taken place in February 1990 between Baker and Mikhail Gorbachev and between Gorbachev and German chancellor Helmut Kohl.[12] The United States and Russia also parted company over the intensifying conflicts in the Balkans.

The Clinton administration in effect was adopting the basic strategy developed after the fall of the Wall. This policy was designed to help Russia's leaders as long as they acquiesced to U.S. preferences in world politics. The Clinton team wanted to avoid a Russian nationalist backlash against that policy. Yet the pursuit of a winner-take-all diplomacy and the existence of a populist tide within the newly democratic Russia ensured strategic failure. Conditions ripened for an entrepreneurial Russian politician to exploit popular passions and resentment against U.S. policy. Vladimir Putin, an intelligence service bureaucrat, became that politician. By pursuing a total victory after 1989–90, the United States sowed the seeds of confrontation that would take root and grow over the next ten years.

As Slocombe notes, Clinton's Russia strategy was coherent. The president was personally engaged and he assigned resources to its achievement. Moreover, the strategy helped sustain a number of diplomatic successes, including the enlargement of NATO and the resolution of the Balkan wars. Yet, ultimately, the difficulty of reforming Russia's internal governance, the clash over NATO enlargement and democracy promotion in Eastern Europe, and the unreliable Boris Yeltsin undermined the central goal of the administration: a long-term strategic partnership with America's former foe in pursuit of a Europe whole and free.

9/11

By the time George W. Bush was elected president, his advisers were beginning to recognize that political instability abroad, even in smaller states, was a major challenge for the post–Cold War era. As Philip Zelikow recounts, in the summer of 2001—before 9/11—National Security Adviser Condoleezza Rice began drafting a national strategy with the premise "that in a globalized world where great power rivalries were fading, the main problems would come from states imploding from within."[13] This, of course, was a distinct change from the "no nation-building" rhetoric of the campaign as well as from Rice's summary of Bush's campaign philosophy in her 2000 *Foreign Affairs* article in which she had emphasized the need to focus on great power rivals and the importance of alliances. But in July 2001 she was not yet grappling with strategies to reconstitute failed states. Even today, these many years after 9/11, U.S. officials are still struggling to design capabilities and policies to deal with this challenge, for example, the development of counterinsurgency forces within the military establishment and the design of governance-building capabilities within the State Department.

The attacks on September 11, 2001, like the fall of the Berlin Wall, shattered expectations and impelled new thinking. The international landscape, however, was no longer one of geopolitical possibility (like after 11/9), but fraught with peril emanating from nonstate actors. Suddenly, a problem that had been simmering, but had not been embraced as a top challenge by the George W. Bush administration, now shaped its entire global outlook. In Rice's 2000 article, "terrorism" was mentioned only three times, all minor asides. But she was not alone in slighting this threat. Subsequently, the 9/11 Commission would call this neglect a "failure of imagination"—an inability to think beyond a Cold War mind-set in a new environment.[14]

Bush and his advisers effectively managed the immediate aftermath of the attack. Even as they struggled to make sense of what occurred, comfort the bereaved, reassure the public, overcome their own humiliation, and seek revenge, they successfully identified al Qaeda as the key source of the 9/11 attack. They admonished the Taliban government in Afghanistan that it must expel the terrorist organization from its territory or face war. When it refused, U.S. officials quickly took action, routed the Taliban forces, and sent al Qaeda members fleeing for safety. As Zelikow notes, this reactive effort was at times chaotic and ad hoc, but it worked.

The record of the United States' medium- and longer-term approach to the post 9/11 world, however, was more mixed. On the positive side, the United States continued to expand trade and promote economic liberalization, themes of all post–Cold War administrations, but goals that could easily have been sublimated in response to fears about globalization in the wake of the 9/11 attacks. Zoellick shows how those efforts in the Americas, in Asia, and elsewhere served U.S. interests.

In political-military terms, however, many of the scholars here argue that U.S. officials erred. Policymakers attacked Iraq without first addressing the unstable situations in Afghanistan and Pakistan and without preparing effectively for the management of a postconflict Iraq. John Mueller contends that Bush administration officials (like their predecessors during the Cold War) exaggerated the threat and clumsily framed the problem as a "war on terror." Odd Arne Westad says that they learned the wrong lessons from the past. Bruce Cumings believes that they could not escape their hardened mind-sets.

Pathologies of Uncertainty

Notwithstanding these criticisms, the chapters in this book demonstrate that the United States effectively shaped and adapted to parts of the new environment spawned by 11/9 and 9/11. Real achievements and partial successes should not be ignored: the reunification of Germany within NATO; the rollback of Saddam's armies in the Gulf War; the reorientation of strategic thinking; NATO enlargement; an end to conflict in the Balkans; and the defeat of the Taliban. But there were shortcomings as well: opportunities were missed to create and reform international institutions; political, military, and economic initiatives were not well coordinated; the dangers emanating from failed states, nonstate terrorists, Islamic fundamentalists, and Russian revanchists were not sufficiently understood.

How can we account for the failures or inadequacies of strategic planning? Insightful recommendations for the future depend on analysis of past problems and achievements. Extrapolating from the chapters in this book, we can group the main impediments to high-quality planning into five categories: nearsighted vision, faulty assumptions, domestic priorities, bureaucratic infighting, and procedural shortcomings.

Nearsighted Vision

Overall, U.S. policymakers did reasonably well in responding to the immediate challenges faced in the wake of both 11/9 and 9/11. This is true in two senses. First, desirable outcomes were achieved, at least initially: Germany was unified peacefully within NATO and the Taliban and al Qaeda were defeated in Afghanistan. Second, as Wohlforth points out, actions by government officials were different than those proposed by knowledgeable nongovernmental experts and the outcomes were better than many independent scholars predicted.

The record for the medium term and longer term is less impressive. Although we see things more clearly after the fact, there was too little focus on and analysis of emerging and foreseeable problems such as a revanchist Russia, the fallout from failed states, the rise of terrorism, and the tribulations of postwar Iraq. Outside experts (who generally have a bad track record on short-term choices and consequences) displayed a much better understanding of these matters.[15]

How can we account for this variation in outcomes? Wohlforth suggests that information and cognitive style make a difference. The pace of change in Europe was startling in the fall of 1989 as were the pressures to respond to the 9/11 attacks. Wohlforth's analysis proposes that U.S. officials may do better adjusting to immediate dangers and opportunities because they have fresher and more complete information than their counterparts in other countries (and more than nongovernmental experts). When officials plan for the long term, however, they face more uncertainty and, therefore, immediate access to information and resources are less decisive. It may also be that the scholarly experts' hedgehog style of deductive reasoning is more appropriate for designing longer-term strategy than for handling immediate crises.

Another possible explanation for the difference is that short-term success has a blowback effect that impairs longer-term results. Immediate success leads to overconfidence, dangerous risk-taking, and insufficient attention to newly emerging problems. Gorbachev's willingness to go along with U.S. desires, for example, may subsequently have encouraged American policymakers to believe that the Russians would bend to U.S. determination. Likewise, in the Bush 43 administration, the early success in Afghanistan, according to Zelikow, became "a stimulant to action" that "loosened inhibitions about experiments with new ideas." This dynamic encouraged the United States to invade Iraq, an operation that had previously been deemed too risky.[16]

Sarotte raises another possible answer. Perhaps it is the case that governmental leaders need to react to immediate challenges and, having done so, those choices make it much harder to go in a different direction at a later time, even if it seems desirable to do so. Bets have been made, reputations staked, and conditions no longer invite big changes.

In these accounts, government officials, in effect, may behave like corporate leaders: the desire for short-term returns may crowd out optimal longer-term strategy.

Faulty Assumptions

Several of the contributors believe that the problems the United States encountered were due to assumptions from U.S. culture or lessons derived from experience that diminished the U.S. ability to read situations accurately. In his analysis of why the Iraq War went so poorly and why the United States got mired in Afghanistan, Westad argues that American leaders "misinterpreted the societies into which they intervened and overestimated the U.S. capacity for forcing change."[17] They were wrong, in Westad's view, because U.S. decision makers operated according to a set of lessons about interventions and political change that came from the Cold War in Europe, but did not apply to the situations in Iraq and Pakistan. If U.S. officials had assessed the conditions on terms appropriate to the cultural and geographic context of Southwest Asia and the Persian Gulf, they either would not have intervened (Iraq) or would have done so differently (Afghanistan/Pakistan) and with better results.

Lack of understanding, Slocombe argues, is not always the problem and was not the central cause of the Clinton administration's troubles in its Russia policy: "Knowledge of Russia was greater than that of the Balkans, the Arab world, North Korea, or Afghanistan." If there was a flawed understanding at work, it was a general one about how easy it would be to influence another country's internal political and economic order in an era of American dominance. "It is very hard for outsiders to shape a basic transformation in attitudes and practices in a foreign society and culture."[18]

Bruce Cumings also believes that the ways policymakers encounter an uncertain world are bounded by systems of axiomatic presuppositions that skew their understanding and action. If states respond to crises with "what is on the shelf," then leaders respond to crises with what is in their head.[19] Both Acheson after World War II and Bush 41 after the Berlin Wall came down were driven by an uncritical belief in the importance of an open, liberal world economy for U.S. well-being; the interventions after 9/11 were molded by flawed presuppositions from the post–World War II era about the appeal of freedom, the efficacy of force, and the success of military occupation (in Germany, Japan, and South Korea); and estimates of North Korea's demise have been consistently wrong because they are not based on an understanding of Korean history and culture.

A clear vision of the future demands an unbiased analysis of current and emerging conditions. Such an analysis, according to Cumings, is impossible. U.S. officials cannot help but err; success is accidental. Westad's analysis is more hopeful. Intelligent extrapolations, he suggests, are possible if situations are better understood.

John Mueller describes a different phenomenon that has haunted U.S. strategy in times of uncertainty: the need to conjure an existential threat. In his view, the United States goes in "quest of monsters" that do not exist. After 1945, it was global communism; after 1989, it was proliferation of nuclear weapons; and, after 9/11, it was global terrorism. In all cases, the threat was exaggerated beyond realistic proportions, causing a pervasive and unnecessary sense of insecurity. In this view, the U.S. approach to uncertainty is addicted to threat mongering and war making except in rare circumstances when the adversary's toughness (for example, Vietnam) chastens policymakers (and the American people)—until they forget.

Domestic Priorities

When the international arena is opaque, domestic political priorities can loom large in the making of U.S. strategy. From the day the Berlin Wall came down, domestic opinion figured prominently in shaping the actions of U.S. leaders.

Bush 41 immediately recognized that in the aftermath of the Cold War new dangers loomed: the U.S. public might no longer support large defense expenditures and the United States "forward defense" strategy might have to be reversed. The specter of American isolationism reared its ugly head once again. Bush's solution was to embed the newly unified Germany inside NATO, an institution that required a continued U.S. presence in Europe.[20]

In chapter 2, Robert Zoellick notes that a motive for the U.S. pursuit of regional cooperation in Asia in 1989 was "to counter a potential resurgence of U.S. economic isolationism."[21] Successful strategy, he stresses, had to be "connected to the 'Home Front.'"[22] The American people needed to be shown that U.S. international activity helped further U.S. jobs, competitiveness, and values. "Without public support, any U.S. administration will not be able to maintain a strategy of global American engagement."[23]

Concerns about domestic support not only revolved around foreign economic policy; they were focused on the heart of U.S. power abroad: the defense budget. As Wolfowitz and Edelman recount, the original impetus for the Defense Planning Guidance process was to provide the United States with a compass in the wake of the Cold War. But they also stress that the planning document was an effort to fend off calls for even greater cuts in the defense budget by legislators who no longer saw dangerous threats in the world.[24]

When the Clinton administration had to choose between the possibility of alienating Russia through NATO enlargement and the certainty of alienating domestic constituencies with ethnic roots in the countries of Eastern Europe or in the Baltic states of Estonia, Latvia, and Lithuania, the president and his advisers decided to assign priority to enlargement. They did not want to lose voters who were critical to reestablishing and preserving a Democratic coalition that the Republicans had undone in the 1994 congressional elections.[25]

John Mueller's chapter does not explore deeply why threat exaggeration occurs. To the extent it does happen, leaders may be attempting to mobilize against imminent threats that they believe would not be countered effectively in the absence of public alarm.[26] But leaders may also be manipulating threats to increase their domestic political popularity and to achieve their domestic political agendas, as many allege Bush 43 tried to do and as often was the case during the Cold War. In other words, strategy under uncertainty may be shaped as much by domestic politics as by the evolving international landscape.

Bureaucratic Battles

From the view of Washington insiders there is one central factor that shapes the way that the United States responds to the external world: the struggle for influence among competing bureaucracies and policymakers. Such dynamics haunt the dreams of those who aspire to integrate national strategy.

Differences in opinion across bureaucracies, leaks to sabotage plans, hesitancy to voice opinions, and enmity among top decision makers shaped the ways in which the United States adapted to the post–Cold War and 9/11 worlds. Even in the Bush 41 presidency, an administration renowned for its relative cohesiveness, the Defense Planning Guidance was almost gutted by a leak that revealed a preliminary and yet to be vetted draft. Edelman calls it "particularly vociferous bureaucratic infighting" that in part was fueled by a policy dispute, examined by Wolfowitz, between Defense and State over Ukraine leaving the Soviet Union.[27]

Philip Zelikow recalls that the start of the Bush 43 administration was "fractious" and encouraged "factional rivalry."[28] Bush's style was that of the business manager who allocated authority to particular bureaucracies depending on the issue. Decisions were made in different subunits with limited coordination. The vice president handled some matters, Defense others, and the State Department had its portfolio. But there were poisonous relations among top officials, and incessant interlopings across bureaucratic boundaries. Secretary of State Colin Powell and CIA director George Tenet struggled to preserve the autonomy and influence of their organizations while National Security Adviser Rice tried to safeguard her special relationship with the president. The famous National Security Strategy of 2002, in fact, was drafted by Rice, assisted by Zelikow working as an outside consultant, and had little input from the neoconservatives in the administration.

Zoellick's integrated strategy was not coordinated across the bureaucratic landscape of Washington. It was coherent in his own mind but he was not inclined to lay it out in a strategy statement. Pragmatic, experienced, and skillful bureaucratic players such as Baker and Zoellick were not prone to spend their time writing elaborate strategy papers, nor was it part of the culture of the State Department to generate a fully worked out strategic plan for a new world order.[29]

In all these cases, the response to complex rapid changes in world politics was molded by intragovernmental bickering and maneuvering. In most cases, bureaucratic conflict was a formidable impediment to integrated strategy.

Distorted Process

Scholars can imagine an ideal scheme for how U.S. strategy should be made in changing and uncertain circumstances. The president convenes a group of the nation's top foreign policy officials such as the heads of the NSC, State, CIA, Defense, and Treasury. They are tasked to gather information and formulate a set of options across policy domains (economic, military, diplomatic, intelligence, and so forth). A well-greased interagency process then reconciles divergent views. After weighing costs and benefits, risks and opportunities, officials present the president with alternative strategic options. The president then selects the most effective overall strategy for immediate and continuing challenges. This strategy is communicated to the bureaucracy, the country, and the world (as needed) to guide the various efforts (departmental, regional, functional, international, and so forth) that constitute the nation's foreign policy.

In reality, U.S. foreign policy often strayed considerably from this ideal as leaders confronted tumultuous times and faced a murky international arena after

11/9 and 9/11. The record reveals a planning process that involved both rational routine and ad hoc artistry. The actual day to day policymaking was at times coherent and well managed, as seemed to have been the case during Brent Scowcroft's tenure as national security adviser during the Bush 41 administration.[30] Managing day-to-day policy, however, is different than long-term strategic planning, which requires presidential input, good personal relationships across bureaucracies, excellent intelligence assessments, and visionary thinkers as well as policy entrepreneurs who are able to seize the opportunity and guide issues in one direction or another.

In the period after the dismantling of the Berlin Wall, the core of governmental planning was a group of decision makers in the State Department under Secretary Baker and in the NSC under Brent Scowcroft. People such as Zoellick, Robert Blackwill, Rice, Robert Hutchings, and Zelikow mapped out the options. They had thought about alternative scenarios. Some contingency planning for the breakup of the Soviet Union seems to have been done in a secret task force headed by Rice (who was in charge of Soviet and Eastern European affairs for the National Security Council) in the fall of 1989.[31] Laggards in the process included Cheney in Defense and Robert Gates at the CIA, both of whom were skeptical about the quick deal making with Gorbachev. The administration, however, decided to increase the pace of diplomacy in order to bolster Gorbachev's stature inside the Kremlin, but also to prevent him from seizing the initiative.[32] Close relationships between Bush and Scowcroft and Bush and Baker enabled officials in those organizations to shape short-term outcomes in timely and competent ways.

Longer-term planning in the Bush 41 administration, to the extent it occurred, took place in the Pentagon. The president and his national security adviser were not inclined toward strategic thinking. As Edelman writes, they "lacked the inclination to engage in speculative 'grand strategy' or the 'vision thing' . . . they had minimal interest in the debate over a new strategy."[33] Spurred by the Persian Gulf War, Bush and Scowcroft did reflect on general principles for a "new world order." They wanted to act in ways that fostered cooperation with the Soviet Union, enhanced the legitimacy of international institutions and rule of law, and preserved old and new alliances and coalitions (for example, by not marching to Baghdad to overthrow Saddam).[34] But they had little patience or interest in putting their ideas on paper in a systematic way and communicating them to the bureaucracy and the world.

In the meantime, officials in the Defense Department went to work on a document that would provide direction for the contraction, reconfiguration, and use of U.S. military forces. Their plan, as described by Edelman, was more than simply military guidance. It incorporated the same "geoeconomic" assumptions that were then shaping Zoellick's thinking in the State Department, but the ideas of State and Defense officials were not joined in a single document.[35] As Wolfowitz notes, "the Regional Defense Strategy was not a grand strategy."[36] Department of Defense officials were not inclined to share their work with other departments. When it was leaked, it caused consternation in the White House. The final draft of the DPG was never championed by the White House. It was released by Secretary of Defense Cheney at the very end of the Bush 41 administration in January 1993.

The Clinton administration lacked a strong strategic focus. To the extent it conducted grand strategy, it did so out of the White House. Clinton wanted an overall approach to the world, but he was not disciplined enough in his own thinking and leadership style to make it happen, and the world was too complicated.[37] Slocombe shows that the administration did have a strategy at least in one area—Russia. Again, the development of this strategy built not on institutionalized process but on circumstances surrounding the fact that the president was a college friend of his main Russia adviser, Strobe Talbott, the deputy secretary of state. Otherwise, Clinton and his aides embraced much of the military strategy and many of the same geoeconomic assumptions of their Republican predecessors.

Bush 43 was intent on avoiding the critique of his father for lacking "the vision thing," but floundered until the attacks of 9/11. He possessed a different approach to policymaking than his father. The president's preferred CEO management style positioned his key advisers like "the heads of the subsidiary companies seeing themselves less as part of a team, more as executives with their own responsibilities to discharge." Although Bush may have been seeking a "team of rivals," he encouraged unruly competition. Effective strategic planning in such a framework was impossible for Rice to orchestrate.[38] The immediate response to 9/11 was generated by an ad hoc group dominated by officials in the Defense Department, the CIA, and the Office of the Vice President (at least insofar as Afghanistan was concerned). This group remained at the heart of efforts that would lead the United States into Iraq, but, paradoxically, this was not the group that authored the notorious 2002 National Security Strategy statement.

Zelikow describes how that long-term strategy was developed within the National Security Council under Secretary Rice and her outside consultants (especially Zelikow himself). The coordination between the war planning for Iraq and the overall strategy was not tight. Nonetheless, the immediate demands of the situation (the desire to remove Saddam Hussein) shaped the drafting of the broader National Security statement, for example, the emphasis on preemption versus prevention. The strategy statement was a relatively consistent and coherent vision of overall strategy, but Zelikow also argues that it reflected the exigencies of the moment.

The record indicates the absence of a standard process for interpreting dramatic change and reacting to it. Although administrations were configured similarly, officials came together in different ways depending on the predilections of the president, the expertise and inclinations of his chief advisers, and the relationships among them and their subordinates.[39] The classic model of hierarchical and integrated policymaking captures only a partial picture of what actually occurred. Instead, different bureaucratic actors competed as much as they collaborated. Strategy was often highly segregated and responsive to domestic political pressures and priorities. Overall there appears to have been little coordinated political-military-economic strategy in the U.S. government in the post–Cold War period.

Managing the Murky Future

In many ways, we are still in the post-11/9 and 9/11 eras. Barack Obama introduced his administration's first national strategy statement in May 2010 by highlighting that the world is in a moment of transition, "a time of sweeping change," which the United States must seek to shape.[40] The United States still struggles to perceive the future of a shifting and complex world in which there are, as John Mueller quotes, "many snakes to slay, but no dragons." As terrifying as the prospect of nuclear war was during the Cold War, the Soviet threat had the advantage of providing an overarching focus to governmental foreign policy, a dominant threat around which to focus, and particular opportunities to pursue when possible.

The priority that should be assigned to different dangers and opportunities as we look ahead is much less clear. The United States must make sense of how threats from nation-states compare with dangers from terrorists; how the spread of nuclear weapons technologies rates in relation to the rise of global warming or the movement of deadly viruses; and how many resources should be devoted to building international institutions or alternative energy supplies versus building effective institutions within troubled countries abroad—or even at home. Officials must also avoid fostering Mueller's "self-licking" threats that misrepresent the actual danger.

The authors here are agreed that how the United States plans for the future affects its competence in the world arena. The policymakers—Zoellick, Wolfowitz, Edelman, Zelikow, and Slocombe—believe that the United States often responded effectively to the dramatic changes in the world over the past twenty years. They are certainly right in noting some achievements such as German unification, the expansion of NATO, and the growth of a global economy based on more open markets and freer enterprise. The academicians, on the other hand, see flaws that have produced costly losses of treasure and lives at home and abroad. They, too, are right. The record has been mixed, and, to their credit, all the authors point in varying degrees to both achievements and mistakes in U.S. performance.

Looking across the chapters, patterns emerge. U.S. leaders have tended to deal with short-run challenges well, but have had more difficulty in managing longer-term feedback and change. They often have relied on outdated and faulty assumptions. In the absence of pressing external demands, they have allowed domestic political pressures to skew policy; they have not effectively managed bureaucratic infighting; and they have not always organized an efficient policy process. Most of these maladies are endemic and enduring; each deserves attention.

There are no absolute cures, but partial remedies are possible. Awareness of the pathologies is an important step in itself. If policymakers understand what can go wrong (and right), they can avoid pitfalls and can inspire efforts to take compensatory actions. For example, an administration that shares Zoellick's vision of an integrated policy could design a process that does a more effective job of coordinating the different policy domains. Organizational changes may also foster that sort of planning. Zelikow, while advising Condi Rice, was worried about the lack of attention to long-term planning in government. He recommended that an office be established within the NSC to help bring a longer-term perspective to planning.[41]

In the midst of our contemporary angst, we should not ignore some instructive lessons from the record of U.S planning since the end of the Cold War. Planning is not always the key source of effective action and entails its own set of risks. Lengthy reviews can be undermined and gutted, as seen in Bush 41's initial strategic review of 1989, a review that Secretary of State Baker called "mush."[42] Others note the dangers of big planning exercises. Paul Wolfowitz concludes that "large interdepartmental reviews inevitably tend to kill innovative ideas."[43] Edelman contends that "any document that must go through the bureaucratic maw ends up being dumbed down to the lowest common denominator."[44]

Yet it is also clear that improvising the nation's foreign policy cannot endure for long. Focused forethought, alternative scenario consideration, and contingency planning are necessary. As seen in the work of the small Rice group in the fall of 1989, in the labors of those crafting the Defense Planning Guidance between 1990 and 1993, and in the efforts of those designing the National Security Strategy of 2002, top decision makers require strategic planning, and policy outcomes in the long run depend, at least in part, on the quality of such efforts.

Strategy is important for developing governmental capabilities and communicating purpose to audiences both within and outside of the national government.

Wolfowitz points out that planning is absolutely essential for making resource decisions to shape U.S. military capabilities.[45] And Zoellick argues that articulating a coherent policy has a potent public affairs function since success may depend on public support both within the United States and abroad. This was the case with the Bush administration's diplomacy in 1989–90, which needed the support of citizens in the two Germanys as well as from those in other Central and Eastern European countries.[46]

Of course, the key to strategy in any U.S. administration is the president and other top officials who have the ability to organize and invest in a system that manages complexity and change in ways that mitigate the pathologies above. Leadership is a critical component of effective national planning. Leadership necessarily involves quick and decisive action, but, as Wolfowitz counsels, it must also allow time for strategic thinking, debate, and reflection.

Finally, U.S. planning under uncertainty may benefit from studying the experience of other countries. There is no question that the United States is in some respects a unique country as a result of its preponderant global power, particular democratic political system, and geographic location. Yet there are still useful things planners may learn from other nations in at least two respects. The first involves the organization and process of planning. Other nations also have to deal with uncertainty—indeed, in many cases, countries that are smaller and possess less control over the external world face even more unknowns and risks. Examining how they have organized themselves to deal with that complexity may be useful to the United States as it is increasingly intertwined with other countries and shaped by external factors. U.S. policymakers using intergovernmental networks could explore these comparative dimensions for useful insights relatively quickly.

The United States might also profit from studying how other nations extrapolate strategy from their planning processes. Countries around the world have had to deal with the threats and opportunities of a globalizing world. They too have had to transition away from a long-ingrained Cold War pattern of thought and decision making. Have some countries done better at this than others? Russia, the members of the EU, China, and Japan have clearly made different choices in terms of their emphasis on military development, the integration of security and economic decision making, and the priority accorded to energy and environmental factors. To what extent have these choices been effective and how have they been shaped by planning efforts? Looking beyond the American experience might usefully benefit future American competence. This is a longer-term task that is perhaps particularly suited to scholarly research.

Strategy requires moving from the knowns to the unknowns and back again. We know that the United States today faces a world that is uncertain and complex.

We also know that there will be events that will occur that we cannot foresee but that will cause further confusion and uncertainty.

Our hope is that a better understanding of how the United States has reacted in the past will help illuminate the way forward—that has been the goal of bringing together the views of former policymakers and scholars. In this book the personal recollections of key decision makers add significantly to the historical record of strategic adaptation—in ways that are both reassuring and troubling. The chapters by scholars provide critical analysis. Both former officials and nongovernmental experts have a role to play in improving future performance in a changing world fraught with peril and opportunity.

Notes

INTRODUCTION

1. Hans-Hermann Hertle, "The Fall of the Wall: The Unintended Self-Dissolution of East Germany's Ruling Regime," Cold War International History Project *Bulletin* 12/13 (Fall–Winter 2001): 134–37; Mary Elise Sarotte, *1989: The Struggle to Create Post–Cold War Europe* (Princeton: Princeton University Press, 2009), 28–47.

2. See, for example, Jane Mayer, *The Dark Side: The Inside Story of How the War on Terror Turned into a War on American Ideals* (New York: Doubleday, 2008), 1–5.

3. For more on the different forms uncertainty can take, see Brian C. Rathbun, "Uncertain about Uncertainty: Understanding the Multiple Meanings of a Crucial Concept in International Relations Theory," *International Studies Quarterly* 51, no. 3 (August 2007): 533–57. For a study of uncertainty and military planning, see Talbot C. Imlay and Monica Duffy Toft, eds., *The Fog of Peace and War Planning: Military and Strategic Planning Under Uncertainty* (New York: Routledge, 2006).

4. Introductory statement by Barack Obama, 27 May 2010, http://www.whitehouse.gov/sites/default/files/rss_viewer/national_security_strategy.pdf.

5. David Halberstam, *War in a Time of Peace: Bush, Clinton, and the Generals* (New York: Simon and Shuster, 2002), 500.

6. Warren I. Cohen, *America's Failing Empire: U.S. Foreign Relations since the Cold War* (Malden, Mass.: Blackwell Publishing, 2005), quotations on pages 38, 121, 186.

7. See, for example, Michael Cox, *U.S. Foreign Policy after the Cold War* (London: Royal Institute of International Affairs, 1995); Timothy Naftali, *George H. W. Bush* (New York: Times Books, 2007); Thomas H. Henriksen, *American Power after the Berlin Wall* (New York: Palgrave/Macmillan, 2007); Hal Brands, *From Berlin to Baghdad: America's Search for Purpose in the Post–Cold War World* (Lexington: University Press of Kentucky, 2008); Derek Chollet and James Goldgeier, *America between the Wars: From 11/9 to 9/11* (New York: Public Affairs, 2008); Jeffrey A. Engel, "A Better World . . . but Don't Get Carried Away: The Foreign Policy of George H. W. Bush Twenty Years On," *Diplomatic History* 34 (January 2010): 25–46.

8. George Bush and Brent Scowcroft, *A World Transformed* (New York: Vintage Books, 1998), 150.

9. Bartholomew H. Sparrow, "Realism's Practitioner: Brent Scowcroft and the Making of the New World Order, 1989–1993," *Diplomatic History* 34 (January 2010): 174.

10. Brands, *From Berlin to Baghdad,* 336.

11. Sarotte, *1989,* 214.

12. See, for example, Brands, *From Berlin to Baghdad,* 262–76, 335–40.

13. The full text may be found at http://www.commondreams.org/headlines02/0920-05.htm.

14. Bush's second inaugural address is at http://www.presidency.ucsb.edu/ws/index.php?pid=58745.

15. See, for example, Jim Mann, *Rise of the Vulcans: The History of Bush's War Cabinet* (New York: Viking, 2004); A. J. Bacevich, *American Empire: The Realities and Consequences*

of U.S. Diplomacy (Cambridge: Harvard University Press, 2002); Chollet and Goldgeier, *America Between the Wars*, 304.

16. Quoted in chapter 2 of this book, 26.
17. See chapter 3 of this book, 57.
18. Quoted in chapter 4 of this book, 69.
19. Quoted in chapter 5 of this book, 93.
20. Quotes are from chapter 6 of this book, 96–97, 115, 97.
21. Ibid., 114, 99, 115, 107.
22. Ibid., 105.
23. Quotes are from chapter 1 of this book, 25.
24. Ibid., 24.
25. Quotes are from chapter 8 of this book, 131, 146.
26. Quoted in chapter 9, 160–61.
27. Quoted in chapter 10, 165.
28. Bush and Scowcroft, *A World Transformed*, 564.

1. THE WALL COMES DOWN

The author is grateful to the following institutions for funding for the research and writing of this chapter: the Alexander von Humboldt Foundation, Bonn; the Institute for Advanced Study, Princeton; the National Endowment for the Humanities, Washington, D.C.; the Mershon Center of The Ohio State University, Columbus; St. John's College, Cambridge; and the University of Southern California. She thanks the editors of the book and Kathleen Conley for their help in producing this essay.

1. Robert M. Gates, *From the Shadows: The Ultimate Insider's Story of Five Presidents and How They Won the Cold War* (New York: Touchstone, 1996), 492.

2. Daniel Deudney and G. John Ikenberry, "The Unraveling of the Cold War Settlement," *Survival* 51, no. 6 (December 2009–January 2010): 42.

3. One of the strengths of the academic field of international relations is that it is willing to draw from a number of disciplines and methodologies: economics, history, political science, as well as other social and quantitative sciences. Historian John Lewis Gaddis has rightly pointed out, however, that in its attempts to address these issues, the field does not make sufficient use of a potentially useful body of scholarship: biological theory. See John Lewis Gaddis, "History, Science, and the Study of International Relations," *Explaining International Relations since 1945*, ed. Ngaire Woods (Oxford: Oxford University Press, 1996), 32–48. Gaddis has also looked at the impact of dramatic change on U.S. foreign policy; see his *Surprise, Security, and the American Experience* (Cambridge: Harvard University Press, 2004). On the topic of biology and security, see Jonathan Renshon, "Leadership Differences: What We Don't (Yet) Know about National Security Decision-Making," *H-Diplo/ISSF Roundtable on "Biology and Security"* 1, no. 1 (30 March 2010), http://www.h-net.org/~diplo/ISSF/roundtables/rt1-1-renshon.html.

4. The original paper, entitled "Models in Paleobiology" and presented to the 1971 Annual Meeting of the Geological Society of America, is summarized in Stephen Jay Gould, *Punctuated Equilibrium* (Cambridge: Belknap Press of Harvard University, 2007), 49–50.

5. Ibid., 55.

6. See, for example, Verne Grant, "Punctuated Equilibria: A Critique," *Biologisches Zentralblatt* 101, no. 2 (1982): 175–84.

7. The practice of focusing in-depth on a short but critical period of time is an approach that I have found rewarding; see Mary Elise Sarotte, *1989: The Struggle to Create Post–Cold War Europe* (Princeton: Princeton University Press, 2009). For the extensive literature examining the end of the Cold War, see, for example, Don Oberdorfer, *The*

Turn: From the Cold War to a New Era (New York: Simon and Schuster, 1991); Stephen Szabo, *The Diplomacy of German Unification* (New York: St. Martin's Press, 1992); Philip Zelikow and Condoleezza Rice, *Germany Unified and Europe Transformed* (Cambridge: Harvard University Press, 1995); Robert L. Hutchings, *American Diplomacy and the End of the Cold War: An Insider's Account of U.S. Policy in Europe, 1989–1992* (Washington, D.C.: Wilson Center, 1997); Charles S. Maier, *Dissolution: The Crisis of Communism and the End of East Germany* (Princeton: Princeton University Press, 1997); Angela Stent, *Russia and Germany Reborn: Unification, the Soviet Collapse, and the New Europe* (Princeton: Princeton University Press, 1999); Archie Brown, *The Rise and Fall of Communism* (New York: HarperCollins, 2009); Andreas Rödder, *Deutschland Einig Vaterland* (München: Beck, 2009); Jeffrey A. Engel, ed., *The Fall of the Berlin Wall: The Revolutionary Legacy of 1989* (New York: Oxford University Press, 2009); Stephen Kotkin with a contribution by Jan T. Gross, *Uncivil Society: 1989 and the Implosion of the Communist Establishment* (New York: Modern Library, 2009); Michael Meyer, *The Year That Changed the World: The Untold Story behind the Fall of the Berlin Wall* (New York: Scribner, 2009); Constantine Pleshakov, *There Is No Freedom without Bread! 1989 and the Civil War That Brought Down Communism* (New York: Farrar, Straus and Giroux, 2009); David Priestland, *The Red Flag: A History of Communism* (New York: Grove Press, 2009); Victor Sebestyen, *Revolution 1989: The Fall of the Soviet Empire* (New York: Pantheon Books, 2009). See also the four-volume study *Geschichte der deutschen Einheit* by a group of German professors who received early access to West German documents. The volume most relevant to this chapter is the fourth, Werner Weidenfeld, with Peter M. Wagner and Elke Bruck, *Außenpolitik für die deutsche Einheit: Die Entscheidungsjahre 1989/90* (Stuttgart: Deutsche Verlags-Anstalt, 1998).

8. For example, see George Herring, *From Colony to Superpower: U.S. Foreign Relations since 1776* (Oxford: Oxford University Press, 2008), 905; or Campbell Craig and Fredrik Logevall, *America's Cold War: The Politics of Insecurity* (Cambridge: Belknap Press of Harvard University, 2009), 341. Both are impressive works of scholarship, so their inclusion of this mistaken assumption shows how pervasive it is.

9. This summary is updated from my book, *1989: The Struggle to Create Post–Cold War Europe* (Princeton: Princeton University Press, 2009); for even more recent accounts, see Hans-Hermann Hertle and Maria Nooke, *Die Todesopfer an der Berliner Mauer 1961–1989: Ein biographisches Handbuch* (Berlin: Links Verlag, 2009); and Hans-Hermann Hertle und Kathrin Elsner, *Der Tag, an dem die Mauer fiel: Die wichtigsten Zeitzeugen berichten vom 9. November 1989* (Berlin: Nicolai, 2009).

10. He has published a memoir about the experience, together with a journalist: Gerhard Haase-Hindenberg, *Der Mann, der die Mauer öffnete: Warum Oberstleutnant Harald Jäger den Befehl verweigerte und damit Weltgeschichte schrieb* (München: Heyne, 2007).

11. For more information on the Cold War context of these events, see Melvyn P. Leffler, *For the Soul of Mankind: The United States, the Soviet Union, and the Cold War* (New York: Hill and Wang, 2007); and Odd Arne Westad, *The Global Cold War: Third World Interventions and the Making of Our Times* (Cambridge: Cambridge University Press, 2005).

12. Hutchings, *American Diplomacy,* 6.

13. Comment made on National Public Radio, 27 July 2008, by Paul Light, in a discussion of his book, *A Government Ill Executed* (Cambridge: Harvard University Press, 2008).

14. Gates, *From the Shadows,* 460.

15. See my *1989,* 230, note 44.

16. See my *1989,* 24, for more discussion of this point.

17. Raymond Garthoff, *The Great Transition: American-Soviet Relations and the End of the Cold War* (Washington, D.C.: Brookings, 1994), 376.

18. Michael Beschloss and Strobe Talbott, *At the Highest Levels: The Inside Story of the Cold War* (Boston: Little, Brown, 1993), 45.

19. James A. Baker with Thomas A. DeFrank, *The Politics of Diplomacy* (New York: G. P. Putnam's Sons, 1995), 68.

20. Gates, *From the Shadows,* 460.

21. For more analysis of these developments, see Sarotte, "Not One Inch Eastward: Bush, Baker, Kohl, Genscher, Gorbachev, and the Origins of Russian Resentment toward NATO Enlargement," *Diplomatic History* 34, no. 1 (January 2010): 119–40.

22. "Gespräch des Bundeskanzlers Kohl mit Präsident Bush, Camp David, 24. Feb. 1990," Dok. 192, DESE, 868–69; see also George H. W. Bush and Brent Scowcroft, *A World Transformed* (New York: Knopf, 1998), 253; Sarotte, *1989,* 128; and Zelikow and Rice, *Germany Unified,* 215.

23. Gates, *From the Shadows,* 492.

24. For more information on transatlantic relations following the end of World War II, see William Hitchcock, *The Bitter Road to Freedom: A New History of the Liberation of Europe* (New York: Free Press, 2008). For more on the topic of U.S. foreign policy, see my "Perpetuating U.S. Preeminence: The 1990 Deals to 'Bribe the Soviets Out' and Move NATO In," *International Security* 35, no. 1 (Summer 2010): 110–37, and the H-DIPLO Roundtable on my book, vol. 11, no. 16 (February 2010).

25. Craig and Logevall, *America's Cold War,* 91.

26. For more on this topic, see my "Perpetuating U.S. Preeminence."

27. Bush and Scowcroft, *A World Transformed,* 253. For an analysis of this particular comment, see Stephen G. Brooks and William C. Wohlforth, "Economic Constraints and the Turn towards Superpower Cooperation in the 1980s," in *The Last Decade of the Cold War: From Conflict Escalation to Conflict Transformation,* ed. Olav Njølstad (New York: Routledge, 2004), 105–6.

28. *The 9/11 Commission Report: Final Report of the National Commission on Terrorist Attacks upon the United States* (New York: Norton, 2004), 399.

29. See my *1989* for more discussion of this point.

30. For an insightful account on the challenges that great powers face in shaping international order, see Jeffrey W. Legro, *Rethinking the World: Great Power Strategies and International Order* (Ithaca: Cornell University Press, 2005).

31. Baker with DeFrank, *Politics of Diplomacy,* 84.

2. AN ARCHITECTURE OF U.S. STRATEGY AFTER THE COLD WAR

1. For more detail about our plans and execution, see Robert Zoellick, "Two Plus Four, Ten Lessons about German Unification," *National Interest* 61 (Fall 2000): 17–28; Philip D. Zelikow and Condoleezza Rice, *Germany Unified and Europe Transformed: A Study in Statecraft* (Cambridge: Harvard University Press, 1995).

2. Mary Elise Sarotte's book, *1989: The Struggle to Create Post–Cold War Europe* (Princeton: Princeton University Press, 2009), raises these questions as does her chapter in this book.

3. See chapter 3 in this book.

4. See chapter 5 in this book.

5. Robert Zoellick, "Happily Ever AAFTA," *Wall Street Journal,* 8 January 2007.

6. Hector Calvo-Pardo, Caroline Freund, and Emanuel Ornelas, *The ASEAN Free Trade Agreement: Impact on Trade Flows and External Trade Barriers* (Washington, D.C.: World Bank Group, 2009); Philip Levy, *The United States–Peru Trade Promotion Agreement: What Did You Expect?* Working Paper Series on Development Policy, no. 1 (Washington, D.C.: American Enterprise Institute, October 2009); Antoni Estevadeordal, Carolina Freund,

and Emanuel Ornelas, *Does Regionalism Affect Trade Liberalization toward Non-Members?* Policy Research Working Paper Series 4751 (Washington, D.C: World Bank Group, 2008); Bernard Hoekman and Alan L. Winters, *Multilateralising Preferential Trade Agreements: A Developing Country Perspective* (Geneva: World Trade Organization, 2007).

7. Excluding European Union member states.

3. SHAPING THE FUTURE

1. Surprisingly early on, Reagan had a notion that Soviet weakness could be used to force a turn away from military confrontation and possibly even force fundamental internal changes. Equally surprising was the priority he assigned to removing the specter of nuclear holocaust. In their new book, Martin and Annelise Anderson show that he assigned great priority to this goal, despite the skepticism of some close advisers. Over the objections of Secretary of State Alexander Haig, he included an unusual handwritten letter, affirming his concern about avoiding nuclear war, along with his stern first official letter to Leonid Brezhnev. See Martin Anderson and Annelise Anderson, *Reagan's Secret War: The Untold Story of His Fight to Save the World from Nuclear Disaster* (New York: Crown Publishers, 2009), 49–55. He personally insisted that the administration's policy on the Soviet Union, finalized in January 1983, should "include nothing that would forego compromise and quiet diplomacy." See Richard Pipes, *Vixi* (New Haven: Yale University Press, 2006), 201–2.

2. See François Jullien, *A Treatise on Efficacy: Between Western and Chinese Thinking* (Honolulu: University of Hawaii Press, 2004), 116, quoting Lao Tzi, and 175, quoting Sun Tzu. Jullien, a remarkable scholar of Chinese art and philosophy, as well as strategy, devotes an entire chapter of *Treatise on Efficacy* to "Water Images."

3. Robert Gates, *From the Shadows: The Ultimate Insider's View of Five Presidents and How They Won the Cold War* (New York: Simon and Schuster, 1984), 449, writes "truth be told, the American government, including the CIA, had no idea in January 1989 that a tidal wave of history was about to break upon us."

4. Michael R. Beschloss and Strobe Talbott, *At the Highest Levels: The Inside Story of the End of the Cold War* (Boston: Little Brown, 1993).

5. President Bush's role in strongly supporting German unification from the very beginning helped to head off opposition not only from the Soviet Union but also from some of our NATO allies. Although German unification in some form may have been inevitable, continued German membership in NATO was not, nor even was the preservation of NATO itself.

6. For more detail on this point see Paul Wolfowitz, "Victory Came Too Easily," *National Interest* 35 (Spring 1994): 91–92. President Bush's boldness is underscored by the fact that only a bare majority of the Congress supported the decision to go to war in 1991, and a majority of Democrats in both the Senate and the House opposed it.

7. The phrase "new world order" made its first public appearance in President Bush's speech to the Joint Session of Congress on September 11, 1990. Former National Security Adviser Brent Scowcroft has since lamented that the term new world order was later "broadened beyond recognition," whereas it was originally conceived as applying "only to a narrow aspect of conflict—aggression between states." Even in this narrower sense, however, the phrase raised excessive expectations about the role of the United Nations. And President Bush went far beyond that in his speech to the Congress, presenting a vision of a new world order in which "the nations of the world, East and West, North and South, can prosper and live in harmony ... where the rule of law supplants the rule of the jungle ... in which nations recognize the shared responsibility for freedom and justice . . . where the strong respect the rights of the weak." See George H. W. Bush and Brent Scowcroft,

A World Transformed (New York: Vintage Books, 1998), 355 and 370. The "no dog" quote is attributed to Baker by Scowcroft. See Laura Silber and Alan Little, *Yugoslavia: Death of a Nation* (London: Penguin Books, 1997), 201.

8. As quoted in Jim Mann, *The Rebellion of Ronald Reagan: a History of the End of the Cold War* (New York: Viking, 2009), 320.

9. Bush and Scowcroft, *A World Transformed,* 43.

10. Beschloss and Talbott, *At the Highest Levels,* 48–49. Not long afterward, Cheney presented a gloomier view, that Gorbachev would "ultimately fail" and be replaced by someone "far more hostile." Ibid., 54–55.

11. Perhaps Scowcroft did not press his suggestion more vigorously because he was principally trying to provoke new thinking from a bureaucracy that he viewed as sluggish.

12. Gorbachev had spoken the year before of "cutting back drastically conventional forces and arms in Europe" in the joint New Year's messages that he and Reagan addressed to the American and Soviet people. *Public Papers of the Presidents of the United States: Ronald Reagan 1988, Book 1* (Washington, D.C.: United States Government Printing Office, 1990), 1–3.

13. Cheney was not enthusiastic about Lance modernization, but an SNF negotiation would open a divisive debate in NATO about the possibility of eliminating all short-range nuclear forces, with the United Kingdom already nervous about the elimination of intermediate-range nuclear missiles by the Intermediate Nuclear Force (INF) treaty.

14. James A. Baker III with Thomas M. Defrank, *The Politics of Diplomacy: Revolution, War, and Peace, 1989–1992* (New York: G. P. Putnam's Sons, 1995), 82.

15. Admiral William Crowe and the Joint Chiefs, particularly the Army and Air Force, wanted to preserve a large number for U.S. military manpower in Europe while Scowcroft pressed, on behalf of the president, for a reduction that would look more dramatic.

16. Our ability to review military contingency plans and to do budget analysis also proved invaluable in the work done by Libby and Henry Rowen, my assistant secretary for international security affairs, in enabling Cheney to encourage the development of the western flanking movement in Operation Desert Storm and in orchestrating what we nicknamed "Operation Tin Cup," the initiative that generated more than $50 billion to pay for the cost of that military operation.

17. Bartholomew was undersecretary of state for arms control and international security affairs. Participants in these discussions included, among others, Dennis Ross and Bartholomew from State, Stephen Hadley, Admiral David Jeremiah, and Libby from Defense, and Arnold Kanter from the NSC staff. The group was never intended to be a decision-making body.

18. My recollection is more detailed than Bartholomew's, though not necessarily more accurate. Bartholomew remembers simply that there was a substantial language problem that concerned the future of the alliance and that the two of us went to Baker who quickly agreed to change the language.

19. In much the same vein, he would tell an interviewer a year later, "I'm running out of demons. I'm running out of villains. I'm down to Castro and Kim Il Sung." *Army Times,* 5 April 1991.

20. One pundit, paraphrasing Stalin's comment about the pope, asked "how many divisions does unpredictability have?"

21. In opposing that change I was joined by the Central Command commander, a not-yet-famous general named Norman Schwarzkopf, who later became a strong supporter of the strategy to deter or defeat an Iraqi attack on the smaller Gulf countries.

22. The UN consensus was valuable, but its importance was frequently exaggerated. When Cheney visited Saudi Arabia after the invasion of Kuwait—and King Fahd surprised the world, including most Middle East experts, by agreeing to accept U.S. forces—a senior

Saudi official explained to us that the decision would have been different if they were still dealing with a United States that "left helicopters burning in the desert" after the failed attempt to rescue the hostages in Iran in 1980 or which "fled Lebanon" after the bombing of the Marine barracks in 1983.

23. Earlier that year General Powell had proposed eliminating NATO'S short-range tactical nuclear weapons, a proposal that was opposed by Assistant Secretary Stephen Hadley's NATO and arms control staff. Powell reports teasing Cheney at the time that his civilian advisers were "all right-wing nuts like you." Colin Powell with Joseph Persico, *My American Journey* (New York: Ballantine Books, 1995), 526. However, although Powell was right that nuclear artillery was no longer needed—arguably it had long ceased to be useful—making that move at the time he suggested would have had far less impact than it did when eventually proposed.

24. During the SALT II negotiations in 1976 Kissinger and Scowcroft wanted to ban all submarine-launched cruise missiles (SLCMs), which would have killed the conventional Tomahawk missile, a move that was blocked by Secretary of Defense Donald Rumsfeld—fortunately so, since the conventional Tomahawk proved so effective in the first Gulf War (and subsequently).

25. Scowcroft mistakenly calls this a South Korean proposal: see Bush and Scowcroft, *A World Transformed*, 545. It was an important piece of the Bush administration's plan to confront North Korea on its nuclear program. However, the Clinton administration retreated in 1994 and dispatched former President Jimmy Carter to Pyongyang when a confrontation loomed over the possible imposition of relatively mild sanctions against North Korea.

26. Powell, *My American Journey*, 527.

27. Beschloss and Talbott, *At the Highest Level*, 170.

28. Ibid., 422, 429.

29. Following Cheney's direction, Hadley insisted that the White House statement must "condemn" the coup. See Gates, *From the Shadows*, 523.

30. Beschloss and Talbott, *At the Highest Level*, 418. In the United States, the columnist William Safire famously labeled it the "Chicken Kiev speech."

31. Gates, *From the Shadows*, 530. The second part of Baker's statement is inconsistent with the first. Baker wanted to avoid the kind of conflict that had engulfed Yugoslavia, but it is hard to see how this ambiguity would have been helpful. To the contrary, Baker's ambiguous position in Belgrade the previous June—supporting both the "unity of Yugoslavia" and a peaceful resolution—arguably contributed to the subsequent violence, or at least failed to prevent it. Warren Zimmermann, who was the U.S. ambassador to Yugoslavia at the time, described Baker's position then as "no green light," but also "no red light." Warren Zimmermann, *Origins of a Catastrophe* (New York: Crown, 1996), 137.

32. Baker, *Politics of Diplomacy*, 560–62.

33. Testimony of Secretary of Defense Dick Cheney, Hearing of the House Armed Services Committee, *Fiscal Year '92–'93 Defense Authorization*, 6 February 1992, as quoted in Donald Kagan and Frederick W. Kagan, *While America Sleeps* (New York: St. Martin's Griffin, 2000), 288–96. The Kagans' account of Cheney's new defense strategy is the only one I'm aware of that bases its analysis on Cheney's very important testimony of February 1992, rather than the draft DPG of the following month that was leaked to the press before it had even been reviewed at senior levels. Both historians, they describe Cheney's presentation as "impressive strategic thinking at an unusually high level" and lament that "so clear an exposition of the true lessons of the past at such a critical time should have fallen on truly deaf ears." Ibid., 294, 292.

34. Kagan and Kagan, *While America Sleeps*, 285–88. Still others believed that the Desert Storm experience demonstrated that the United Nations could now be an effective instrument of collective action, as an earlier generation had hoped after World War II.

Senator Joseph Biden suggested that the United States should pursue "the next big advance in civilization," which he described as "collective power through the United Nations" (as quoted by Patrick Tyler, "Lone Superpower Plan: Ammunition for Critics," *New York Times*, 10 March 1992). In the same article, Tyler himself presents this astonishing mischaracterization of postwar history: "The Pentagon document articulates the clearest rejection to date of collective internationalism, the strategy that emerged from World War II when the five victorious powers sought to form a United Nations that could mediate disputes and police outbreaks of violence." At least when Bush spoke of a "new world order," he understood that the initial hopes for the United Nations had not yet been realized. See note 7 above.

35. Kagan and Kagan, *While America Sleeps*, 288–96, quoting from Cheney's House Armed Services Committee testimony. Similar testimony was given to the Senate.

36. See note 7 above.

37. See note 22 above.

38. See *Defense Strategy for the 1990's: The Regional Defense Strategy*, 2: "These reductions will reduce force structure to its lowest level in terms of manpower since before the Korean War and spending to the lowest percentage of GNP since before the attack on Pearl Harbor."

39. See chapter 4 in this book.

40. The collection of related documents posted by the National Security Archive does not include the president's Aspen speech, any of the documents or briefings by General Powell and myself that preceded that speech, any of Cheney's subsequent testimony, or any of the considerable material available on the development of the "Base Force." In fairness to the National Security Archive, however, it is not clear why DOD, so long after the fact, is still redacting the documents it declassified. For the materials on the National Security Archive website, see http://www.gwu.edu/~nsarchiv/nukevault/ebb245/.

41. We tried to get the final document cleared through an interagency approval process, but none of the other departments would either clear it or state any disagreements. Finally, as the administration was about to end, Cheney decided to publish it under his own signature as *Defense Strategy for the 1990s: The Regional Defense Strategy*.

42. Ibid., 1.

43. During the last year of the Bush administration, the State Department sent "minders" along with Scooter Libby and Eric Edelman when they traveled to Central and Eastern Europe, quite evidently to make sure that they didn't entertain the possibility of NATO membership in case these newly independent countries raised it. And, during the Clinton administration, Scowcroft, unlike Cheney, opposed NATO enlargement.

44. For more on these predictions, see chapter 4 in this book.

45. Some might even say with excessive equanimity, but certainly we are better off, because the new members of NATO in Central and Eastern Europe are not reacting with panic to the emergence of a Russian hard line.

4. THE STRANGE CAREER OF THE 1992 DEFENSE PLANNING GUIDANCE

1. "Frontline: The War behind Closed Doors," http:/www.pbs.org/wgbh/pages/front line/Iraq/.

2. Nicholas Lemann, "Letter from Washington: The Next World Order. The Bush Administration May Have a Brand-New Doctrine of Power," *New Yorker*, 1 April 2002; Frances Fitzgerald, "George Bush and the World," *New York Review of Books* 49, no. 14 (26 September 2002).

3. Eugene Jarecki, *The American Way of War: Guided Missiles, Misguided Men, and a Republic in Peril* (New York: Free Press, 2008), 12; Joan Hoff, *A Faustian Foreign Policy from Woodrow Wilson to George W. Bush: Dreams of Perfectibility* (New York: Cambridge

University Press, 2007), 137–38. The argument that the neoconservatives were seized by anger at the failure to overthrow Saddam at the end of the Gulf War is echoed in French polemics about the end of the Cold War; see Daniel Vernet, *1989–2009: Les tribulations de la liberté* (Paris: Buchet/Chastel, 2009), 55. The issue of whether or not the Gulf War's end was a long-term strategic failure is a subject that goes beyond the scope of this chapter, but I do not recall anyone suggesting at the time that it was a motivation for those involved in the DPG exercise. Michael Lind, *The American Way of Strategy: U.S. Foreign Policy and the American Way of Life* (New York: Oxford University Press, 2006), 128–29; Francis Fukuyama, "Soft Talk, Big Stick," in *To Lead the World: American Strategy after the Bush Doctrine*, ed. Melvyn P. Leffler and Jeffrey W. Legro (New York: Oxford University Press, 2008), 220; see also Francis Fukuyama, "The Beginning of Foreign Policy," *New Republic* (17–24 August 1992).

4. Several of the key documents (but not all) were declassified in redacted form in December 2007. They are available at the National Security Archive website: National Security Archive, "The Nuclear Vault: The Making of the Cheney Regional Defense Strategy, 1991–1992," http://www.gwu.edu/~nsarchiv/nukevault/ebb245/index.htm. The editorial commentary is hardly sympathetic to the authors of the DPG but does note that the word "pre-empt" does not appear in the document.

5. Walter LaFeber, *America, Russia, and the Cold War, 1945–2006*, tenth edition (New York: McGraw-Hill, 2008), 103; Robert R. Bowie and Richard Immerman, *Waging Peace: How Eisenhower Shaped an Enduring Cold War Strategy* (New York: Oxford University Press, 1998), 22; the classic study of NSC-68 is Paul Y. Hammond, "NSC-68: Prologue to Rearmament," in *Strategy, Politics and Defense Budgets*, ed. Warner R. Schilling, Paul Y. Hammond, and Glenn H. Snyder (New York: Columbia University Press, 1962), 267–78; see also Samuel Huntington, *The Common Defense: Strategic Programs in National Politics* (New York: Columbia University Press, 1961), 47–64; John Lewis Gaddis, *Strategies of Containment: A Critical Appraisal of Postwar American National Security Policy* (New York: Oxford University Press, 1982), 88–126. Gaddis is quite critical of NSC-68, which he believes "provided less than adequate guidance as to how objectives and capabilities were to be combined to produce coherent strategy," 106. The best, and most balanced, short treatment is Melvyn P. Leffler, *A Preponderance of Power: National Security, the Truman Administration, and the Cold War* (Stanford: Stanford University Press, 1992), 355–60; for Solarium, see Bowie and Immerman, *Waging Peace;* for the American strategic synthesis, see the outstanding study by Aaron L. Friedberg, *In The Shadow of the Garrison State: America's Anti-Statism and Its Cold War Grand Strategy* (Princeton: Princeton University Press, 2000), 62–81 and 107–15; for Nixon and Kissinger's "grand design," see George F. Herring, *From Colony to Superpower: U.S. Foreign Relations since 1776* (New York: Oxford University Press, 2008), 770–79.

6. Although Gellman reported, later in the spring, the final draft repudiated important elements of the leaked February 18 draft. As I suggest below, a careful reading of the documents does not support such a conclusion. To be fair to Gellman, it is not clear that he had access to later drafts.

7. National Security Archive, "The Nuclear Vault: The Making of the Cheney Regional Defense Strategy, 1991–1992," Document 1.

8. Ibid.; George H. W. Bush and Brent Scowcroft, *A World Transformed* (New York: Vintage Books, 1998), 302–22.

9. George H. W. Bush, "Remarks at the Aspen Institute Symposium in Aspen, Colorado," 2 August 1990, http://bushlibrary.tamu.edu/research/public_papers.php?id=21288&year=1990&month=8.

10. James J. Tritten, "America Promises to Come Back: The President's New National Security Strategy," *Security Studies* 1, no. 2 (1991): 173–234, quotations 174–75.

11. Federation of American Scientists, "National Security Strategy of the United States, August 1991," http://www.fas.org/man/docs/918015-nss.htm; the statement on the NSS was made in a private interview with a Bush 41 administration NSC Official, Washington, D.C., 19 September 2009. In *A World Transformed,* Bush and Scowcroft write about the opportunity for the United States to reshape the world, but they do not suggest a strategy or mention the Aspen speech. Nor do they mention the flap over the DPG. See Bush and Scowcroft, *A World Transformed,* 564–66. For Zoellick's views, see chapter 2 in this book.

12. National Security Archive, "The Nuclear Vault: The Making of the Cheney Regional Defense Strategy, 1991–1992," Document 1; for the importance of the revolution in military affairs, see Andrew F. Krepinevich Jr., *The Military-Technical Revolution: A Preliminary Assessment* (Washington, D.C.: Center for Strategic and Budgetary Assessments, 2002); Michael Vickers and Robert C. Martinage, *The Revolution in War* (Washington, D.C.: Center for Strategic and Budgetary Assessments, 2004).

13. National Security Archive, "The Nuclear Vault: The Making of the Cheney Regional Defense Strategy, 1991–1992," Documents 2 and 3.

14. The point that the document was Cheney's is made in Adrian Wooldridge and John Micklethwait, *The Right Nation: Conservative Power in America* (New York: Penguin Press, 2004), 211.

15. National Security Archive, "The Nuclear Vault: The Making of the Cheney Regional Defense Strategy, 1991–1992," Documents 2 and 3.

16. Ibid., Documents 4, 6a, and 6b.

17. Ibid., Documents 8 and 12.

18. James A. Baker III, with Thomas M. DeFrank, *The Politics of Diplomacy: Revolution, War, & Peace, 1989–92* (New York: G. P. Putnam's Sons, 1995), 560.

19. David Callahan, *Between Two Worlds: Realism, Idealism, and American Foreign Policy after the Cold War* (New York: Harper Collins, 1994), 90–94; for studies that discuss the issues connected with the danger of renationalization of defense in Europe and Japan, see Jan Willem Honig, "The 'Renationalization' of Western European Defense," *Security Studies* 2, no. 1 (1992): 122–138, and Peter Liberman, "Ties That Bind: Will Germany and Japan Rely Too Much on the United States?," *Security Studies* 10, no. 2 (2000): 98–138.

20. James Mann, *The Rise of the Vulcans: The History of Bush's War Cabinet* (New York: Viking, 2004), 213–15, 199; the Tony Lake speech at Johns Hopkins School of Advanced International Studies can be found at www.mtholyoke.edu/acad/intrel/lakedoc.html. Other accounts that argue that the DPG underpinned U.S. policy throughout the decade are Christopher Layne, "From Preponderance to Offshore Balancing: America's Future Grand Strategy," *International Security* 22, no. 1 (Summer 1997): 86–124; William C. Wohlforth, "The Stability of a Unipolar World," *International Security* 24, no. 1 (Summer 1999): 5–41; Melvyn P. Leffler, "Dreams of Freedom, Temptations of Power," in *The Fall of the Berlin Wall: The Revolutionary Legacy of 1989,* ed. Jeffrey A. Engel (New York: Oxford University Press, 2009), 132–69.

21. Derek Chollet and James Goldgeier, *America between The Wars: From 11/9 to 9/11, The Misunderstood Years between the Fall of the Berlin Wall and the Start of the War on Terror* (New York: Public Affairs Press, 2008), 43–47, the Scowcroft quote is at 45; National Security Archive, "The Nuclear Vault: The Making of the Cheney Regional Defense Strategy, 1991–1992," Document 12.

22. Chollet and Goldgeier, *America between the Wars,* 46; Stefan Halper and Jonathan Clarke, *America Alone: The Neo-Conservatives and Global Order* (New York: Cambridge University Press, 2004), 145–46. Michael Lind makes a similar argument on "coercive nonproliferation" in Lind, *American Way of Strategy,* 158–59.

23. Paul Wolfowitz, "Remembering the Future," *National Interest* 59 (Spring 2000).

24. National Security Archive, "The Nuclear Vault: The Making of the Cheney Regional Defense Strategy, 1991–1992," Document 2; Charles Krauthammer, "The Unipolar Mo-

ment," *Foreign Affairs* 70, no. 1 (1991); Samuel P. Huntington, "Why International Primacy Matters," *International Security* 17, no. 4 (Spring 1993): 83.

25. Jack Snyder, "Averting Anarchy in the New Europe," *International Security* 14, no. 4 (Spring 1990); John Mearsheimer, "Back to the Future: Instability in Europe after the Cold War," *International Security* 15, no. 1 (Summer 1990); Stephen Van Evera, "Primed for Peace: Europe after the Cold War," *International Security* 15, no. 3 (Winter 1990–91); Charles A. Kupchan and Clifford A. Kupchan, "Concerts, Collective Security, and the Future of Europe," *International Security* 16, no. 1 (Summer 1991); Christopher Layne, "The Unipolar Illusion: Why New Great Powers Will Rise," *International Security* 17, no. 4 (Spring 1993); Kenneth N. Waltz, "The Emerging Structure of International Politics," *International Security* 18, no. 2 (Autumn 1993). For a more thorough review of the academic world's poor record in predicting the post–Cold War international system, see William C. Wohlforth's excellent chapter in this book.

26. Huntington, "Why International Primacy Matters?" stresses the continuity of the themes in the DPG and the Clinton administration's "democratic realism;" Vernet, *1989–2009*, 163; Mann, *Rise of the Vulcans*, 199; Herring, *From Colony to Superpower*, 922.

27. Peter Rodman, *Presidential Command: Power, Leadership, and the Making of Foreign Policy from Richard Nixon to George W. Bush* (New York: Alfred A. Knopf, 2009); Andrew F. Krepinevich and Barry D. Watts, *Regaining Strategic Competence* (Washington, D.C.: Center for Strategic and Budgetary Assessments, 2009); Nicholas Thompson, *The Hawk and the Dove: Paul Nitze, George Kennan, and the History of the Cold War* (New York: Henry Holt, 2009), 111–18; Leffler, *Preponderance of Power*, 355–60.

28. The general role of ideas in the elaboration of great power strategies is treated well in Jeffrey W. Legro, *Rethinking the World: Great Power Strategies and International Order* (Ithaca: Cornell University Press, 2005); Mark Haas, "The United States and the End of the Cold War: Reactions to Shifts in Soviet Power, Policies, or Domestic Politics?" *International Organization* 61 (Winter 2007): 145–79.

29. Richard Betts, "Is Strategy an Illusion?" *International Security* 25, no. 2 (Fall 2000): 5–50.

5. A CRISIS OF OPPORTUNITY

1. White House, *A National Security Strategy of Engagement and Enlargement* (February 1996), http://www.fas.org/spp/military/dcops/national/1996stra.htm.

2. In the early 1990s, Japan, not China, appeared to be the big problem case in Asia, because of its economic success, then barely starting to falter. Whatever issues there were with China were expected to be about trade and human rights, not security.

3. *1996 National Security Strategy.*

4. Bill Clinton, *My Life* (New York: Vintage, 2005), 502.

5. *1996 National Security Strategy.*

6. Talbott writes that Clinton told him, just before the inauguration, that "what was happening in Russia . . . was 'the biggest and toughest thing out there. . . . There is stuff starting—stuff that's new. Figuring out what it is, how we work with it, how we keep it moving in the right direction: that's what we've got to do.'" Strobe Talbott, *The Russia Hand* (New York: Random House, 2003), 42.

7. Ibid.

8. Ibid., 52.

9. Clinton, *My Life*, 504.

10. "Clinton would build on what he regarded as Bush's good work, not only in arms control, but across the board." Talbott, *The Russia Hand*, 34.

11. "Defense Strategy for the 1990s: The Regional Defense Strategy," Department of Defense (20 January 1993), 20. The statement went on to say that "a democratic partnership with Russia, Ukraine, and the other new states would be the best possible outcome."

Ibid., 21. Many Bush administration statements could be cited to describe its successor's approach. The principal difference is that the Bush line was more explicit about "the possibility that undemocratic regimes could emerge in some of the new states and seek to remilitarize their policies and societies" and the corresponding need to plan for "timely and realistic responses to unanticipated reversals in our relations." Ibid., 21, 13. But even this aspect found some echo in Clinton-era statements. For example, the 1993 Defense Department "Bottom Up Review" referred to the need to "hedge against the possibility that a future adversary might one day confront us with a larger-than-expected threat." DOD, *Report on the Bottom-Up Review* (October 1993), http://fas.org/man/docs/bur/index.html.

12. Talbott, *The Russia Hand*, 34, 46, 51.

13. The Clinton administration's justification for continued U.S. support for Russian reform focused heavily on the relationship between Russia's "historic" economic transformation and U.S. interests. See the *1996 National Security Strategy*.

14. Regarding Yeltsin's personal behavior, Talbott writes that "what we [his Russia advisers] found appalling in Yeltsin's conduct Clinton found amusing." Talbott, *The Russia Hand*, 184.

15. The Bush administration had been careful—if discreet—to avoid giving Russia any assurance against former satellites joining NATO, but it had not had to face whether, or on what terms, any new allies would actually be accepted into the alliance.

16. There were, of course, many in the United States who were, for a variety of reasons, hostile to the idea that it was even, in principle, desirable to center U.S. policy on building a partnership with Russia. Other than NATO enlargement, the public did not have much interest in the Clinton administration's policies toward Russia.

17. Talbott, *The Russia Hand*, 99.

18. "A National Security Strategy of Engagement and Enlargement," White House (February 1996), http://fas.org/spp/military/docops/national/1996strat.htm (quoted language in final paragraph).

19. Talbott, *The Russia Hand*, 225.

20. Ibid., 206.

21. Quoted in Talbott, *The Russia Hand*, 371.

6. U.S. STRATEGIC PLANNING IN 2001–02

1. Condoleezza Rice, "Rethinking the National Interest," *Foreign Affairs* 87, no. 4 (July–August 2008).

2. Michael Mandelbaum, "Foreign Policy as Social Work," *Foreign Affairs* 75, no. 1 (January–February 1996): 16–32. On Bush's focus on domestic affairs, see also Karen DeYoung, *Soldier* (New York: Knopf, 2006), 298–99.

3. Transcript of the Second Gore-Bush Presidential Debate, Commission on Presidential Debates (11 October 2000), http://www.debates.org/pages/trans2000b_p.html.

4. For example, James Mann's claim that the United States sought global dominance along the lines of the 1992 Defense Policy Guidance is highly suspect. For Mann's view, see James Mann, *Rise of the Vulcans* (New York: Viking, 2004), 199; for a persuasive rejoinder, see chapter 4 in this book.

5. See Richard Berke, "A Safe Pick Is Revealing," *New York Times*, 26 July 2000, A1; Editorial, "Dick Cheney's Political Resume," *New York Times*, 26 July 2000, A22. The most useful books on Cheney, offering contrasting perspectives, are Barton Gellman, *Angler* (New York: Penguin, 2008), and Stephen Hayes, *Cheney* (New York: HarperCollins, 2007). Even in June 2002, Cheney's former colleague Brent Scowcroft thought that the vice president was "not ideological, in my mind. He's been very conservative, but I never had any trouble with him. I think the problem [in the current Bush administration] is at the second echelons." Mann, *Rise of the Vulcans*, 170.

6. "President Bush's defining private characteristic is discipline." Michael Gerson, *Heroic Conservatism* (New York: HarperOne, 2007), 80.

7. See the campaign working papers drafted by Rice and Stephen Hadley and sent to Powell in May 2000, summarized and quoted in DeYoung, *Soldier,* 290.

8. Christopher Meyer, recounting his December 2000 meetings with Rice and Karl Rove, in testimony to the British government's Iraq Inquiry (chaired by Sir John Chilcot), (hereinafter referred to as the *Iraq Inquiry*), Meyer transcript, 4–5. Testifying under oath, these witnesses knew the Inquiry had wide access to the contemporary records to check their testimony. The Inquiry's evidence is posted online at http://www.iraqinquiry.org.uk/transcripts.aspx.

9. Editorial, "A National Humiliation," *Weekly Standard,* 16–23 April 2001, 11.

10. DeYoung, *Soldier,* 335–37; Bradley Graham, *By His Own Rules* (New York: Public Affairs, 2009), 248–50.

11. A virtual memoir/oral history of O'Neill's experience is Ron Suskind, *The Price of Loyalty* (New York: Simon and Schuster, 2004).

12. "Transcript of Bush Speech at World Bank," (17 July 2001), http://www.presidency.ucsb.edu/ws/index.php?pid=73621&st=&st1=.

13. Draft "National Security Strategy," 23 July 2001, unclassified but apparently produced by the NSC staff, given to me at the time and available in a set of my papers deposited at the University of Virginia, accessible online at http://faculty.virginia.edu/zelikow/documents/nationalsecuritypolicy.pdf (hereinafter referred to as Zelikow Papers). The unclassified document has no authorial markings and I can no longer remember who worked on this. I may have helped. Rice appears to have directly drafted much of it; certainly the whole draft bears the stamp of her thought and style.

14. See Strobe Talbott, *The Russia Hand* (New York: Random House, 2002), 155; Taylor Branch, *The Clinton Tapes* (New York: Simon and Schuster, 2009), 235.

15. Draft "National Security Strategy," 23 July 2001, in Zelikow Papers (emphasis added).

16. For more examples of this casting about, soliciting ideas for a major presidential address, see the kind of ideas being discussed in Zelikow paper for Rice, "Themes for General Foreign Policy Address," 27 August 2001, with an annex, "Critique of International Law," in Zelikow Papers. The theme is how to adapt best to unprecedented global forces. The concept emphasizes loose international frameworks around core principles that empower/encourage local experiments and adaptation to these challenging forces.

17. Morton Abramowitz, "So Quiet at the Top," *Washington Post,* 11 September 2001, A27. See also the pungent description in *Iraq Inquiry,* Meyer transcript, 17–18.

18. Condoleezza Rice, "Campaign 2000: Promoting the National Interest," *Foreign Affairs* 79, no. 1 (January–February 2000).

19. See *9/11 Commission Report* (New York: Norton, 2004), 14–46; see also John Farmer, *The Ground Truth* (New York: Riverhead, 2009).

20. Bob Woodward, *Bush at War* (New York: Simon and Schuster, 2002), 17.

21. Hayes, *Cheney,* 351; Woodward, *Bush at War,* 73.

22. *9/11 Commission Report,* 194, 208, and 332.

23. For the high-level view, see George Tenet with Bill Harlow, *At the Center of the Storm* (New York: HarperCollins, 2007), 207–27; Woodward, *Bush at War,* 143–94; all the CIA leaders of this campaign have published their accounts: Henry Crumpton, "Intelligence and War: Afghanistan 2001–2002," *Transforming U.S. Intelligence,* ed. Jennifer Sims and Burton Gerber (Washington, D.C.: Georgetown University Press, 2005), 162–79, quotation on 168; Gary Schroen, *First In* (New York: Random House, 2005); and Gary Berntsen and Ralph Pezzullo, *Jawbreaker* (New York: Three Rivers Press, 2006).

24. R. W. Apple Jr., "A Military Quagmire Remembered: Afghanistan as Vietnam," *New York Times,* 31 October 2001, B1.

25. A balanced analysis finding that a larger U.S. operation had a decent chance of catching bin Laden, though it would have been risky and costly, is Peter John Paul Krause, "The Last Good Chance: A Reassessment of U.S. Operations at Tora Bora," *Security Studies* 17, no. 4 (October 2008): 644–84. Under Secretary of Defense for Policy Douglas Feith emphasized Afghan forces as the key instrument for fighting al Qaeda. See Feith to Rumsfeld, "Afghanistan Strategy," 11 October 2001, available among papers posted by Douglas Feith at his book's website, http://www.waranddecision.com, hereinafter cited as Feith Papers.

26. As a sign of the attention to new dangers, Bush announced in May 2001 that Cheney would take charge of the task force to work on domestic preparedness for a large attack. For more abstract warnings of what might happen, see, for example, the report of a group of ex-policymakers summarized in Ashton Carter, John Deutch, and Philip Zelikow, "Catastrophic Terrorism," *Foreign Affairs* 77, no. 6 (November–December 1998): 80–94; also see the work of the three commissions that began issuing reports in 2000 and 2001 (Hart-Rudman, Bremer, Gilmore); congressional activity is summarized in *9/11 Commission Report*, 479, notes 113 and 114. On the "Pearl Harbor" diary entry, see Robert Draper, *Dead Certain* (New York: Free Press, 2007), 147.

27. See Draper, *Dead Certain*, 145; Hayes, *Cheney*, 346, 358. See also the personal sense of responsibility Tenet describes in *At the Center of the Storm*, 171–174.

28. Eric Edelman was with Cheney that day and has recounted his memory of this episode to me. Rice has also discussed it with me.

29. See also Rice's comments on Cheney's near-obsessive attention to the mass of intelligence reports in Hayes, *Cheney*, 356, 358.

30. One of the main CIA officials responsible for this work at the time has now published a monograph detailing the grounds for this (ongoing) concern. Rolf Mowatt-Larssen, "Al Qaeda Weapons of Mass Destruction Threat: Hype or Reality?" Harvard University Belfer Center, January 2010.

31. The analyst is quoted in Tenet, *At the Center of the Storm*, 342, also see 229–80. On how the daily alarms affected Bush and Rice, see also Elizabeth Bumiller, *Condoleezza Rice: An American Life* (New York: Random House, 2007), 167–69; Ron Suskind, *The One Percent Solution* (New York: Simon and Schuster, 2006).

32. See the seven sets of issues summarized in the *9/11 Commission Report*, 326–27; also see Steven Brill, *After* (New York: Simon and Schuster, 2003).

33. Woodward, *Bush at War*, 74–91; see also the drier account, informed by some documentary evidence, in *9/11 Commission Report*, 334–36; for more evidence on what Bush and his aides were telling Blair and his aides about Iraq before 9/11 and immediately afterward, see *Iraq Inquiry*, John Sawers transcript, 11, 17; Jonathan Powell transcript, 14–16; David Manning transcript, 8–9; and Peter Ricketts transcript, 24.

34. Rumsfeld to DoD leadership, "Strategic Guidance for the Campaign Against Terrorism," 3 October 2001, 10, 14, Feith Papers; also see Graham, *By His Own Rules*, 301; for Tenet's worries, see Tenet, *At the Center of the Storm*, 311–14.

35. One of these scenarios, an India-Pakistan war, almost materialized a month later, after Pakistani-trained terrorists attacked India's Parliament. For the scenarios and accompanying memoranda, see Zelikow to Rice and Hadley, "Forward Planning: General Observations," 10 November 2001, Zelikow Papers.

36. The photographs by Annie Leibovitz were taken in December 2001 and were published in the *Vanity Fair* issue of February 2002. On Powell's sense of renewed team unity, see DeYoung, *Soldier*, 364.

37. Gerson, *Heroic Conservatism*, 176, 81; Draper, *Dead Certain*, xii.

38. A relatively early and perceptive academic treatment of this point was Melvyn Leffler, "9/11 and American Foreign Policy," *Diplomatic History* 29, no. 3 (June 2005): 395–413.

39. Gellman, *Angler*, 153.

40. Department of Homeland Security History Office, "Brief Documentary History of the Department of Homeland Security 2001–2008," 5, http://www.dhs.gov/xlibrary/assets/brief_documentary_history_of_dhs_2001_2008.pdf; also see Brill, *After*.

41. The program management and congressional issues that would confront Ridge in his job heading the newly created White House Office of Homeland Security are discussed, along with some other choices, in Zelikow to Ridge, "Developing the Office of Homeland Security (or the Homeland Security Council): Six Topics to Consider," 2 October 2001, in Zelikow Papers. My summary of the March 2002 turn relies on the recollection of a key staffer at the time, Richard Falkenrath.

42. The seven were: "rule of law; limits on the power of the state; respect for women; private property; free speech; equal justice; and religious tolerance." These ideas appear to have been worked up in the White House, especially by Rice and Michael Gerson and their respective staffs. For my input, see "America's Vision for the Postwar World," 30 January 2002 and 4 February 2002, Zelikow Papers.

43. For the critiques of foreign aid, see, for example, Robert Klitgaard, *Tropical Gangsters* (New York: Basic Books, 1991); William Easterly, *The Elusive Limits of Growth* (Cambridge: MIT Press, 2002) and *The White Man's Burden* (New York: Penguin, 2006); and, perhaps most important at the time, World Bank, *Assessing Aid* (New York: Oxford University Press, 1998).

44. Treasury Secretary O'Neill was a key figure pushing forward the debt relief agenda. Suskind, *The Price of Loyalty*. Trade representative Robert Zoellick worked the Africa trade angle, seeking to amend and expand the Africa Growth and Opportunity Act, passed by Congress in 2000.

45. Bush explained his initiative as part of his war strategy, stressing the "nonnegotiable demands of human dignity." Bush address at Virginia Military Institute, Lexington, Virginia, 17 April 2002, in *Public Papers*, http://www.presidency.ucsb.edu/ws/index.php?pid=73000&st=&st1=. For the Millennium Challenge initiative and the new paradigm for aid, see Stephen Krasner, "Conclusion—Garbage Cans and Policy Streams: How Academic Research Might Affect Foreign Policy," *Power, the State, and Sovereignty* (London: Routledge, 2009), 265–68; Steven Radelet, *Challenging Foreign Aid* (Washington, D.C.: Center for Global Development, 2003), 1–18; Robrecht Renard, "The Cracks in the New Aid Paradigm," University of Antwerp Institute of Development Policy and Management Discussion Paper (January 2006), 4; Joshua Busby, "Bono Made Jesse Helms Cry: Jubilee 2000, Debt Relief, and Moral Action in International Politics," *International Studies Quarterly* 51 (2007): 247–75.

46. For Rice's role, see Bumiller, *Condoleezza Rice*, 219; on the development of PEPFAR, see John Dietrich, "The Politics of PEPFAR: The President's Emergency Plan for AIDS Relief," *Ethics and International Affairs* 21, no. 3 (Fall 2007): 277–92; see also Gerson, *Heroic Conservatism*, 1–4, 25; for an early evaluation of PEPFAR by the Institute of Medicine, see Jaime Sepúlveda, et al., eds., *PEPFAR Implementation: Progress and Promise* (Washington, D.C.: National Academies Press, 2007).

47. Carol Lancaster, *George Bush's Foreign Aid* (Washington, D.C.: Center for Global Development, 2008), 4–5; Radelet, *Challenging Foreign Aid*, 13. Using Organization for Economic Cooperation and Development standardized data for overseas development assistance (ODA) and for converting the numbers to constant dollars, my calculations are that by 2008, Bush's last year in office, annual U.S. ODA had doubled since 2001.

48. For the 2002 State of the Union message and for reactions to it, see Matthew Scully, "Present at the Creation," *Atlantic*, September 2007, http://www.theatlantic.com/doc/print/200709/michael-gerson; Draper, *Dead Certain*, 168–169; Bumiller, *Condoleezza Rice*, 173–75.

49. For Rice's view, see Rice, "Promoting the National Interest"; on the draft national security language, see below; for Cheney, see Kenneth Pollack, *The Threatening Storm* (New York: Random House, 2002), 105.

50. *Iraq Inquiry,* Meyer transcript, 18.

51. Rumsfeld to Rice, with copies to Cheney and Powell, "Iraq," 27 July 2001, Feith Papers.

52. *Iraq Inquiry,* Powell transcript, 15.

53. Manning to Prime Minister Blair, "Your Trip to the US," 14 March 2002, http://downingstreetmemo.com/memos.html; also see *Iraq Inquiry,* Manning transcript, 9–16; Powell transcript, 17; Tony Blair transcript, 42–51. On the other hand, CIA director Tenet has said that he does not recall a systematic discussion of whether to go to war against Iraq. See Tenet, *At the Center of the Storm,* 305, 309.

54. Al Gore, "A Commentary on the War against Terror: Our Larger Tasks," address to the Council on Foreign Relations, 12 February 2002, http://www.cfr.org/publication/4343/commentary_on_the_war_against_terror.html; see also Adam Nagourney, "A Nation Challenged: The Democrat—Gore, Championing Bush, Calls for a 'Final Reckoning' with Iraq," *New York Times,* 13 February 2002, A18.

55. Tenet, however, also believes there were other motives besides WMD. See Tenet, *At the Center of the Storm,* 321. He sees other agendas at work for some of Cheney's staffers, such as Libby, and for Rumsfeld's subordinates, such as Paul Wolfowitz and Feith. But the available evidence does not show that wider hopes to remake the Middle East, for example, motivated either Cheney or Rumsfeld. For Cheney, see Hayes, *Cheney,* 393; Gellman, *Angler,* 215–22, 226–27, 239, 249–52; also his January 2009 interview with Jim Lehrer on the PBS Newshour, http://www.pbs.org/newshour/bb/politics/jan-june09/cheney_01–14.html; for Rumsfeld, see Graham, *By His Own Rules,* 336. In March 2002 Wolfowitz acknowledged to the British ambassador that his position was slightly different from others in the administration. He said the others, unlike him, were focused "on Saddam's capacity to develop weapons of mass destruction." Meyer to Manning, "Iraq and Afghanistan: Conversation with Wolfowitz," 18 March 2002, http://downingstreetmemo.com/memos.html.

56. Rice address, SAIS at Johns Hopkins, Washington, D.C., 29 April 2002, http://usinfo.org/wf-archive/2002/020502/epf407.htm.

57. The quote is from the memoir of the Bush administration's Afghan reconstruction envoy, James Dobbins, in *After the Taliban* (Washington, D.C.: Potomac Books, 2008), 125; for his discussion of the revealing debates on Afghan nation-building in early 2002, see 117–44. See also Seth Jones, *In the Graveyard of Empires* (New York: Norton, 2009), 109–39, and the emphasis on relying on Afghan forces in a few declassified documents, such as the paper from Feith's office, "U.S. Role in the Gardez Situation," 6 May 2002, in Feith Papers.

58. On the war planning at this stage, see Bob Woodward, *Plan of Attack* (New York: Simon and Schuster, 2004), 66, 88, 102; Michael Gordon and Bernard Trainor, *Cobra II* (New York: Random House, 2006), 28; Douglas Feith, *War and Decision* (New York: Harper, 2008), 393. The lure of a covert action panacea for Iraq had been part of U.S. deliberations for years. It appears that the CIA finally persuaded the Bush administration of the bankruptcy of this approach in early January 2002. Instead, in February 2002, Bush authorized a broad set of CIA covert actions to support a possible invasion by U.S. armed forces. See Woodward, *Plan of Attack,* 72–74, 108; and the corroboration and comment in Charles Duelfer, *Hide and Seek* (New York: Public Affairs, 2009), 246–47.

59. See Micah Zenko, "Foregoing Limited Force: The George W. Bush Administration's Decision Not to Attack Ansar Al-Islam," *Journal of Strategic Studies* 32, no. 4 (August 2009): 615–49, quotation on 639.

60. Rice asked me to draft a national security strategy, taking into account a prior State drafting effort. My initial draft was submitted to her and Hadley on 5 March 2002. There were a series of drafts reflecting their successive comments, and from other individual officials that I consulted. The various drafts and suggestions can be reviewed and compared. See Zelikow Papers. I was a private citizen and volunteered my time; none of the drafts were classified. From July 2002 onward, the NSC staff took over the drafting. The later drafts were handled as government documents and kept exclusively in the government's custody until the final product was released in September 2002.

All the drafts from March into July 2002 are entitled "The Basic National Security Policy of the United States," not "National Security Strategy." That working title was inspired by Eisenhower's basic national security policy statement of 1953, NSC 162/2. Since this 2002 document was also to be a statement of basic policy, without detailed explanations of just how all these ends were to be achieved (strategies), the older nomenclature seemed more fitting. At the end, though, the White House changed the title back to the default phrase used in the statute.

61. This passage is in the drafts of June 24 and July 12, Zelikow Papers. Bumiller is too generous in attributing to me the authorship of the preemption language that appeared in the final strategy document. Bumiller, *Condoleezza Rice,* 193–94.

62. For an earlier discussion of this problem, see Philip Zelikow, "Offensive Military Options," in *New Nuclear Nations,* ed. Robert Blackwill and Albert Carnesale (New York: Council on Foreign Relations Press, 1993), 162–95.

63. White House, Office of the Press Secretary, "Interview of Senior Administration Official by David Sanger, New York Times," 12 June 2002. Rice later agreed that material from this interview could be used on the record. See David Sanger, "Bush to Formalize a Defense Policy of Hitting First," *New York Times,* 17 June 2002, A1.

64. Rice address at the Manhattan Institute, 1 October 2002, http://www.manhattan-institute.org/html/wl2002.htm. Rice's legal adviser, John Bellinger, helped prepare this address, as he had been the principal drafter of the "preemption" paragraphs that finally appeared in the strategy document itself.

7. QUESTING FOR MONSTERS TO DESTROY

1. Warner R. Schilling, "Surprise Attack, Death, and War," *Journal of Conflict Resolution* 9 (September 1965): 389.

2. For some assessments, see John Mueller, *Overblown: How Politicians and the Terrorism Industry Inflate National Security Threats, and Why We Believe Them* (New York: Free Press, 2006); Jane K. Cramer and A. Trevor Thrall, eds., *Threat Inflation: The Theory, Politics, and Psychology of Fear Mongering in the United States* (London: Routledge, 2009).

3. On this interpretation of the Cold War's end, see John Mueller, "What Was the Cold War About? Evidence from Its Ending," *Political Science Quarterly* 119 (Winter 2004–05): 609–31.

4. See John Mueller, *Capitalism, Democracy, and Ralph's Pretty Good Grocery* (Princeton: Princeton University Press, 1999).

5. See Jong Kun Choi, "Predictions of Tragedy vs. Tragedy of Predictions in Northeast Asian Security," *Korean Journal of Defense Analysis* 18 (Spring 2006): 7–33.

6. Historicus [George Allen Morgan], "Stalin on Revolution," *Foreign Affairs* 27 (January 1949): 198. On these issues, see particularly Frederic S. Burin, "The Communist Doctrine of the Inevitability of War," *American Political Science Review* 57 (June 1963): 337–41. See also John Mueller, *Retreat from Doomsday: The Obsolescence of Major War* (New York: Basic Books, 1989), 99–102; Robert Jervis, "Was the Cold War a Security Dilemma?" *Journal of Cold War Studies* 3 (Winter 2001): 59. On Stalin's caution, see also Melvyn P. Leffler,

A Preponderance of Power: National Security, the Truman Administration, and the Cold War (Stanford: Stanford University Press, 1992), 102, 510.

7. John Lewis Gaddis, *Strategies of Containment* (New York: Oxford University Press, 1982), 35, also 366–67. See also Leffler, *Preponderance,* 499.

8. R. James Woolsey Jr. Testimony before the Senate Intelligence Committee, 2 February 1993; see Douglas Jehl, "C.I.A. Nominee Wary of Budget Cuts," *New York Times,* 3 February 1993.

9. John Mueller, "War Has Almost Ceased to Exist: An Assessment," *Political Science Quarterly* 124 (Summer 2009): 297–321.

10. John Mueller, *The Remnants of War* (Ithaca: Cornell University Press, 2004), chap. 6.

11. On this creative process, see W. Seth Carus, *Defining "Weapons of Mass Destruction"* (Washington, D.C.: National Defense University Press, 2006); John Mueller, *Atomic Obsession: Nuclear Alarmism from Hiroshima to Al Qaeda* (New York: Oxford University Press, 2010), 11–13, 242 note 25.

12. For sources, see Mueller, *Atomic Obsession,* 133–34.

13. John E. Rielly, ed., *American Public Opinion and U.S. Foreign Policy, 1999* (Chicago: Chicago Council on Foreign Relations, 1999), 15.

14. Nikita Khrushchev, *Khrushchev Remembers* (Boston: Little, Brown, 1970), 367–68. William Stueck, *Rethinking the Korean War: A New Diplomatic and Strategic History* (Princeton: Princeton University Press, 2002), 70–75.

15. Stueck, *Rethinking the Korean War,* 73.

16. For an evaluation of the depths of the Soviets' "huge setback," see Vladislav Zubok and Constantine Pleshakov, *Inside the Kremlin's Cold War: From Stalin to Khrushchev* (Cambridge: Harvard University Press, 1996), 69–72.

17. Fawaz Gerges, *The Far Enemy: Why Jihad Went Global* (New York: Cambridge University Press, 2005), 27, 228, 233, also 270; Fawaz Gerges, "Word on the Street," *Democracyjournal.org* (Summer 2008): 71. See also Peter Bergen and Paul Cruickshank, "The Unraveling: The Jihadist Revolt against bin Laden," *New Republic,* 11 June 2008; Lawrence Wright, "The Rebellion Within," *New Yorker,* 2 June 2008.

18. Gerges, *Far Enemy,* 232, and, for a tally of policing activity, 318–19. See also Marc Lynch, "Al Qaeda's Media Strategies," *National Interest* (Spring 2006): 54–55; Marc Sageman, *Leaderless Jihad* (Philadelphia: University of Pennsylvania Press, 2008), 149.

19. Gerges, *Far Enemy,* 153; Marc Sageman, *Understanding Terror Networks* (Philadelphia: University of Pennsylvania Press, 2004), 47. On the generally counterproductive effects for terrorists of targeting civilians, see Max Abrahms, "Why Terrorism Does Not Work," *International Security* 31 (Fall 2006): 42–78; Andrew Mack, "Dying to Lose: Explaining the Decline in Global Terrorism," in *Human Security Brief 2007* (Vancouver, B.C.: Human Security Report Project, School for International Studies, Simon Fraser University, 2008), 8–21.

20. Mueller, *Atomic Obsession,* chap. 15.

21. David Callahan, *Dangerous Capabilities: Paul Nitze and the Cold War* (New York: HarperCollins, 1990), 136–37.

22. Quoted in Marshall D. Shulman, *Stalin's Foreign Policy Reappraised* (New York: Atheneum, 1963), 150.

23. Bernard Brodie, *War and Politics* (New York: Macmillan, 1973), 63. See also Fred Kaplan, *The Wizards of Armageddon* (New York: Simon and Schuster, 1983), 39, 81; Glenn D. Paige, *The Korean Decision, June 24–30, 1950* (New York: Free Press, 1968), 166, 171, 173; William Taubman, *Stalin's American Policy* (New York: Norton, 1982), 201–2.

24. Harry S Truman, *Years of Trial and Hope* (Garden City, N.Y.: Doubleday, 1956), 333.

25. Marc Trachtenberg, *History and Strategy* (Princeton: Princeton University Press, 1991), 112–13.

26. Callahan, *Dangerous Capabilities*, 120–23. See also Paige, *Korean Decision*, 137, 174; Taubman, *Stalin's American Policy*, 214; Jervis, "Was the Cold War a Security Dilemma?" 48; Stueck, *Rethinking the Korean War*, 82.

27. On Korea as an important turning point, see also John Lewis Gaddis, "Was the Truman Doctrine a Real Turning Point?" *Foreign Affairs* 52, no. 2 (January 1974): 386–401; Ernest R. May, "The Cold War," in *The Making of America's Soviet Policy*, ed. Joseph S. Nye Jr. (New Haven: Yale University Press, 1984), 209–30; Trachtenberg, *History and Strategy*, 107–15; and especially Robert Jervis, "The Impact of the Korean War on the Cold War," *Journal of Conflict Resolution* 24 (December 1980): 563–92.

28. Bernard Brodie, *Escalation and the Nuclear Option* (Princeton: Princeton University Press, 1966), 71–72; see also Kaplan, *Wizards*, 339.

29. Jervis, "Was the Cold War a Security Dilemma?" 59.

30. Robert H. Johnson, *Improbable Dangers: U.S. Conceptions of Threat in the Cold War and After* (New York: St. Martin's, 1994), 29, 78. On exaggerations of Soviet military capabilities, see Richard Rhodes, *Arsenals of Folly: The Making of the Nuclear Arms Race* (New York: Knopf, 2007); Andrew Cockburn, *The Threat: Inside the Soviet Military Machine* (New York: Random House, 1983). See also Mueller, *Atomic Obsession*, 63–69.

31. For rare, perhaps unique, exceptions, see John Mueller, "Harbinger or Aberration? A 9/11 Provocation," *National Interest* (Fall 2002): 45–50; Russell Seitz, "Weaker Than We Think," *American Conservative* (6 December 2004).

32. "Dr. Condoleezza Rice Discusses President's National Security Strategy," Washington, D.C.: Office of the Press Secretary Press Release, White House (1 October 2002), http://www.hsdl.org/?view&doc=80320&coll=public.

33. Speech at the National Cathedral, 14 September 2001, http://www.opm.gov/guidance/09-14-01gwb.htm. This preposterous goal was blandly accepted by press and public alike, although the *New Orleans Times-Picayune* did modestly suggest that "perhaps the President over-promised." Mueller, *Overblown*, 216, note.

34. Shane Harris and Stuart Taylor Jr., "Homeland Security Chief Looks Back, and Forward," governmentexecutive.com, 17 March 2008.

35. Brian Michael Jenkins, *Will Terrorists Go Nuclear?* (Amherst, N.Y.: Prometheus, 2008), 250–51.

36. Ammunition: James Fallows, "Why Iraq Has No Army," *Atlantic* (December 2005): 72. Heavy weapons: Maggie O'Kane, "Saddam Wields Terror—and Feigns Respect," *Guardian*, 25 November 1998. See also Michael R. Gordon and Bernard E. Trainor, *Cobra II: The Inside Story of the Invasion and Occupation of Iraq* (New York: Pantheon, 2006), 55–66, 505.

37. David Holloway, *Stalin and the Bomb: The Soviet Union and Atomic Energy, 1939–1956* (New Haven: Yale University Press, 1994), 138–44, 222, 283, 366; Mueller, *Atomic Obsession*, 49–50.

38. For example, a group of German émigré writers living in the United States and Mexico were deemed a potential danger to the republic and were under FBI surveillance for decades. None was ever found to pose much of a subversive threat, and what impresses Alexander Stephan is the essential absurdity of the situation: the "high efficiency and gross overkill" as hundreds of agents were paid to intercept and catalogue communications, to endlessly record goings and comings, and to sift enterprisingly through trash bins at taxpayers' expense. Alexander Stephan, *"Communazis": FBI Surveillance of German Emigré Writers* (New Haven: Yale University Press, 2000), xii.

39. Thus, in a best-selling memoir, FBI informant Herbert Philbrick at no point documents a single instance of Communist violence or planned violence—although violence became a central focus of nearly every episode when his story was transmuted into a popular television series. Herbert A. Philbrick, *I Led Three Lives: Citizen, "Communist," Counterspy* (New York: Grosset and Dunlap, 1952).

40. Bill Gertz, "5,000 in U.S. Suspected of Ties to Al Qaeda; Groups Nationwide under Surveillance," *Washington Times*, 11 July 2002, A1.

41. Brian Ross, "Secret FBI Report Questions Al Qaeda Capabilities: No 'True' Al Qaeda Sleeper Agents Have Been Found in U.S.," *ABC News* (9 March 2005); Michael Isikoff and Mark Hosenball, "The Flip Side of the NIE," www.newsweek.com, 15 August 2007. Bill Gertz, "Al Qaeda Seen in Search of Nukes: Defense Official Warns U.S. Still Group's Target," *Washington Times*, 26 July 2007, 4.

42. Jervis, "Was the Cold War a Security Dilemma?" 36.

43. John Lewis Gaddis, *We Now Know: Rethinking Cold War History* (New York: Oxford University Press, 1997), 221. See also Mueller, *Overblown*, 77–78. Eisenhower does seem to have grasped the fundamental reality that the Soviets had no interest whatever in a direct military confrontation and therefore that an ever-enlarged military was scarcely required to deter them. He never summoned the political courage to say this openly, however, choosing instead to flail at the "military-industrial complex" rather than at the faulty and underexamined premise that gave that complex its political potency.

44. The importance of this issue can be seen not only in its prominence in Kennan's 1947 article but in his notion that containment might have to be continued for "ten or fifteen years," a time frame very likely suggested by the fact that Stalin was nearing seventy when Kennan was formulating the policy: George F. Kennan, "The Sources of Soviet Conduct," *Foreign Affairs* 25 (July 1947): 576.

45. Kennan, "Sources," 580.

46. Cited from a tape of the original CSPAN telecast. Transcripts from the debate (in a slightly different translation) can be found at http://en.wikiquote.org/wiki/kitchen. Debate.

47. Gaddis, *Strategies of Containment*, 47.

48. George W. Breslauer, "Ideology and Learning in Soviet Third World Policy," *World Politics* 39 (April 1987): 436–37. Jervis, "Was the Cold War a Security Dilemma?" 50.

49. On the rising costs of the Soviet overseas empire at the time, see Charles Wolf Jr., K. C. Yeh, Edmund Brunner Jr., Aaron Gurwitz, and Marilee Lawrence, *The Costs of Soviet Empire* (Santa Monica, Calif.: Rand Corporation, 1983); Valerie Bunce, "The Empire Strikes Back: The Evolution of the Eastern Bloc from a Soviet Asset to a Soviet Liability," *International Organization* 39, no. 1 (Winter 1985): 1–46; Stephen Kotkin, "The Kiss of Debt: The East Goes Borrowing," *The Shock of the Global: The 1970s in Perspective*, ed. Niall Ferguson, Charles Maier, Erez Manela, and Daniel Sargent (Cambridge: Harvard University Press, 2010); for Soviet policy, also see Vladislav Zubok, *A Failed Empire: The Soviet Union in the Cold War from Stalin to Gorbachev* (Chapel Hill: University of North Carolina Press, 2008); Christopher M. Andrew, *The World Was Going Our Way* (New York: Basic Books, 2005).

50. On this process, see Mueller, "What Was the Cold War About?" See also Nigel Gould-Davies, "Rethinking the Role of Ideology in International Politics during the Cold War," *Journal of Cold War Studies* 1 (Winter 1999): 90–109. Jervis, "Was the Cold War a Security Dilemma?" 60. It does not follow, however, that economic and social travail would *necessarily* lead to a mellowing of ideology. Leaders, in this case Mikhail Gorbachev, had to *choose* that policy route. Faced with the same dilemmas, a conservative leader might have stuck to the faith while suffering gradual decline (like the Ottoman Empire) or might have adopted more modest reforms to maintain the essential quality of the system and the privileges of its well-entrenched elite. On this point, see also Myron Rush, "Fortune and Fate," *National Interest* (Spring 1993): 19–25; Archie Brown, *The Rise and Fall of Communism* (New York: Ecco, 2009), 486, 587–92.

8. THE ASSUMPTIONS DID IT

1. William Pfaff, "Mac Bundy Said He Was 'All Wrong,'" *New York Review of Books*, 10 June 2010, 61, citing Gordon M. Goldstein, *Lessons in Disaster: McGeorge Bundy and the Path to War in Vietnam* (New York: Times Books, 2008).

2. Clive Thompson, "Can Game Theory Predict When Iran Will Get the Bomb?" *New York Times Magazine*, 16 August 2009.

3. His theories have also foretold another Great American Depression in every decade going back at least to 1980; he was wrong for thirty years, appeared right in late 2008, but today he seems wrong again.

4. This tendency was perhaps most pronounced in John Lukacs's self-important *The End of the Twentieth Century and the End of the Modern Age* (Boston, Mass.: Houghton Mifflin Harcourt, 1993).

5. In the 1960s, Mao Tse-tung was asked to comment on the real meaning of the French Revolution. He responded that not enough time had yet passed to know.

6. I had written this section before listening to Virginia's David Waldron pose this question at a Princeton conference on October 10, 2009—and now I have appropriated it for myself, with apologies to David.

7. Didier Eribon, *Foucault 1926–1984* (New York: Mass Market, 1993), 19–20.

8. Dean Acheson, "An American Attitude toward Foreign Affairs," 28 November 1939, in Dean Acheson, *Morning and Noon: A Memoir* (Boston: Beacon Press, 1965), 267–75; see also Acheson's reflections on the speech, 216–17.

9. Bruce Cumings, *The Origins of the Korean War*, vol. 2, *The Roaring of the Cataract, 1947–1950* (Princeton: Princeton University Press, 1991), 57–58.

10. Robert Latham, *The Liberal Moment* (New York: Columbia University Press, 1997).

11. Bruce Cumings, "The End of the Seventy-Years' Crisis," *World Policy Journal* 7 (Spring 1991): 195–226.

12. Joseph Conrad, *The Secret Agent* (New York: Penguin Books, 1980), 8–9.

13. Gordon Prange, *At Dawn We Slept: The Untold Story of Pearl Harbor* (New York: Penguin Books, 1981), 539.

14. Quoted in Jonathan Power, "The Arm of the Terrorists," *Jordan Times*, 6 November 2009, http://www.jordantimes.com/?news=21352.

15. Eric Schmitt and James Dao, "U.S. Is Building Up Its Military Bases in Afghan Region," *New York Times*, 9 January 2002, A1.

16. For example, Reuters News Service, "War on Terrorism Spreads around the Globe," *New York Times*, 24 January 2002.

17. Clive Thompson, "Can Game Theory Predict When Iran Will Get the Bomb?" *New York Times Magazine*, 16 August 2009.

18. Bruce Bueno de Mesquita, David Newman, and Alvin Rabushka, *Forecasting Political Events: The Future of Hong Kong* (New Haven, Conn.: Yale University Press, 1988).

19. Naewoe Press, *North Korea: Uneasy, Shaky Kim Jong-il Regime* (Seoul: ROK Government, 1997), 143.

20. In the spring of 2009 I attended a number of conferences and meetings in Washington, and was pleased to hear yet again that the North was deeply embroiled in a "succession struggle" and might therefore "explode or implode."

21. See his "The Coming Collapse of North Korea," *Wall Street Journal*, 25 June 1990.

22. Robert A. Wampler introduced the collection with his essay, "North Korea's Collapse? The End is Near—Maybe" (26 October 2006). I am part of Dr. Wampler's declassification project at the National Security Archive, and appreciate his making these documents available to me. The CIA's 21 January 1998 report (about the 1997 conference) is entitled "Exploring the Implications of Alternative North Korean Endgames:

Results from a Discussion Panel on Continuing Coexistence between North and South Korea," which is mostly declassified except for some redacted names.

23. Nicholas Eberstadt, "Tear Down This Tyranny," *Weekly Standard,* 29 November 2004.

24. The best account of the knock-down, drag-out internal struggles is Mike Chinoy, *Meltdown: The Inside Story of the North Korean Nuclear Crisis* (New York: St. Martin's Press, 2008).

25. Friedrich Nietzsche, *Philosophy and Truth: Selections from Nietzsche's Notebooks of the Early 1870s,* ed. and trans. Daniel Breazeale (Atlantic Highlands, N.J.: Humanities Press, 1979), 81–91, quotation on 83.

9. FAULTY LEARNING AND FLAWED POLICIES IN AFGHANISTAN AND IRAQ

1. See, for instance, E. H. Carr's discussion in *The Twenty Years Crisis,* ed. Michael Cox (London: Palgrave Macmillan, 2001), 209–20.

2. This is not, of course, the same as saying that the overthrow of the existing regimes will have no long-term positive consequences at all. The chances for people in Iraq to have relatively stable societies sometime over the next decade are fairly good, and in Afghanistan the opportunities for different communities to choose their own fates will probably improve during the same period, if political compromises can be found.

3. From a Pakistani point of view, see Ahmed Rashid, *Descent into Chaos: The World's Most Unstable Region and the Threat to Global Security* (London: Penguin, 2009), 24–60 and 145–68, and Zahid Hussain, *Frontline Pakistan: The Struggle with Militant Islam* (New York: Columbia University Press, 2007), 89–101.

4. Kim Gamel, "AP IMPACT: Secret Tally Shows Violence Has Killed at Least 87,215 Iraqis since 2005," Associated Press newswire, 23 April 2009, http://abcnews.go.com/International/WireStory?id=7411522. For a good discussion of the impact the Iraq War had on operations in Afghanistan, see the U.S. Army's draft official history, Donald P. Wright et al., *A Different Kind of War: The United States Army in Operation ENDURING FREEDOM (OEF) October 2001–September 2005* (Ft. Leavenworth, Kan.: Combat Studies Institute Press, U.S. Army Combined Arms Center, 2009), 245–271, http://documents.nytimes.com/a-different-kind-of-war#p=255.

5. For discussion of some of these (mis)interpretations, see Melvyn P. Leffler and Odd Arne Westad, eds., *The Cambridge History of the Cold War,* 3 vols. (Cambridge: Cambridge University Press, 2010), especially vol. 3.

6. Wright et al., *A Different Kind of War,* draft version, http://documents.nytimes.com/a-different-kind-of-war#p=38.

7. Max Boot, "The New American Way of War," *Foreign Affairs* 82, no. 4 (2003): 41. For an overview of the reliance on military technology in Iraq, see Michael R. Gordon and Bernard E. Trainor, *Cobra II: The Inside Story of the Invasion and Occupation of Iraq* (New York: Vintage, 2007), 43–62.

8. For Reagan, see Bob Woodward and Don Oberdorfer, "State Dept. Acted to Block U.S.-Egypt Attack on Libya," *Washington Post,* 20 February 1987; for Clinton's usage, see the Iraq Liberation Act, passed by Congress on 31 October 1998, http://frwebgate.access.gpo.gov/cgi-bin/getdoc.cgi?dbname=105_cong_public_laws&docid=f:publ338.105.pdf.

9. Ron Suskind, "Faith, Certainty, and the Presidency of George W. Bush," *New York Times Magazine,* 17 October 2004.

10. Deputy Secretary Wolfowitz interview with the *New York Times,* 18 April 2002, http://www.defenselink.mil/transcripts/transcript.aspx?transcriptid=3409.

11. *Rebuilding America's Defenses: Strategy, Forces and Resources for a New Century.* A Report of the Project for the New American Century, September 2000, 76.

12. By early 2009 larger numbers of Afghans believed that the United States, NATO, or the Afghan government were responsible for the country's travails than those who blamed the Taliban. See Jon Cohen and Jennifer Agiesta, "Poll of Afghans Shows Drop in Support for U.S. Mission," *Washington Post,* 10 February 2009.

13. See the discussion of the effects of 1989 in Jeffrey Engel, ed., *The Fall of the Berlin Wall: The Revolutionary Legacy of 1989* (New York: Oxford University Press, 2009), esp. the chapter by Melvyn Leffler.

14. Rumsfeld to Shultz, 21 December 1983, http://www.gwu.edu/~nsarchiv/NSAEBB/NSAEBB82/iraq31.pdf.

15. Statement of Howard Teicher in *US vs. Cardoen et al.,* U.S. District Court, South Florida, 31 January 1995, http://www.gwu.edu/~nsarchiv/NSAEBB/NSAEBB82/iraq61.pdf.

16. Deputy Secretary Wolfowitz Briefing with Arab/Muslim Media, 25 April 2003, http://www.defense.gov/Transcripts/Transcript.aspx?TranscriptID=2507.

17. See chapter 1 in this book.

18. It is worth quoting Wolfowitz on how the situation appeared in the summer of 2003: "Does democracy mean that overnight countries are going to achieve what it took us two centuries and the British four centuries and we're very far from perfect? Of course not. But the Rumanians are so much better off today with an imperfect democracy than they were under the totalitarianism of Ceaucescu. And I feel absolutely certain the Iraqis will be better off, much better off five years from now than they were under that brutal, sadistic, abusive regime. To me it's almost beyond argument. My impression from talking to quite a large number of Arabs is that while they care about the Arab-Israeli issue and they care deeply if they live under a dictatorship, and unfortunately most of them do, that is the principal political complaint they have. And very often the complaint is you, the United States, either helped bring the dictatorship into power, or you support it today. I don't think Iraq is the only Arab country that is capable of democracy. You cited King Abdullah of Jordan. He's made some very bold statements that are just reported in the *Washington Post* today about the importance of democracy in Jordan. And he acknowledged that they have a long way to go, but that it is very important to move forward. And that what's happening in Iraq is part of that forward movement." Deputy Secretary Wolfowitz, interviewed by Jeffrey Goldberg, *New Yorker* Festival, 21 September 2003, http://www.defenselink.mil/transcripts/transcript.aspx?transcriptid=3172.

19. Odd Arne Westad, *The Global Cold War: Third World Interventions and the Making of Our Times* (Cambridge: Cambridge University Press, 2005).

20. Wilson quoted in Carr, *Twenty Years' Crisis,* 215.

21. G. John Ikenberry, "The Rise of China and the Future of the West," *Foreign Affairs* 87, no. 1 (2008): 23–37.

10. HOW DID THE EXPERTS DO?

1. See, for example, Jack Snyder, *Myths of Empire: Domestic Politics and Political Ambition* (Ithaca: Cornell University Press, 1991), 32–55; Jack Snyder, *From Voting to Violence: Democratization and Nationalist Conflict* (New York: W. W. Norton, 2000), 56–66; and Stephen Van Evera, *The Causes of War* (Ithaca: Cornell University Press, 1999), chaps. 2 and 5.

2. On the problems of predicting from statistical findings, see Michael D. Ward, Brian D. Greenhill and Kristin Bakke, "The Perils of Policy by P-Value: Predicting Civil Conflicts," *Journal of Peace Research* 47, no. 4 (March 2010): 1–13. On overcertainty and hindsight in case studies, see John Gerring, *Case Study Research: Principles and Practices* (New York: Cambridge University Press, 2006).

3. For an illuminating discussion, see Albert S. Yee, "Realist Analyses of China's Rise: Theory-Specific Derivations of Core Defenses and Auxiliary Emendations," unpublished manuscript, Dartmouth College.

4. Philip E. Tetlock, *Expert Political Judgment: How Good Is It? How Can We Know?* (Princeton: Princeton University Press, 2005).

5. Ibid., 20–22; Isaiah Berlin, "The Hedgehog and the Fox," in the *Proper Study of Mankind*, ed. Henry Hardy and Roger Hausheer (New York: Farrar, Straus and Giroux, 1997), 436–98.

6. See Mary Elise Sarotte, *1989: The Struggle to Create Post–Cold War Europe* (Princeton: Princeton University Press, 2009); and Philip Zelikow and Condoleezza Rice, *Germany Unified and Europe Transformed: A Study in Statecraft* (Cambridge: Harvard University Press, 1995).

7. Zelikow and Rice, *Germany Unified*, 197.

8. George H. W. Bush and Brent Scowcroft, *A World Transformed* (New York: Vintage, 1999), 252.

9. See Zelikow and Rice, *Germany Reunified*, chap. 5–6.

10. See CIA, "Soviet National Security Policy: Responses to the Changing Military and Economic Environment," Doc. No. 59 in Brown University, "Understanding the End of the Cold War: Reagan/Gorbachev Years," a briefing book prepared for an oral history conference by the National Security Archive.

11. The document is excerpted and analyzed in Hans Hermann Hertle, "Staatsbankrott: Der ökonomische Untergang des SED-Staates," *Deutschland Archiv* 25, no. 10 (October 1992): 1019–30. Overall, see Jeffrey Kopstein, *The Politics of Economic Decline in East Germany, 1945–1989* (Chapel Hill: University of North Carolina Press, 1997).

12. John J. Mearsheimer, "Back to the Future: Instability in Europe after the Cold War," *International Security* 15, no. 1 (Summer 1990): 125. See also Steven (*sic*) Walt, "Sokhranenie mira v Evrope: Podderzhanie status-kvo" (The Preservation of Peace in Europe: Support for the Status Quo), *S Sh A-EPI* 2 (February 1990).

13. Kurt M. Campbell, "Prospects and Consequences of Soviet Decline," in *Fateful Visions: Avoiding Nuclear Catastrophe*, ed. Joseph S. Nye, Graham T. Allison, and Albert Carnesale (Cambridge, Mass.: Ballinger, 1988), and the interviews reported in G. R. Urban, *End of Empire: The Demise of the Soviet Union* (Washington, D.C.: American University Press, 1993).

14. See Edward Hallett Carr, *The Twenty Years' Crisis, 1919–1939: An Introduction to the Study of International Relations* (New York: Harper and Row, 1939), chap. 13. The most important modern statement of the problem is Robert Gilpin, *War and Change in World Politics* (New York: Cambridge University Press, 1981). See also Arie M. Kacowicz, *Peaceful Territorial Change* (Columbia: University of South Carolina Press, 1994).

15. Kenneth Waltz, for example, only made the distinction between these two concepts clear in his *Theory of International Politics* (Reading, Mass.: Addison-Wesley, 1979).

16. Paul F. Diehl and Gary Goertz, "Territorial Change and Militarized Conflict," *Journal of Conflict Resolution* 32, no. 1 (March 1988): 103–22.

17. Paul Kennedy, *The Rise and Fall of the Great Powers* (New York: Random House, 1987), 514.

18. Eric Pace, "Scholars Say Veneer of Nonchalance Masks Worry over German Unification," *New York Times*, 26 November 1989, A21; Andrew Borowiec, "Unified Germany Not Given All Raves," *Washington Times*, 23 October 1989, A11. See also citations in Zelikow and Rice, *Germany Reunified*, 407, note 45.

19. Anne-Marie Burley, "The Once and Future German Question," *Foreign Affairs* 68, no. 5 (1989–90): 82.

20. Bush and Scowcroft, *A World Transformed*, 230–31.

21. See, especially, Sarotte, *1989*, chap. 4.

22. Ibid., 203.

23. See, for example, Christopher Layne, "Superpower Disengagement," *Foreign Policy* 77 (Winter 1989–90): 17–40.

24. George Kennan, "The Wall Falls: This Is No Time to Talk of German Reunification," *Washington Post*, 12 November 1989, D1.

25. James M. Goldgeier, *Not Whether but When: The U.S. Decision to Enlarge NATO* (Washington, D.C.: Brookings Institution, 1999).

26. John Lewis Gaddis, "History, Grand Strategy, and NATO Enlargement," *Survival* 40, no. 1 (Spring 1998): 145.

27. George Kennan, "A Fateful Error," *New York Times*, 5 February 1997.

28. See, for example, William C. Wohlforth, "German Reunification: A Reassessment" in *The Cold War—Reassessments*, ed. Arthur L. Rosenbaum and Chae-Jin Lee (Claremont, Calif.: Keck Center, 2000); Bruce Russett and Allan C. Stam, "Courting Disaster: An Expanded NATO vs. Russia and China," *Political Science Quarterly* 113, no. 3 (Fall 1998): 361–82; Dan Reiter, "Why NATO Expansion Does Not Expand Democracy," *International Security* 25, no. 4 (Spring 2001): 41–67; Michael Mandelbaum, "Preserving the New Peace: The Case against NATO Expansion," *Foreign Affairs* 74, no. 3 (May–June 1995): 9–13; Michael E. Brown, "Minimalist NATO: A Wise Alliance Knows When to Retrench," *Foreign Affairs* 78, no. 3 (May–June 1999): 204–18; editorial, "The Debate over NATO Expansion: A Critique of the Clinton Administration's Responses to Key Questions," *Arms Control Today* 27, no. 7 (September 1997): 3–10; Charles A. Kupchan, "Expand NATO—And Split Europe," *New York Times*, 27 November 1994, E11; Kenneth W. Thompson, ed., *NATO Expansion* (Lanham, Md.: University Press of America, 1998); Ted Galen Carpenter and Barbara Conry, *NATO Enlargement: Illusions and Reality* (Washington, D.C.: CATO Institute, 1998). As always, the consensus was widespread but not universal. See, for example, Christopher L. Ball, "Nattering NATO Negativism? Reasons Why Expansion May Be a Good Thing," *Review of International Studies* 24, no. 1 (January 1998): 43–67.

29. Kenneth N. Waltz, "NATO Expansion: A Realist's View," *Contemporary Security Policy* 21, no. 2 (August 2000): 23–38; and "Structural Realism after the Cold War," *International Security* 25, no. 1 (Summer 2000): 5–41.

30. Gaddis, "History, Grand Strategy," 147; see also Russett and Stam, "Courting Disaster: An Expanded NATO vs. Russia and China."

31. Quoted in Thomas Friedman, "Now a Word from Mr. X," *New York Times*, 2 May 1998.

32. Paul Kennedy, "Let's See the Pentagon's Plan for Defending Poland," *Los Angeles Times*, 16 May 1997.

33. Quoted in Friedman, "Now a Word from Mr. X."

34. Gaddis, "History, Grand Strategy," 147–48.

35. See Reiter, "Why NATO Expansion Does Not Expand Democracy"; Kennan, "A Fateful Error"; R. T. Davies, "Should NATO Grow?—A Dissent," *New York Review of Books*, 21 September 1995, 74–75; Stanley Kober, "The United States and NATO Expansion," *Transition*, 15 December 1995, 6–10; Stephen F. Cohen, "If Not Yeltsin: Four Voices of the Russian Opposition," *Washington Post*, 3 December 1995, C3.

36. See, for example, Bobo Lo, *Axis of Convenience: Moscow, Beijing, and the New Geopolitics* (Washington, D.C.: Brookings, 2008); Stephen Kotkin, "The Unbalanced Triangle: What Chinese-Russian Relations Mean for the United States," *Foreign Affairs* 88, no. 5 (September–October 2009), http://www.foreignaffairs.com/articles/65230/stephen-kotkin/the-unbalanced-triangle; S. G. Brooks and W. C. Wohlforth, *World Out of Balance: International Relations and the Challenge of American Primacy* (Princeton: Princeton University Press, 2008), chap. 3.

37. See William C. Wohlforth, "The Stability of a Unipolar World," *International Security* 21, no. 1 (1999): 1–36; and Brooks and Wohlforth, *World Out of Balance*.

38. Some cautioned against relying on local actors as proxies, suggesting the need for larger U.S. ground operations (see, for example, Andrew Bacevich, "Not So Special Operation," *National Review*, 20 November 2001, 20–22), while others warned against large troop deployments (see John J. Mearsheimer, "Guns Won't Win the Afghan War," *New York Times*, 4 November 2001). See also Samina Ahmed, "The US and Terrorism in Southwest Asia: September 11 and Beyond," *International Security* 26, no. 3 (Winter 2001–02): 79–93; Barry R. Posen, "The Struggle against Terrorism: Grand Strategy, Strategy and Tactics," *International Security* 26, no. 3 (Winter 2001–02): 39–55. Some international legal scholars did question the legality of the use of force without explicit UN Security Council authorization. See Jonathan I. Charney, "The Use of Force against Terrorism and International Law," *American Journal of International Law* 95, no. 4 (October 2001): 835–39. See also Timothy P. Carney, "Leftist Peaceniks Want More UN, Less U.S.," *Human Events* 57, no. 37 (8 October 2001): 7.

39. Though it included many nonexperts, the major antiwar petition discussed in Lindsay Bosslett, "13,000 Professors Sign Petition Opposing War With Iraq," *Chronicle of Higher Education*, 1 November 2002, was indicative of the mood in academe.

40. Security Scholars for a Sensible Foreign Policy, http://www.sensibleforeignpolicy.net/letter.html

41. Jim Lobe, "Security Scholars Say Iraq War Most Misguided Policy since Vietnam," *Foreign Policy in Focus*, http://www.fpif.org/fpiftxt/528.

42. See, for example, Robert J. Lieber, "Foreign-Policy 'Realists' Are Unrealistic on Iraq," *Chronicle of Higher Education*, 18 October 2002, 22; Michael Ignatieff, "American Empire: The Burden," *New York Times Magazine*, 5 January 2003; Michael Howard," The Case against Saddam is Strong, but Bush is Failing to Convince," *Scotsman*, 3 February 2003, 15.

43. See John J. Mearsheimer and Stephen M. Walt, "An Unnecessary War," *Foreign Policy*, no. 134 (January–February 2003): 50–59; "'Realists' Are Not Alone in Opposing War with Iraq," *Chronicle of Higher Education*, 15 November 2002; John Baylis and Steve Smith, "IR Theory in Practice Case Study: The Iraq War, 2003," *The Globalization of World Politics*, 3rd ed., (Oxford University Press, 2005); Coalition for a Realistic Foreign Policy advertisement, "War With Iraq is not in America's Interest," *New York Times*, 26 September 2002; Richard Kohn, "Attacking Iraq: Weighing the Means and Ends," *Chronicle of Higher Education*, 20 September 2002, 10; Adeed Dawisha and Yitzhak Nakash, interviewed in Kir Roane and Robert Ingrassia, "Lurking Peril for U.S.: Tribal Fighting in Iraq," *New York Daily News*, 23 February 2003, 22; R. K. Ramazani, interviewed in Robert Ingrassia, "Ethnic Tensions Cloud a Post-Saddam Region," *New York Daily News*, 9 February 2003, 34; Paul Wilkinson, interviewed in Christopher Andreae, "His Answer to Terrorism Lies Not in War," *Christian Science Monitor*, 6 March 2003, 17; Murray Dubin, "Conversations on War: Current Facts Don't Justify an Attack, a Professor Says," *Philadelphia Inquirer*, 29 January 2003, C1; Tom Allard, "Cornered Saddam Could Bring Economy Down, Academic Warns," *Sydney Morning Herald*, 3 October 2003, 10; Francis Fukuyama, interviewed in Sid Maher, "After the War: The Real Battle," *Courier Mail*, 18 January 2003; Shibley Telhami, "A Hidden Cost of War on Iraq," *New York Times*, 7 October 2002, 19; Sean Kay and Joshua Spero, "The Risks of Going to War against Iraq," *Boston Globe*, 3 November 2002, D12.

44. Robert Jervis, "Reports, Politics, and Intelligence Failures: The Case of Iraq," *Journal of Strategic Studies* 29, no. 1 (February 2006): 3–52.

CONCLUSION

1. See chapter 10, 169.

2. See G. John Ikenberry's *After Victory: Institutions, Strategic Restraint, and the Rebuilding of Order after Major Wars* (Princeton: Princeton University Press, 2001) and

Liberal Order and Imperial Ambition: Essays on American Power and International Order (London: Polity Press, 2006).

3. Stephen G. Brooks and William C. Wohlforth, *World Out of Balance: International Relations and the Challenge of American Primacy* (Princeton: Princeton University Press, 2008).

4. Hurd quote is from Mary E. Sarotte, *1989: The Struggle to Create Post–Cold War Europe* (Princeton: Princeton University Press, 2009), 4.

5. George Bush and Brent Scowcroft, *A World Transformed* (New York: Knopf, 1998).

6. Quoted in chapter 3, 52.

7. For the Defense Policy Guidance, see chapters 3 and 4 in this book. The many drafts of the DPG can be found on the website of the National Security Archive. See http://www.gwu.edu/~nsarchiv/nukevault/ebb245/index.htm.

8. Chapter 4, 75.

9. Chapter 2, 41.

10. Charles A. Kupchan and Peter L. Trubowitz, "Dead Center: The Demise of Liberal Internationalism in the United States," *International Security* 32, no. 2 (Fall 2007): 7–44.

11. Chapter 5, 78.

12. Sarotte, *1989: The Struggle to Create Post-Cold War*, 204–8.

13. Chapter 6, 101 (note 13); see Draft "National Security Strategy," 23 July 2001, in Zelikow Papers, http://faculty.virginia.edu/zelikow/documents/nationalsecuritypolicy.pdf.

14. *Final Report of the National Commission on Terrorist Attacks upon the United States* (New York: W. W. Norton, 2004), 339–50.

15. On the record of expert judgment, see Philip Tetlock, *Expert Political Judgment: How Good Is It? How Can We Know?* (Princeton: Princeton University Press 2005).

16. Chapter 6, 107.

17. Chapter 9, 151.

18. Chapter 5, 92 and 94.

19. Chapter 6, 105.

20. See Bush and Scowcroft, *A World Transformed*.

21. Chapter 2, 38.

22. Ibid., 27.

23. Ibid., 42.

24. See chapters 3 and 4.

25. Chapter 5, 86–87.

26. See Jack Snyder, *Myths of Empire: Domestic Politics and International Ambition* (Ithaca: Cornell University Press, 1991); Thomas Christensen, *Useful Adversaries: Grand Strategy, Domestic Mobilization, and Sino-American Conflict, 1947–58* (Princeton: Princeton University Press, 1996).

27. Chapter 4, 71–72; chapter 3, 56–57.

28. Chapter 6, 99.

29. In the waning days of the Bush administration, Secretary of State Lawrence Eagleburger apparently sent a twenty-two page memo evaluating world affairs to incoming secretary of state Warren Christopher. In contrast to the emphasis on traditional state threats in the Defense Planning Guidance, the memo focused more on the new dangers of a globalizing world. See Derek Chollet and James Goldgeier, *America between the Wars* (New York: PublicAffairs, 2008), 47–51.

30. Bartholomew Sparrow, "Realism's Practitioner: Brent Scowcroft and the Making of the New World Order," *Diplomatic History* 34, no 1 (January 2010): 149–52.

31. Ibid., 153.

32. See chapter 1, 22.

33. Chapter 4, 69, 76.

34. See Bush and Scowcroft, *A World Transformed.*

35. See chapter 4, 69.

36. Chapter 3, 60.

37. Strobe Talbott, deputy secretary of state and friend of President Clinton, wrote, "He never felt that he had quite found the right word to explain what he was trying to do in his foreign policy." *The Great Experiment: The Story of Ancient Empires, Modern States, and the Quest for a Global Nation* (New York: Simon and Schuster, 2008), 325. On the general search for strategy in the Clinton administration, see Chollet and Goldgeier, *America between the Wars.*

38. Chapter 6, 99. There are many accounts of Bush administration decision making. See, for example, David Rothkopf, *Running the World: The Inside Story of the National Security Council and the Architects of American Power* (New York: Public Affairs, 2006); Ron Suskind, *The One Percent Doctrine: Deep inside America's Pursuit of Its Enemies since 9/11* (New York: Simon and Schuster, 2007).

39. The National Security Council Project, Oral History Roundtables, The Bush Administration National Security Council (29 April 1999), http://www.brookings.edu/projects/archive/nsc/19990429.aspx.

40. Introduction to the *National Security Strategy, May 2010* (White House), http://www.whitehouse.gov/sites/default/files/rss_viewer/national_security_strategy.pdf.

41. Memorandum, Philip Zelikow to Condoleezza Rice and Steve Hadley, "Proposal for NSC Office of Strategic Planning," 5 December 2001, See Zelikow papers, 211, n.13.

42. Chapter 1, 21.

43. Chapter 3, 46.

44. Chapter 4, 76.

45. Chapter 3, 50–51, 60–61.

46. Chapter 2, 28.

Notes on Contributors

Bruce Cumings is the Gustavus F. and Ann M. Swift Distinguished Service Professor in History and the College at the University of Chicago. His book, *The Origins of the Korean War*, won the John King Fairbank Book Award of the American Historical Association and the Quincy Wright Book Award of the International Studies Association. He is the editor of the modern volume of the *Cambridge History of Korea* (forthcoming), and is a frequent contributor to the *London Review of Books*, the *Nation*, *Current History*, the *Bulletin of the Atomic Scientists*, and *Le Monde Diplomatique*. In 2007 he won the Kim Dae Jung Prize for Scholarly Contributions to Democracy, Human Rights and Peace. Cumings's newest book, *Dominion from Sea to Sea: Pacific Ascendancy and American Power*, was published by Yale University Press in 2010.

Eric S. Edelman was U.S. Under Secretary of Defense for Policy from 2005 to 2009, and Principal Deputy Assistant to the Vice President for National Security Affairs from 2001 to 2003. A career Foreign Service Officer, he has held ambassadorships to Turkey and the Republic of Finland. Edelman received the Secretary of Defense's award for Distinguished Civilian Service in 1993, and is a two-time recipient of the State Department's Superior Honor Award (in 1990 and 1996). In 2009, Edelman was awarded the Secretary of Defense award for Distinguished Public Service. He is currently a distinguished fellow at the Center for Strategic and Budgetary Assessments, working on national security policy, strategy, and alliance issues.

Melvyn P. Leffler is Edward R. Stettinius Professor of American History in the Department of History at the University of Virginia. He served as the Dean of the College of Arts and Sciences at U.Va. from 1997 to 2001, and is now a Faculty Associate in the Miller Center's Governing America in a Global Era Program. In 1993 he won the Bancroft Prize for *A Preponderance of Power: National Security, the Truman Administration, and the Cold War* and, in 2008, the George Louis Beer Prize for *For the Soul of Mankind: The United States, the Soviet Union, and the Cold War*. His other books include *Specter of Communism: The United States and the Origins of the Cold War, 1917–1953* and *The Elusive Quest: America's Pursuit of European Stability and French Security, 1919–1933*. In 2010, along with Odd Arne Westad, he coedited the three-volume *Cambridge History of the Cold War*. He is a former president of the Society of Historians of American Foreign Relations and was Harmsworth Professor at the University of Oxford in 2002–03.

Jeffrey W. Legro is Randolph P. Compton Professor at the Miller Center of Public Affairs and Professor in the Department of Politics at the University of Virginia. He is a Faculty Associate in the Governing America in a Global Era Program at the Miller Center. Legro is the author of *Rethinking the World: Great Power Strategies and International Order* and *Cooperation under Fire: Anglo-German Restraint during World War II*. He is coeditor, with Melvyn Leffler, of *To Lead the World: American Strategy after the Bush Doctrine*. Legro chaired the American Political Science Association (APSA) Task Force on U.S. Standing in the World and is past president of APSA's International History and Politics section.

John Mueller is the Woody Hayes Chair of National Security Studies at the Mershon Center and Professor of Political Science at Ohio State University. His most recent books are *Atomic Obsession: Nuclear Alarmism from Hiroshima to al Qaeda* and *Overblown: How Politicians and the Terrorism Industry Inflate National Security Threats, and Why We Believe Them.* He has been a visiting fellow at the Brookings Institution and the Cato Institute in Washington, D.C., the Hoover Institution at Stanford University, and the Norwegian Nobel Institute in Oslo. He is a member of the American Academy of Arts and Sciences, has been a John Simon Guggenheim Fellow, and has received grants from the National Science Foundation and the National Endowment for the Humanities.

Mary Elise Sarotte holds a joint appointment as Professor of History and Professor of International Relations in the History Department and School of International Relations at the University of Southern California. In 2006–07, Sarotte was a National Endowment for the Humanities fellow at the Institute for Advanced Study in Princeton, where she worked on her prize-winning Princeton University Press book, *1989: The Struggle to Create Post–Cold War Europe.* Her other publications include *Dealing with the Devil: East Germany, Détente, and Ostpolitik* and *German Military Reform and European Security,* as well as numerous scholarly articles. She has worked as a journalist for the *Economist, Time,* and *Die Zeit;* served as a White House Fellow in 2001–02; and is a member of the Council on Foreign Relations.

Walter B. Slocombe was Under Secretary of Defense for Policy from 1994 to 2001. He was Senior Adviser for National Defense in the Coalition Provisional Authority for Iraq in 2003. In 2004, President George W. Bush appointed him to the Commission on the Intelligence Capabilities of the United States Regarding Weapons of Mass Destruction. Slocombe served on the staff of the National Security Council in 1969–70. He is a four-time recipient of the Defense Department's Award for Distinguished Public Service and Secretary of the Atlantic Council of the United States.

Odd Arne Westad is Professor of International History and Director of IDEAS, the Centre for International Affairs, Diplomacy and Strategy at the London School of Economics and Political Science. He is editor of the journal *Cold War History* and coeditor, with Melvyn Leffler, of the three-volume *Cambridge History of the Cold War.* His 2006 book, *The Global Cold War: Third World Interventions and the Making of Our Times,* was awarded the Bancroft Prize, the Akira Iriye International History Book Award, and the Michael Harrington Award from the American Political Science Association. In 2000, Westad was awarded the Bernath Lecture Prize from the Society of Historians of American Foreign Relations.

William C. Wohlforth is the Daniel Webster Professor of Government at Dartmouth College. He is the author of *Elusive Balance: Power and Perceptions during the Cold War,* and editor of *Witnesses to the End of the Cold War* and *Cold War Endgame: Oral History, Analysis, and Debates.* His newest book is *World Out of Balance: International Relations Theory and the Challenge of American Primacy.* He is editor in chief of *Security Studies* and a member of the editorial board of *International Security.*

Paul Wolfowitz was U.S. Deputy Secretary of Defense from 2001 to 2005 and President of the World Bank from 2005 to 2007. From 1989 to 1993, he served as Undersecretary of Defense for Policy in the administration of George H. W. Bush. He was appointed Ambassador to Indonesia in 1986, and was Professor of International Relations and Dean of the Paul H. Nitze School of Advanced International Studies (SAIS) at Johns Hopkins University from 1994 to 2001. He is currently a visiting scholar at the American Enterprise Institute for Public Policy Research. He is chairman of the U.S.-Taiwan Business Council.

Philip Zelikow is White Burkett Miller Professor of History and Director of Graduate Studies in the Department of History at the University of Virginia. A former career diplomat who was detailed to the National Security Council staff in the administration of George H. W. Bush, he has taught and directed research programs at Harvard University and at Virginia since 1991. He has directed three national bipartisan commissions, including the 9/11 Commission. His most recent full-time government service was as the Counselor of the Department of State, a deputy to Secretary Rice, from 2005 to 2007.

Robert B. Zoellick is President of the World Bank Group. He served as U.S. Deputy Secretary of State from 2005 to 2006 and as the U.S. Trade Representative from 2001 to 2005. He held various positions at the Treasury Department under Secretary James A. Baker and was Under Secretary of State for Economic and Agricultural Affairs and White House Deputy Chief of Staff under George H. W. Bush. He served from 2006 to 2007 as Vice Chairman, International, of the Goldman Sachs Group, and Managing Director and Chairman of Goldman Sach's Board of International Advisors. He was appointed the John M. Olin Professor of National Security at the U.S. Naval Academy (1997–98) and was a Research Scholar at the Belfer Center for Science and International Affairs at Harvard's John F. Kennedy School of Government.

Index

Abdullah (king of Jordan), 221n18
ABM Treaty, 90, 173
academic policy advice, 10, 163–78; on
  Afghanistan War, 174, 224n38; conventional
  wisdom regarding, 163–64; on enlargement
  of NATO, 170–74, 177, 178; on German
  reunification within NATO, 166–70,
  177, 178; "hedgehogs" versus "foxes,"
  166, 177–78; on Iraq War, 174–78, 186;
  predictive success of analysts and social
  scientists, 118, 132–33, 145–47, 163–66,
  177–78; uncertainty levels affecting value
  of, 163–66
Acheson, Dean, 133, 137–39, 148, 189
Adenauer, Konrad, 18
Afghanistan, Soviet invasion of, 20, 53, 129,
  155, 158
Afghanistan War (2001–), 9–10, 150–62;
  academic policy advice on, 174, 224n38;
  alliances, Regional Defense Strategy
  dependent on, 60; as consequence of 9/11,
  142, 174; initial success in, 103–4, 106, 112,
  151; limits of American power in, 144–45;
  reasons for failures of intervention in,
  151–52; short-term versus middle-term
  and long-term responses, 187–88; Taliban,
  103–4, 112, 118, 142, 151–53, 155, 159,
  174, 186–87, 221n12; Vietnam Syndrome
  and, 129. *See also* Cold War lessons for
  Afghanistan and Iraq
The Agenda for American Renewal (1992),
  41–42
aid as part of Bush 43 war on terror strategy,
  108–9, 115–16
Aidid, Mohamed Farrah, 153
AIDS/HIV, 101, 109
al Qaeda: bin Laden, Osama, 103, 125, 141–44,
  152, 212n25; counterproductive results of
  9/11 for, 123; Iraq War, consequences of,
  152, 176; overestimation of threat posed by,
  123, 125, 127, 144; Pakistan, retrenchment
  in, 151–52, 159; short-term versus middle-
  term and long-term responses, 187; war on

terror strategy and, 104, 105, 112, 113, 114,
  186. *See also* Afghanistan War
alliances: in Cold War, 138; DPG 92 on, 66, 70;
  Regional Defense Strategy dependent on,
  60–61; Rice, Condoleezza, on coalitions, 101
Andean Trade Preference Act (ATPA), 36
Andropov, Yuri, 90
anthrax attacks, post-9/11, 104–5
anticolonialism, 9, 129, 133, 137, 146
ANZUS treaty, 35
APEC (Asia-Pacific Economic Cooperation),
  39–40, 181
Apple, R. W. "Johnny," 103
Aquino, Corazon, 19
Arab-Israeli conflict, 79, 99, 106, 142, 221n18
Aron, Raymond, 135
ASEAN (Association of Southeast Asian
  Nations), 35, 39, 42
Asia-Pacific Economic Cooperation (APEC),
  39–40, 181
Asia-Pacific region, post-Cold War U.S.
  strategy for, 27, 38–40
Aspen speech, by George H. W. Bush, 1990, 53,
  58, 59, 68–69
Aspin, Les, 58, 61
Association of Southeast Asian Nations
  (ASEAN), 35, 39, 42
assumptions, danger of, 9, 131–49, 188–89;
  American power, limits of, 143–45; end of
  WWII, forecasting world order at, 136–40;
  life or history as means of detecting falsehood
  of assumptions, 133–36, 150–51; metaphor,
  importance of escaping, 9, 131, 132, 148–49;
  mètis or rules of thumb, advantages of,
  145–47; North Korea, predicted collapse of,
  9, 134, 146–48; numbers, doing history by,
  132, 145–47; predictive success of analysts
  and social scientists, 118, 132–33, 145–47,
  163–66, 177–78; September 11, 2001,
  significance of, 140–43; Soviet Union at
  end of WWII, 137–38, 140; Soviet Union,
  predictions/interpretation of collapse of,
  132–33, 135–36, 140

Jäger, Harald, 17
Japan: assumptions regarding post-WWII
     world order and, 138, 139; in Bush 43
     policy agenda prior to 9/11, 98; continuing
     presence of U.S. troops in, 145; as economic
     threat, 74, 121, 209n2; foreign policy lessons
     from, 196; renationalization of defense,
     concerns regarding, 61, 72, 183; as security
     threat in early 20th century, 117, 118, 119;
     security treaty with, 35–36, 38, 52; U.S.
     strategy during Cold War and, 180
Jarecki, Eugene, 64
Jeremiah, David, 204n17
Jervis, Robert, 125, 127, 176
Johnson, Robert, 125
Joulwan, George, 85

Kagan, Donald and Frederick W., 205n33
Kanter, Arnold, 204n17
Karzai, Hamid, 104, 152, 157
Kazakhstan, 89
Kennan, George F., 120, 128–29, 133, 138, 139,
     156, 171–72, 218n44
Kennedy, John F., 19, 38, 114
Kennedy, Paul, 169, 172
Keohane, Robert, 174
Khalilzad, Zalmay, 49
Khrushchev, Nikita, 122, 128, 143
Kim Il Sung, 51, 122, 140, 154, 204n19
Kim Jong Il, 147
Kissinger, Henry, 65, 205n24
kitchen debate, 128
Kohl, Helmut, 8, 13, 18–19, 20–24, 166–67,
     169, 184
Kolt, George, 49
Korea. See North Korea; South Korea
Korean War, 117, 122–27, 139, 152, 154–55
Kosovo, 62, 83–85, 88–89, 90, 103, 153
Krauthammer, Charles, 74
Krenz, Egon, 14
Kuwait: Iraq War, academic policy advice on,
     175; Iraqi invasion of (see Persian Gulf War)
Kyoto climate treaty, 99
Kyrgyzstan, 143, 144

Lake, Tony, 73
Lance, 47, 204n13
Latham, Robert, 138
Latin America: neoliberalism rejected in, 135;
     post-Cold War U.S. strategy for, 27, 33–38
Latvia (Baltic state), 89, 190
Layne, Christopher, 75
Lebanon, bombing of Marine barracks in, 118,
     205n22

Leibovitz, Annie, 107
Lemann, Nicolas, 63–64
Lenin, Vladimir, 120
Libby, Lewis "Scooter": as Cheney's chief
     of staff, 214n55; Department of Defense
     planning, 1989–93, and, 49, 51, 52, 54, 58,
     59, 204nn16–17, 206n43; DPG 92 and, 66,
     67, 69, 70; as neoconservative, 5
liberalization of trade, 33–38
Libya, 155
Lieberman, Joe, 108
Lieberthal, Kenneth, 147
Lind, Michael, 64, 208n22
Lithuania (Baltic state), 89, 190
Logevall, Fredrik, 22
Louvre accords, 40–41
Lovett, Robert, 139
Luck, Gary, 146
Lula da Silva, Luiz Inácio, 135

Madrid agreements, 79
Mann, James, 72–73, 75, 210n4
Mao Tse-tung, 134, 219n5
Marshall, Andy, 49
Marshall Plan, 22, 24, 35, 38, 109, 137, 138
MBFR (Mutual and Balanced Force
     Reduction) talks, 32, 47
Mearsheimer, John J., 75, 139, 168, 175, 177
Merleau-Ponty, Maurice, 135
metaphor, importance of escaping, 9, 131, 132,
     148–49
mètis or rules of thumb, advantages of,
     145–47
Mexico: Bush 43 and, 99, 109; illegal
     immigration from, 118; post-Cold War
     strategy toward, 34–35, 37
Meyer, Christopher, 211n8
military-industrial complex, 218n43
"Millennium Challenge" program, 109, 115
Milošević, Slobodan, 88–89, 90, 118
Mitterrand, François, 23, 30–31, 48
Momper, Walter, 18–19
Mongolia, 146
moral absolutes and national values, U.S.
     predilection for, 156–58
Mueller, John, 8–9, 10, 186, 189, 190, 194
Mugabe, Robert, 118
Mullah Omar, 174
multilateralism: in Cold War period, 73; post-
     Cold War U.S. strategy of, 27, 40–41
Musharraf, Pervez, 152, 159
Mutual and Balanced Force Reduction
     (MBFR) talks, 32, 47
Myanmar (Burma), 118

Russia: in Bush 43 policy agenda prior to 9/11, 98; Central Asia, intersection of major nuclear powers in, 145; end of Cold War, role of Russians generally in, 45; enlargement of NATO and, 83, 86–88, 170–74; foreign policy lessons from, 196; internal disorder and economic crisis in, 83, 90–91, 92–93; post-Cold War U.S. strategy regarding, 32–33. *See also* Soviet Union

Russian policy of Clinton administration, 6, 78–95, 184–85; assumptions, problem of, 188; Balkans, unrest in, 83–85, 88–89, 90, 184; benign situations, problems peculiar to, 78–80; Central and Eastern Europe in NATO, 83, 86–88, 184; failure of strategy, analysis of, 89–95; formation of strategy, 80–81; implementation of strategy, 82–83; NATO alliance, role of, 83, 85–89; process of policy making and, 193; recognition of opportunities afforded by, 79–80

Salinas, Carlos, 34
SALT II negotiations, 205n24
Sandinista regime, Nicaragua, 36–37
Sarotte, Mary Elise, 4, 8–9, 10, 96, 170, 182, 188
Sartre, Jean-Paul, 135
Saudi Arabia: counterproductivity of 9/11 for perpetrators, 123; Iraq War, academic policy advice on, 175; in Persian Gulf War, 54, 204–5n22; war on terror strategy and, 106
Schabowski, Günter, 15–17
Schilling, Warren, 117
Schmidt, Helmut, 20
scholarly experts. *See* academic policy advice
Schwarzkopf, Norman, 204n21
Scott, James, 145
Scowcroft, Brent: changes brought about by end of Cold War, responding to, 10–11; on Cheney, 210n5; Defense Department planning, 1989–93, and, 46–47, 53, 55, 56, 59; DPG 92 and, 68–70, 73, 76; on National Security Review 3, 21; on NATO enlargement, 171, 206n43; on "new world order," 46, 203–4n7; process of policy making under, 192; SALT II negotiations, 1976, 205n24; standard assessments of, 4
SEATO (Southeast Asia Treaty Organization), 35
Second World War. *See* World War II, end of
The Secret Agent (Conrad), 140–41
September 11, 2001, 1–3, 102, 185–86; Afghan War as consequence of, 142, 174; Berlin Wall, legacy of fall of, 23–24; change, ability

to respond to, 11; counterproductivity for perpetrators, 123; fear as strategic motivator inspired by, 7, 105; incomparability to other crises, 142–43; interpretation of significance of, 140–43; Iraq, alleged link to, 111; Korean War compared, 122–27; *9/11 Commission Report,* 23–24, 182, 186; Pearl Harbor compared to, 1, 104, 143; personal experience of, 104–6. *See also* war on terror strategy
Serbia, 84, 88, 118, 153, 173
Sestanovich, Steve, 48–49
Shevardnadze, Eduard, 20, 56, 72
Shilling, Dave, 70
short-range nuclear forces (SNF) negotiations, 47, 48, 204n13
Shultz, George, 20, 33, 48, 98
Singapore, 39
Slocombe, Walter B.: on post-Cold War U.S. strategy, 6, 7, 184, 185, 188, 193, 194
Smoot-Hawley Tariff Act, 38
SNF (short-range nuclear forces) negotiations, 47, 48, 204n13
Snyder, Jack, 75
Solarium project, 65, 67, 77
Somalia, 79, 129, 153
South Africa, end of Apartheid in, 79
South America: neoliberalism rejected in, 135; post-Cold War U.S. strategy for, 27, 33–38
South Korea: APEC and, 39; assumptions regarding post-WWII world order and, 138; during Clinton administration, 79; FTAs, 42; Korean War, 117, 122–27, 139, 152, 154–55; security treaty with, 35–36, 38; U.S. nuclear arsenal, withdrawal of, 55
Southeast Asia Treaty Organization (SEATO), 35
Soviet Union: in Afghanistan, 20, 53, 129, 155, 158; assumptions at end of WWII regarding, 137–38, 140; as Cold War era threat, 117–18, 119–20, 122, 123–25, 128, 180; conventional arms control, shift of U.S. priorities toward, 46–48; DPG 92 and collapse of, 69, 76; failed coup against Gorbachev (1991), 56, 58; German reunification within NATO and, 166–67; in Persian Gulf War, 59; in post-Cold War U.S. strategy, 28, 29, 31–33, 35–37. *See also* Russia; Russian policy of Clinton administration; *entries at* Cold War
Soviet Union, collapse of, 183–84; assumptions associated with, 132–33, 135–36, 140; Berlin Wall, fall of, 13, 19, 20, 22–25, 50; Defense Department strategy response to, 52, 53, 55–57, 58, 60, 61; nuclear weapons and,

CPSIA information can be obtained
at www.ICGtesting.com
Printed in the USA
LVHW042354210920
666686LV00004B/10

9 780801 476198